Michael K. Sullivan, PhD
Editor

Sexual Minorities: Discrimination, Challenges, and Development in America

Sexual Minorities: Discrimination, Challenges, and Development in America has been co-published simultaneously as *Journal of Human Behavior in the Social Environment* Volume 8, Numbers 2/3 2003.

Pre-publication REVIEWS, COMMENTARIES, EVALUATIONS . . .

Sexual Minorities: Discrimination, Challenges, and Development in America

Sexual Minorities: Discrimination, Challenges, and Development in America has been co-published simultaneously as *Journal of Human Behavior in the Social Environment*, Volume 8, Numbers 2/3 2003.

The *Journal of Human Behavior in the Social Environment*™ Monographic "Separates"

Below is a list of "separates," which in serials librarianship means a special issue simultaneously published as a special journal issue or double-issue *and* as a "separate" hardbound monograph. (This is a format which we also call a "DocuSerial.")

"Separates" are published because specialized libraries or professionals may wish to purchase a specific thematic issue by itself in a format which can be separately cataloged and shelved, as opposed to purchasing the journal on an on-going basis. Faculty members may also more easily consider a "separate" for classroom adoption.

"Separates" are carefully classified separately with the major book jobbers so that the journal tie-in can be noted on new book order slips to avoid duplicate purchasing.

You may wish to visit Haworth's Website at . . .

http://www.HaworthPress.com

. . . to search our online catalog for complete tables of contents of these separates and related publications.

You may also call 1-800-HAWORTH (outside US/Canada: 607-722-5857), or Fax 1-800-895-0582 (outside US/Canada: 607-771-0012), or e-mail at:

docdelivery@haworthpress.com

Sexual Minorities: Discrimination, Challenges, and Development in America, edited by Michael K. Sullivan, PhD (Vol. 8, No. 2/3, 2003). *"This timely and readable book offers stimulating insights to the casual or serious reader/student/professional. . . . Presents richly diverse and encouraging information about acceptance, self-acceptance, and the ability to cope with minority sexuality." (Horace Lethbridge, MA, School Psychologist (Retired), Rochester, NY)*

Charting the Impacts of University-Child Welfare Collaboration, edited by Katharine Briar-Lawson, PhD, and Joan Levy Zlotnik, PhD, ACSW (Vol. 7, No. 1/2, 2003). *"An excellent comprehensive compilation of Title-IVE collaborations between public child welfare agencies and university settings at both BSW and MSW levels . . ." (Rowena Fong, MSW, EdD, Professor of Social Work, The University of Texas at Austin)*

Latino/Hispanic Liaisons and Visions for Human Behavior in the Social Environment, edited by José B. Torres, PhD, MSW, and Felix G. Rivera, PhD (Vol. 5, No. 3/4, 2002). *"An excellent example of scholarship by Latinos, for Latinos. . . . Quite useful for graduate social work courses in human behavior or social research." (Carmen Ortiz Hendricks, DSW, Associate Professsor, Hunter College School of Social Work, New York City)*

Violence as Seen Through a Prism of Color, edited by Letha A. (Lee) See, PhD (Vol. 4, No. 2/3, 4, 2001). *"Incisive and important. . . . A comprehensive analysis of the way violence affects people of color. Offers important insights. . . . Should be consulted by academics, students, policymakers, and members of the public." (Dr. James Midgley, Harry and Riva Specht, Professor and Dean, School of Social Welfare, University of California at Berkeley)*

Psychosocial Aspects of the Asian-American Experience: Diversity Within Diversity, edited by Namkee G. Choi, PhD (Vol. 3, No. 3/4, 2000). *Examines the childhood, adolescence, young adult, and aging stages of Asian Americans to help researchers and practitioners offer better services to this ethnic group. Representing Chinese, Japanese, Filipinos, Koreans, Asian Indians, Vietnamese, Hmong, Cambodians, and native-born Hawaiians, this helpful book will enable you to offer clients relevant services that are appropriate for your clients' ethnic backgrounds, beliefs, and experiences.*

Voices of First Nations People: Human Services Considerations, edited by Hilary N. Weaver, DSW (Vol. 2, No. 1/2, 1999). *"A must read for anyone interested in gaining an insight into the world of Native Americans. . . . I highly recommend it!" (James Knapp, BS, Executive Director, Native American Community Services of Erie and Niagara Counties, Inc., Buffalo, New York)*

Human Behavior in the Social Environment from an African American Perspective, edited by Letha A. (Lee) See, PhD (Vol. 1, No. 2/3, 1998). *"A book of scholarly, convincing, and relevant chapters that provide an African-American perspective on human behavior and the social environment . . . offer[s] new insights about the impact of race on psychosocial development in American society." (Alphonso W. Haynes, EdD, Professor, School of Social Work, Grand Valley State University, Grand Rapids, Michigan)*

Sexual Minorities: Discrimination, Challenges, and Development in America

Michael K. Sullivan, PhD
Editor

Sexual Minorities: Discrimination, Challenges, and Development in America has been co-published simultaneously as *Journal of Human Behavior in the Social Environment*, Volume 8, Numbers 2/3 2003.

THSWPP

The Haworth Social Work Practice Press
An Imprint of
The Haworth Press, Inc.
New York • London • Oxford

Published by

The Haworth Social Work Practice Press, 10 Alice Street, Binghamton, NY 13904-1580 USA

The Haworth Social Work Practice Press is an imprint of The Haworth Press, Inc., 10 Alice Street, Binghamton, NY 13904-1580 USA.

Sexual Minorities: Discrimination, Challenges and Development in America has been co-published simultaneously as *Journal of Human Behavior in the Social Environment*, Volume 8, Numbers 2/3 2003.

The development, preparation, and publication of this work has been undertaken with great care. However, the publisher, employees, editors, and agents of The Haworth Press and all imprints of The Haworth Press, Inc., including The Haworth Medical Press® and The Pharmaceutical Products Press®, are not responsible for any errors contained herein or for consequences that may ensue from use of materials or information contained in this work. Opinions expressed by the author(s) are not necessarily those of The Haworth Press, Inc.

Cover design by Lora Wiggins.

Library of Congress Cataloging-in-Publication Data

Sexual Minorities: Discrimination, Challenges and Development in America / Michael K. Sullivan editor.
    p. cm.
    "Co-published simultaneously as Journal of human behavior in the social environment, Volume 8, Numbers. 2/3, 2003."
    Includes bibliographical references and index.
    ISBN 0-7890-0230-2 (hard cover: alk. paper)–ISBN 0-7890-0235-3 (soft cover: alk. paper)
    1. Gay–United States–Social conditions. 2. Transsexuals–United State–Social conditions. 3. Homophobia–United States. 4. Social work with gays–United States. I. Sullivan, Miahael (Michael K.) II. Journal of human behavior in the social environment.
HQ76.25.S497 2004
306.76´6´0973–dc22   2003023602

Indexing, Abstracting & Website/Internet Coverage

This section provides you with a list of major indexing & abstracting services. That is to say, each service began covering this periodical during the year noted in the right column. Most Websites which are listed below have indicated that they will either post, disseminate, compile, archive, cite or alert their own Website users with research-based content from this work. (This list is as current as the copyright date of this publication.)

Abstracting, Website/Indexing Coverage . . . . Year When Coverage Began

- *Cambridge Scientific Abstracts, Risk Abstracts*
  <http://www.csa.com> **1998**

- *CareData: the database supporting social care management
  and practice <http://www.elsc.org.uk/caredata/caredata.htm>* . . . **2003**

- *Child Development Abstracts & Bibliography
  (in print & online) <http://www.okans.edu>* **1998**

- *CINAHL (Cumulative Index to Nursing & Allied Health
  Literature), in print, EBSCO, and SilverPlatter, Data-Star,
  and PaperChase. (Support materials include Subject Heading
  List, Database Search Guide, and instructional video)
  <http://www.cinahl.com>* **1998**

- *Criminal Justice Abstracts* **1998**

- *Environmental Sciences and Pollution Management
  (Cambridge Scientific Abstracts Internet Database
  Service) <http://www.csa.com>* **2003**

- *e-psyche, LLC <http://www.e-psyche.net>* **2002**

- *Family & Society Studies Worldwide <http://www.nisc.com>* **1998**

- *Family Index Database <http://www.familyscholar.com>* **2003**

(continued)

*Exact start date to come

Special Bibliographic Notes related to special journal issues (separates) and indexing/abstracting:

- indexing/abstracting services in this list will also cover material in any "separate" that is co-published simultaneously with Haworth's special thematic journal issue or DocuSerial. Indexing/abstracting usually covers material at the article/chapter level.
- monographic co-editions are intended for either non-subscribers or libraries which intend to purchase a second copy for their circulating collections.
- monographic co-editions are reported to all jobbers/wholesalers/approval plans. The source journal is listed as the "series" to assist the prevention of duplicate purchasing in the same manner utilized for books-in-series.
- to facilitate user/access services all indexing/abstracting services are encouraged to utilize the co-indexing entry note indicated at the bottom of the first page of each article/chapter/contribution.
- this is intended to assist a library user of any reference tool (whether print, electronic, online, or CD-ROM) to locate the monographic version if the library has purchased this version but not a subscription to the source journal.

ABOUT THE EDITOR

Dr. Michael K. Sullivan received his PhD from The University of Georgia's School of Social Work. He currently teaches foundations of social work practice courses, research, and clinical evaluation. His research area focuses on barriers to development in late adolescence and young adulthood. He has written on the subject of coming out issues with gay adolescents, self-esteem perceptions of adolescents living in public housing, welfare reform barriers for young mothers, and effects of children who witness violence.

Dr. Sullivan worked in direct practice for 15 years in a variety of capacities before obtaining his PhD. His career history in direct practice included a mixture of administrative positions and direct service positions in the areas of emergency services, crisis intervention, public health, death and dying, and counseling and facilitating groups for gay men focused on self-esteem and personal growth. He has been teaching in the social work curriculum since 1992.

Sexual Minorities: Discrimination, Challenges, and Development in America

CONTENTS

Homophobia, History, and Homosexuality: Trends for Sexual Minorities

Michael K. Sullivan

SUMMARY. This paper explores the cultural, religious, and sociological underpinnings of homophobia and intolerance toward homosexuals. Theories of homosexual causation are also explored as well as a brief historical accounting of the rise of modern gay culture in Western society. Empirical findings or regional attitudinal differences toward homosexuals both recently and over time are presented in graphical format. Finally, changing attitudes are explored, and conclusions suggest that although homophobia is still very prevalent, tolerance and support from social institutions for GLBT individuals are slowly increasing over time. *[Article copies available for a fee from The Haworth Document Delivery Service: 1-800-HAWORTH. E-mail address: <docdelivery@haworthpress.com> Website: <http://www. HaworthPress.com> © 2003 by The Haworth Press, Inc. All rights reserved.]*

KEYWORDS. Homosexuality, homophobia, history, geography, regional attitudes

---

Michael K. Sullivan, PhD, is Assistant Professor, The University of Tennessee, College of Social Work at Memphis, 822 Beale Street, Room 220, Memphis, TN 38163 (E-mail: msulliv3@utk.edu).

[Haworth co-indexing entry note]: "Homophobia, History, and Homosexuality: Trends for Sexual Minorities." Sullivan, Michael K. Co-published simultaneously in *Journal of Human Behavior in the Social Environment* (The Haworth Social Work Practice Press, an imprint of The Haworth Press, Inc.) Vol. 8, No. 2/3, 2003, pp. 1-13; and: *Sexual Minorities: Discrimination, Challenges, and Development in America* (ed: Michael K. Sullivan) The Haworth Social Work Practice Press, an imprint of The Haworth Press, Inc., 2003, pp. 1-13. Single or multiple copies of this article are available for a fee from The Haworth Document Delivery Service [1-800-HAWORTH, 9:00 a.m. - 5:00 p.m. (EST). E-mail address: docdelivery@haworthpress.com].

Journal of Human Behavior in the Social Environment, Vol. 8(2/3) 2003
http://www.haworthpress.com/web/JHBSE
© 2003 by The Haworth Press, Inc. All rights reserved.
Digital Object Identifier: 10.1300/J137v8n02_01

1

Homophobia broadly defined is characterized by dislike or hatred toward homosexuals, including both cultural and personal biases against homosexuals. Homophobia has dual facets and both need to be considered when working with homosexual clients, including both internalized homophobia, i.e., the internalization of society's antihomosexual sentiments within the psyche of gay and lesbian individuals, as well as external (generally heterosexual) homophobia. It can be measured on a continuum from mild anti-homosexual bias, through overt phobic avoidance of same sex socialization (Fyfe, 1983).

Social control theory suggests that external homophobia is not an isolated individual neurosis but a form of social control that serves psychologically and physically to intimidate sexual minorities and to validate heterosexuality as the only normal sexual identity choice (Radkowsky & Siegel, 1997). Rigid role definitions of gender underpin homophobia, as many heterosexuals believe homosexuality to be gender confusion. Another possible underpinning of homophobia may be misogyny, where society's detestation of gay male sexuality is linked to gays who 'act like a women,' thus abandoning the masculine privilege to which he is entitled, whereas the lesbian is seen as usurping male authority and privilege. The lesbian may be scorned for her behaviors and choices but she is likely to be more understood (Irvine, 1994).

Similarly, role theory suggests that feelings of homophobia are a result of undermining the sex-role stereotypes. A society demands that its members engage in upholding traditional belief systems by exhibiting behaviors concurrent with those teachings including role-modeling behaviors. Therefore, role erosion threatens the orderly spoken and unspoken rules of what is masculine and feminine creating anger in those who may believe there is potential for adolescent confusion and possibly social anarchy because of nonconforming gay behaviors. The belief that homosexuality is a choice helps to support this belief. Because men and women are socialized according to sex-role expectations their experiences that guide them in their life-course does not always follow the similar trajectories.

Homophobia is detrimental to both heterosexuals and homosexuals, and recent evidence suggests a direct relationship between male homophobia and lack of intimacy in heterosexual friendships among men (Devlin & Cowan, 1985). Adams, Wright, and Lohr (1996) found support for a long held belief that homophobia is associated with homosexual arousal, suggesting the homophobic individual is either unaware of, or denies the presence of same-sex erotic feelings. Thus, those who exhibit the most homophobic behaviors may have strong secret desires for same-sex erotic behaviors that are repressed; homophobic attitudes and behaviors arise as a result of reaction formation.

Recent research by Cullen, Wright and Alessandri (2002) suggests that homophobia is similar to traditional fears of ethnic minorities, in that lack of contact with homosexuals fosters significantly more homophobia. In addition, gender was associated with external homophobia as heterosexual men were more homophobic than women studied, but gender was not a predictor of the level of internalized homophobia.

Gay and lesbians also have some psychosocial predisposing factors common to ethnic minorities, and some unique to the homosexual population. In ethnic minorities is the damage done to self-image by the internalization of society's scorn (Erikson, 1959). Internalized homophobic fear has several implications regarding the lack of support for gay adolescents and young adults. Gay adolescents and young adults often need assistance negotiating the effects of personal and institutional homophobia on their identity development. In addition, homophobia may increase reliance upon the family, making it difficult to separate oneself from family sufficiently to develop healthy peer relationships at this life stage (Lock, 1998; Radkowsky & Siegel, 1997).

Gay teachers are often fearful of offering support because of concerns that they would be labeled unfit or worse; as perpetrators who are trying to recruit teenagers into the gay lifestyle. Schools are a primary source of information and socialization and an ideal environment to educate teenagers about homophobia and offer social support for gay youth, but most administrators and teachers are afraid to speak on the subject because of vehement criticism from conservative parents and community leaders who often believe any discussion of gay issues will somehow validate the topic and expand the number of gay adolescents and young adults.

HISTORICAL CONTEXT OF HOMOSEXUALITY

This historical overview concentrates primarily on male homosexuality within Western culture, and suggests society's attitude toward homosexuality has been conflicting across the ages. Various theories of homosexuality are derived from either an essentialist approach or a social constructionalist approach. Essentialism claims that homosexuality is a construct that is both ahistorical and acultural, a part of human civilization for all time; whereas constructionalism suggests homosexuality is defined more by temporal periods and the cultural context.

Halperin (1990) argued a social constructionalist paradigm, suggesting that sexuality is a matter of invention, and before this invention, sexual evaluation was determined by one's sexual acts, not their sexual orientation. However, before Victorian time people did not perceive homosexuality as a distinct identity, but rather thought of all sexuality within the framework of heterosexuality. Some cultures assumed that all persons harbored homoerotic feelings.

Often the active partner was not thought of as a homosexual, only the passive effeminate partner. A variation of this theme was true in Native American culture where the Beardache (gay Indians) were thought of as a third sex. It was acceptable for a man to have sex with a Beardache, but a taboo for a Beardache to have sex with each other (Mondimore, 1996).

These paradigms may both have validity to the extent that history points to both cultural influences as well as acknowledgement that homosexuality has been part of society for all of recorded time. Thirty years ago one author exploring sexuality offered insight on the subject by suggesting the following: "Our information about sexual [norm] deviance is, in the kindest possible judgment, less than adequate, and yet there is no subject about which there are stronger and noisier convictions or more energetic claims to final wisdom" (Kennedy, 1973, p. 129).

Many early accounts of homosexuality indicated that a permissive attitude with same-sex relationships existed in many cultures, and it was considered at least a transitional rite of passage for young men in early Greek and Roman societies. The Bible acquaints us with some of the earliest taboos on the subject from Old Testament tales such as Leviticus admonitions: "If a man also lie with mankind, as he lieth with a woman, both of them have committed an abomination: they shall surely be put to death; their blood shall be upon them" (Holy Bible, Lev. 20.13 KJV). Most sexuality scholars agree that the few references that the Bible makes about homosexuality have become the modern basis for homophobia as the majority of anti-homosexual and homophobic attitudes and behaviors are supported by the major premise that homosexuality is unholy and/or forbidden by the Bible (Sullivan & Wodarski, 2002).

The modern view is that sexual preferences are determinants of personal identity, but premodern societies did not think of sexual preference as a determining feature of identity. Little was written on the subject of homosexuality until the Victorian age when homosexuality became a criminal offense in many European and American societies. The idea of a deviant gay lifestyle arose in this historical context.

The term homosexual was coined in 1869, and before this homosexuality was not thought to be a separate orientation. This new sexual orientation identity began to emerge suggesting that an individual's sexual attraction toward persons of the same sex was an inherent and unchanging aspect of their personality. The word homosexual can mean many things dependent on the culture and temporal period. Some same-sex eroticism would not be classified as homosexual in some modern or Western societies. In fact, the hetero-homosexual binarism, the current sexual paradigm in American culture, is a relatively recent creation (Chauncey, 1995).

Many young people today believe the gay movement began with the Stonewall riot in 1969. In fact, many large cities had a notable gay presence before the turn of the century. For instance, gays in New York City had enclaves in several neighborhoods and many commercial establishments catered exclusively or predominately to gays as far back as 1890 (Chauncey, 1995). American gay life actually flourished in the 1920s in the large cities with a host of commercial establishments catering to gay lifestyles including speak-easies, restaurants, saloons, bathhouses, and neighborhood enclaves.

Most of the prewar history has been forgotten because of a societal backlash that began in prohibition and continued throughout the 1950s. Drag balls were canceled, plays and films were censored, and a host of laws and regulations were enacted prohibiting homosexuals from being served or even working in restaurants, bars, and clubs. In New York, it was illegal to serve known homosexuals liquor until 1970. Anti-gay policing intensified during the cold war, and Senator McCarthy insisted homosexuals were a threat to the U.S. State Department's security. Local police warned that homosexuals threatened the nation's children (Chauncey, 1995).

Two images most associated with gay male relationships up to this point in history were either that of the derogatory 'sissy' or the pathological assumption that gay men were child molesters. Gay males finally reacted to these images and a third pattern of same sex-relationships emerged, a new masculine erotic bond similar to 'buddy' relationships in the armed forces during World War II. This new identity was very different from the former man-boy and gender bending stereotypes of the past, as these men were masculine, consenting, and they easily passed as heterosexual. These men usually assimilated into larger society and often rejected their gay cultural roots. A class system began to emerge, and those most able to assimilate (pass) had high distinction, whereas others less masculine had lower status, and transvestites (drag queens) became the untouchable class scorned both within and outside of this gay culture.

After the war, some movements began to argue against the predominant pathological view of homosexuality. Kinsey's pioneering sexuality work began in the late 1930s for three decades. He ascribed the source of antihomosexual attitudes to Judeo-Christian traditions. This is supported by data suggesting the widely held belief that the more religiously devout harbored the most vehement homophobia (Klassen, Williams, & Levitt, 1989). Kinsey made no assumptions about what was normal but set out to discover what is the realm of human sexual behavior. His scientific findings that homosexuality is commonplace and that gay and lesbian persons are a significant proportion of the population met with criticism and disbelief.

Evelyn Hooker pioneered a study in the late fifties where she contrasted an experimental group of homosexuals with a heterosexual control matched on age, IQ, and education, on a battery of psychological tests. She then asked a panel of experts psychologists to rate the psychological health and predict who was gay versus straight. The adjustment ratings showed no significant differences; if anything, the gay men did better. In addition, the predictions of gayness were no better than chance. Kinsey and Hooker began to utilize empirical research as a foundation for our knowledge base about sexuality that others followed in debunking the myth that homosexuality was a mental illness (Mondimore, 1996). Hooker and Kinsey's empirical findings and conclusions provided some assistance in the movement to have homosexuality eliminated as a psychiatric disorder.

Until the early 1970s the American Psychiatric Association (APA) classified homosexuality as a disease, based on Freudian concepts of arrested sexual development that lead to a loveless life. Homosexuality was originally classified as a mental illness in the APA's *Diagnostic and Statistical Manual* (DSM). The classification was referred to as ego-dystonic homosexuality, or negative homosexual identity, characterized by guilt, shame, anxiety, and depression. The age of onset was thought to be adolescence, and one of the predisposing factors was the presence of anti-social attitudes (Nungesser, 1983). In December 1973, the APA ended the classification of homosexuality as a mental illness by removing it from the DSM.

Today a class system still exists based on the degree of the gay individual's ability to pass as heterosexual and assimilate into the broader culture. Many heterosexuals and those within the gay community still harbor resentment toward gender-bending identities. This class system has changed somewhat, as many gays are no longer as interested in assimilation. There has been the addition of transsexuals with surgical advances and a greater understanding of bisexuals as an identity rather than merely a transitional phase. Sadly, however, many heterosexuals still believe that homosexuals have natural tendencies toward pedophilia even though research clearly demonstrates heterosexual men comprise the vast majority of known pedophiles (Stevenson, 2002a; Stevenson, 2002b).

THEORIES OF CAUSATION

Theories abound to attempt explanatory causes of homosexuality. Many early theories suggested environmental causation with poor relations with parents as a central theme followed by beliefs that exposure to homosexuals might be an explaining factor. Newer biological theories attribute the expression of sexual orientation to genes that shape the central nervous system's development, organization, and structure via prenatal sex steroids (Huwiler & Remafedi, 1998). Brain chemistry and structure has recently been analyzed suggesting differences in homosexual men in one post-mortem study (Swaab, Chung, Kruijver, Hofman, & Ishunina, 2001). In addition, environmental factors may interact with biological and genetic factors for yet another theory of possible multiple causations with complex interactions.

The original environmental theory was suggested by Freud. He argued an environmental causation for male homosexuality, indicating poor parental relations (mother/son) as the central cause. Most psychoanalytic writers agree to a close connection between homosexuality and narcissism. Lewes (1988) documents that Freud had four theories on homosexuality during his lifetime. His early theories suggested homosexuality was derived from the Oedipus complex, i.e., the young male begins a normal erotic bond with his mother, but she displays excessive tenderness toward the boy and as a consequence he becomes obsessed with the importance of the penis. Another theory suggested the distinction between self and other has not been made by the child, so the child assumes the mother has identical anatomy, but during the narcissistic period the child realizes his separateness from the mother, and he realizes a castration threat might be a punishment for his erotic feelings and becomes obsessed with his penis. Another suggests that when the child discovers the mother is lacking a penis, he is horrified, and his love for the mother turns to loathing. From then on, he chooses a woman with a penis (an effeminate boy). His fourth and last theory was also another Oedipus complex variation that suggested homosexual boys develop an intense love for the mother followed by extreme jealousy for the father. This paternal jealousy is mobilized into death wishes and sadistic fantasies of violence. The child subsequently transforms these feelings through reaction formation into feelings of homosexual love (Lewes, 1988). Although Freud thought homosexuality was acceptable toward the end of his career, he struggled with the concept and considered homosexuality as a perversion at different times during his early career. His successors were mainly responsible for characterizing homosexuality as a perversion, needing professional intervention.

Historically, the medical community was one of the most powerful anti-gay social forces, taking an early stance that gays were, in fact, mentally ill and in need of treatment. Chauncey (1995) documents a quote from one doctor in the 1920s lamenting, [gays were] "Proud to be degenerates and do not want nor care to be cured . . . and it was this problem that made homosexuality so intractable" (p. 6). Beginning in the 1930s and increasingly after the war, sociological viewpoints continued to shape the belief that heterosexuality was the only natural and healthy result of psychosexual development. Homosexuality became defined as a perversion in which individuals suffer from primitive object relations, impaired ego function, and a defective superego.

Recently psychoanalytic theory of causation has been retired in favor of a competing environmental theory suggesting both overt and covert rejection by the father as the cause of homosexuality, with the mother simply filling the void as a defensive response to protect the child. Environmental theories hinge on the premise that homosexuality is an elective choice. This theory has been contested in recent years, and appears to be strongly associated with negative attitudes toward gay lifestyles. A recent finding suggests a correlational dichotomy where those who believe homosexuality is wrong generally believe homosexuality is an individual choice (environmental theory), versus those who believe homosexuality is normal and more often believe in a genetic or biological causation theory (Sullivan & Wodarski, 2002).

SOCIOLOGICAL INFLUENCES

Identity formation can be thought of as self-labeling. Humans have a strong desire to categorize and label themselves. Children are pressured into gender roles at a very young age, possibly beginning with a pink versus blue swaddling blanket. Several models of gay psychosocial development describe the initial stages of awareness and confusion about same-sex attractions, followed by acknowledgment of homosexuality, disclosure to others, and eventual integration of sexual identity into a comprehensive sense of identity. During adolescence, personal identity achievement is a central task for all youth, including gay youth, and is a period of increased risk taking. This often is the most vulnerable period in their lives, with many gay youth facing little support from either the family and/or social institutions (Sullivan & Wodarski, 2002). Social stigmatization hinders the ability of gay adolescents to achieve the tasks of adolescence. Because their sexual identity is denigrated by society, these youth have difficulty forming a positive identity and establishing healthy peer and intimate relationships. Family relations are often painful, and gay adolescents are susceptible to loneliness, isolation, depression, and suicide (Radkowsky & Siegel, 1997).

Most sexuality researchers believe that sexual preference is determined very early in life. If Kinsey's numbers were accurate, that would translate into 1 in 10 adolescents having strong same-sex feelings in high school. Gay and lesbian adolescents tend to be isolated in their family of origin. Most adolescents go through periods of rejecting their parents as an expression of individuality, knowing that their support will be unconditionally available to them when needed. Conversely, the parent sometimes rejects the gay adolescent, and permanent detachment can often materialize as a result of the adolescent's coming out.

Facing this external view of self, it is no wonder that the homosexual person internalizes this hatred and has difficulty with accepting his or her identity, building self-esteem, and expressing sexuality. About 65% of all homosexuals seek therapy and give depression as a reason, which is often a result of adjusting to their homosexuality; and of these, 50% started therapy between the ages of 18-21 (Diamond-Friedman, 1990).

These difficulties lead some gay adolescents to increase their consumption of alcohol and/or other drugs to aid in the coming-out process, or alleviate the anxiety or depression associated with concealing their identity or facing rejection from family and friends, discrimination in employment and housing, physical assault, arrest, or imprisonment. As far back as Colcher (1982), it was hypothesized that homosexuals use substances to dull the pain of feeling "different and alone," to reduce "sexual inhibitions" relating to internalized homophobia, and to reduce the stress of the keen competition for good-looking sexual partners. Nardi (1982) suggested that homosexuals are more at risk of drinking to the point of addiction because the gay lifestyle often revolves around gay bars, which have a history of permissiveness and protectiveness.

Our cumulative knowledge suggests both family support and religion contribute to self-esteem enhancement or self-depravation for those lacking these supports. Family support is perhaps the major influence on adolescents' self esteem. Gay youth often receive messages of worthlessness both overtly and covertly from their family. Often parents will detach themselves emotionally from their gay children early in childhood when they recognize that their child is different, particularly if non-gender conforming issues arise. If the parental bonding diminishes, the gay adolescent often withdraws or begins acting-out behaviors that can often lead to self-destructive behaviors.

CURRENT TRENDS

Attitudes toward homosexuals have changed favorably over time. Although general attitudes toward homosexuals are not a direct measure of homophobia, it represents a surrogate marker for intolerance, a known factor in homophobic attitudes. In a previous publication, an analysis of attitudes toward homosexuality using National Opinion Research Center's (NORC) General Social Survey (GSS) was performed. The dichotomized variable of homosexuality defined as either wrong or not wrong over the time period between 1973 and 1994 was analyzed. Findings indicated an increasing trend in the belief homosexuality was not wrong. The percentage believing homosexuality was not wrong increased from a low of 19% in 1973 to 31% by 1994, and with the exception of the late 1980s (when AIDS deaths were at a peak in the United States), the trend has been in the direction of increasing tolerance of homosexuality over time (Sullivan & Wodarski, 2002). The intent of this new analysis is to follow-up those trends and explores regional differences, as they exist currently.

Data from the GSS (Davis & Smith, 1992) were used again in a secondary analysis to determine current trends. The GSS utilized probability-sampling techniques and large sample sizes; the data set included the additional years of 1996 and 1998. In 1996 and 1998, the percentage of respondents stating 'homosexuality is not wrong' rose to 33% and 34%, respectively.

Regional differences are important to considerations when studying these attitudes as attitudes can vary widely throughout our nation and across other countries. For this analysis, the United States was separated into five regions, and each region was compared to others on the attitude toward homosexuals by region over time, using the cumulative data set. The chi-square statistic indicated regional variations were highly significant ϕ^2 (5, N = 27,763) = 503.98, p = .000. The Southeastern and Mid-south regions tended to have significantly less tolerant attitudes toward homosexuals. Figure 1 illustrates this relationship graphically.

This same analysis was then performed for 1998, the latest year available for analysis. The chi-square statistic indicated regional differences were highly significant, ϕ^2 (5, N = 1,874) = 67.36, p = .000. Figure 2 illustrates this relationship graphically. In all cases, when gender was controlled, females were more tolerant than males.

DISCUSSION AND CONCLUSIONS

In the last few decades, large strides have been made in securing social acceptance of homosexuals. The data presented demonstrate the slow but increasing tolerance toward homosexuals in our society. There still exists strong regional differences, especially in the Bible belt areas, where the attitude lags behind those of the other regions. The Atlantic and Pacific coasts are the areas most tolerant of gays and lesbians. Religious and political influences appear to mediate attitudes in this area as well as geography.

Many liberal churches have made outreach efforts through an all inclusive welcoming mission statement, including the Protestant "More Light" congregations, Unitarian and Universalist churches, and some liberal urban Catholic congregations. Parents, Families, and Friends of Lesbians and Gays (PFLAG) is an organization for parents of gay and lesbian children, which assists parents in acceptance and affirmation of their gay children. Many more books are

FIGURE 1. Cumulative Attitudes Toward Same Sex Relations by Region

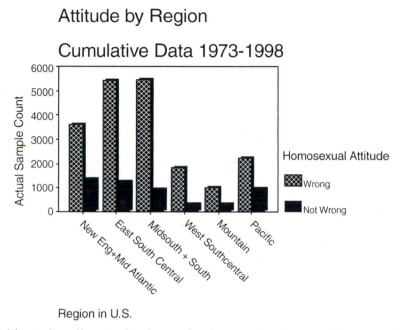

Attitude by Region
Cumulative Data 1973-1998

Region in U.S.

available, and media attention has assisted many Americans with a more objective view of gay culture. Support groups are available nationally at many colleges and in gay and lesbian outreach centers in metro areas, to assist those coming out and struggling to accept themselves. Recent media coverage involving two cruel gay-related murders has rallied support for new hate crime legislation. Vermont was the first state to legalize same-sex marriage, and many public and private organizations are beginning to offer benefits to unmarried domestic partners regardless of sexual orientation.

Pathology is often defined by an emotional problem's impact on an individual's ability to function, causing an impaired state; in this regard the question of whether homophobia should be considered a diagnosis when functioning is impaired will need to be considered by the American Psychological Association in future revised editions of the *Diagnostic and Statistical Manual* (DSM-IV).

Although it is still true that most persons find it difficult to maintain an open and unprejudiced attitude toward gay persons, there is both increasing tolerance for gays and lesbians and a slow increasing understanding of sexual diversity in our culture. Perhaps in a few short decades, the majority opinion will be in favor of accepting sexual minorities and an understanding that gay, lesbian,

FIGURE 2. Attitudes Toward Same Sex Relations in 1998 by Region

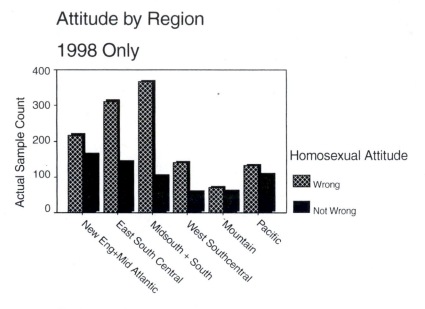

Attitude by Region
1998 Only

Region in U.S.

transgendered, and transsexual persons are equally capable and equally deserving of societal respect and support. Until that time, it will take many pioneers to pave this road of social tolerance and respect.

REFERENCES

Adams, H. E., Wright, L. W., Jr., & Lohr, B. A. (1996). Is homophobia associated with homosexual arousal? *Journal of Abnormal Psychology, 105*(3), 440-445.

American Psychiatric Association (1994). *Diagnostic and Statistical Manual of Mental Disorders* (4th ed.). Washington, DC: American Psychiatric Association.

Chauncey, G. (1995). *Gay New York: The Making of the Gay Male World 1890-1940.* London, England: Flamingo.

Colcher, R.W. (1982). Counseling the homosexual alcoholic. *Journal of Homosexuality, 7*(4), 43.

Cullen, J. M., Wright, L. W., Jr., & Alessandri, M. (2002). The personality variable openness to experience as it relates to homophobia. *Journal of Homosexuality, 42*(4), 119-134.

Davis, J. A., & Smith, T. W. (1992). *The NORC general social survey : A user's guide.* Newbury Park, CA: Sage Publications.

Devlin, P. K., & Cowan, G. A. (1985). Homophobia, perceived fathering, and male intimate relationships. *Journal of Personality Assessment, 49*(5), 467-473.

Diamond-Friedman, C. (1990). A multivariant model of alcoholism specific to gay-lesbian populations. *Alcoholism Treatment Quarterly, 7*(2), 111.

Erikson, E. (1959). *Identity and the Life Cycle.* New York: Norton, 30. Quoted from Greene, R. & Ephross, P. (1991). *Human Behavior Theory and Social Work Practice.* New York: Aldine de Gruyter, 97.

Fyfe, B. (1983). "Homophobia" or homosexual bias reconsidered. *Archives Sex Behavior, 12*(6), 549-554.

Halperin, D. (1990). *One Hundred Years of Homosexuality.* New York: Routledge, Chapman and Hall.

Halwani, R. (1998). Essentialism, Social Constructionism, and the History of Homosexuality. *Journal of Homosexuality, 35*(1), 25-51.

Holy Bible. King James version. [http://bible.gospelcom.net/cgi-bin/bible?language=english&passage=leviticus+20%3A13&version=KJV] Accessed 2 February 2003.

Huwiler, S. M., & Remafedi, G. (1998). Adolescent homosexuality [In Process Citation]. *Advanced Pediatrics, 45,* 107-144.

Kennedy, E. (1973). *The New Sexuality.* New York: Doubleday.

Klassen, A., Williams, C., & Levitt, E. (1989). *Sex and morality in the U.S.* Middletown: Wesleyan University Press.

Lewes, K. (1988). *The Psychoanalytic Theory of Male Homosexuality* (1st ed.). New York: Simon and Schuster.

Lock, J., & Kleis, B. (1998). Origins of homophobia in males. Psychosexual vulnerabilities and defense development. *American Journal of Psychotherapy, 52*(4), 425-436.

Mondimore, F. (1996). *A natural history of homosexuality.* Baltimore: John Hopkins University Press.

Nardi, P. N. (1982). Alcoholism and homosexuality: A theoretical perspective. *Journal of Homosexuality, 7*(4), 9.

Nungesser, L. G. (1983). *Homosexual acts, actors, and identities.* New York: Praeger.

Radkowsky, M., & Siegel, L. J. (1997). The gay adolescent: Stressors, adaptations, and psychosocial interventions. *Clinical Psychology Review, 17*(2), 191-216.

Stevenson, M. R. (2000a). Conceptualizing diversity in sexuality research. In M. W. Wiederman, & B. E. Whitley, Jr. (Eds.), *Handbook for Conducting Research on Human Sexuality.* Mahwah, NJ: Erlbaum.

Stevenson, M. R. (2000). Public policy, homosexuality, and the sexual coercion of children. *Journal of Psychology and Human Sexuality, 12*(4), 1-19.

Sullivan & Wodarski. (2002). Social alienation in gay youth. *Journal of Human Behavior in the Social Environment, 5*(1), 1-17.

Swaab, D. F., Chung, W.C., Kruijver, F. P., Hofman, M. A., & Ishunina, T. A. (2001). Structural and functional sex differences in the human hypothalamus. *Hormonal Behavior, 40*(2), 93-98.

Williams, W. (1992). The Spirit and the flesh: Sexual diversity in American Indian culture. Boston: Beacon Press.

Being Heard on Sexual Orientation:
An Analysis of Testimonies at Public Hearings
on an Anti-Discrimination Bill

Geoffrey L. Greif
Daphne L. McClellan

SUMMARY. In 2001, Maryland became the twelfth state to pass legislation that prohibits discrimination against gays, lesbians, and bi-sexuals in employment, housing, and public accommodations. As part of a ten-year effort to pass such protections, the Governor of Maryland established a Commission to Study Sexual Orientation Discrimination. The Commission held five public hearings throughout the state in 2000 and used the testimonies to prepare a report which helped pave the way for the passage of the legislation. This article is an analysis of 113 oral testimonies, both for and against the legislation. Such information may be helpful in other states where anti-discrimination efforts are on-going.

Geoffrey L. Greif, DSW, LCSW-C, is Associate Dean and Professor, University of Maryland Baltimore, School of Social Work, 525 West Redwood Street, Baltimore, MD 21201 (E-mail: ggreif@ssw.umaryland.edu).

Daphne L. McClellan, PhD, is Assistant Professor, Department of Social Work, University of Maryland Baltimore County.

Address correspondence to: Geoffrey L. Greif, 525 West Redwood Street, Baltimore, MD 21201.

[Haworth co-indexing entry note]: "Being Heard on Sexal Orientation: An Analysis of Testimonies at Public Hearings on an Anti-Discrimination Bill." Greif, Geoffrey L., and Daphne L. McClellan. Co-published simultaneously in *Journal of Human Behavior in the Social Environment* (The Haworth Social Work Practice Press, an imprint of The Haworth Press, Inc.) Vol. 8, No. 2/3, 2003, pp. 15-27; and: *Sexual Minorities: Discrimination, Challenges, and Development in America* (ed: Michael K. Sullivan) The Haworth Social Work Practice Press, an imprint of The Haworth Press, Inc., 2003, pp. 15-27. Single or multiple copies of this article are available for a fee from The Haworth Document Delivery Service [1-800-HAWORTH, 9:00 a.m. - 5:00 p.m. (EST). E-mail address: docdelivery@haworthpress.com].

Journal of Human Behavior in the Social Environment, Vol. 8(2/3) 2003
http://www.haworthpress.com/web/JHBSE
Digital Object Identifier: 10.1300/J137v8n02_02

KEYWORDS. Sexual orientation discrimination, gays, lesbians, bi-sexuals, sexual orientation legislation

When public hearings are held on possible legislation that would ban sexual orientation discrimination in state law, what is the content of the testimony provided by proponents and opponents? What does the testimony tell us about the situation of lesbians, gay men, bi-sexuals, and trans-gendered people (LGBT) and what they encounter in their daily lives? In the fall of 2000, Governor Parris Glendening issued an Executive Order establishing the Special Commission to Study Sexual Orientation Discrimination in Maryland (Executive Order, 2000). The purpose of the Commission was, in part, to examine laws in relation to employment, housing, and public accommodations, gather information, and develop recommendations to eliminate discrimination in those three areas. Five public hearings were held throughout Maryland as part of the information gathering process. The purpose of this article is to describe and analyze the nature of the oral testimony that was received.

The content of these hearings is instructive to social workers for a number of reasons. As other states consider the process of changing anti-discrimination laws, this information may be helpful in anticipating the kind of testimony that will be heard. Social workers and social work students are often key advocates in such civil rights advocacy and legislation. Public testimonies describe both the experiences of the LGBT population as well as the reactions of people who are opposed to legislation and, often by association, are opposed to a homosexual lifestyle. For practitioners working with LGBT clients, knowing the types of experiences these clients may have had may be helpful in understanding the context of their situations. In addition, for those working with people opposed to such legislation, some of whom may be homophobic, having a clearer understanding of their beliefs can be helpful with any issues for which they are seeking assistance.

THE CONTEXT OF ANTI-DISCRIMINATION LAWS AND PUBLIC HEARINGS

No federal law exists that protects citizens from being discriminated against on the basis of sexual orientation. At the time of the initial Executive Order, eleven states (California, Connecticut, Hawaii, Massachusetts, Minnesota, Nevada, New Hampshire, New Jersey, Rhode Island, Vermont, and Wisconsin) and the District of Columbia had passed state laws forbidding discrimination. In Maryland (and as is true in some other states) four local jurisdictions had passed laws prohibiting sexual orientation discrimination. Within these four jurisdictions, 48.5% of the population of Maryland reside. Thus there is protection in some parts of Maryland, but not in all of Maryland.

Attempts to pass a state law had met with partial success in the past. A bill was passed by the House of Delegates in Maryland in 1999 but was held in the Senate's Judicial Proceedings Committee and never came to the floor of the Senate for a vote. A majority of the members of the Committee were opposed to the bill. In 2000, the bill was held again in that Committee. By the fall of 2000, the Governor, working in tandem with activist groups, committed himself once again to passing an anti-discrimination bill and established the Commission. His brother, who was gay, had died of AIDS after serving in the armed forces and living in "the closet" his whole life. The Governor publicly declared that passage of the bill was a top legislative and personal priority.

When the Governor established the Commission, he appointed 23 members that included the Secretary of Health and Mental Hygiene, the Secretary of Housing, the Director of the Human Relations Commission, and a representative from the Attorney General's Office. He asked the Speaker of the House and the President of the Senate to appoint two legislators each who would serve. He also enlisted the aid of 15 private citizens drawn from the business, religious, and educational communities, and the gay and lesbian community. Attempts to get members of those communities (business and religious in particular) who were opposed to the bill to serve so that there would be balance on the Commission failed.

Hearings were advertised in local newspapers, libraries, community centers, and on the Governor's web-site. Newspaper articles appeared after each hearing occurred which alerted Marylanders to the public hearings as well as future hearings. Those who attended hearings could testify for three to four minutes and submit written testimony and any other supporting material they wished. As time allowed, Commissioners asked questions following individual testimonies. Those who could not attend a hearing were also invited to submit written testimony. As there was no limit on written testimony, some citizens submitted reams of information. This information often focused on providing the Commissioners with research from public interest groups and lobbying interests both for and against passage of a gay rights bill, national opinion polls about feelings towards gay men and lesbians, and religious treatises with biblical references concerning the immorality of homosexuality. Anonymous testimony was accepted as it was recognized some people who were the potential targets of discrimination might feel unsafe revealing their identity in public if they were "in the closet."

Activist groups both for and against the potential legislation organized their constituents to attend and speak at the public hearings. To a large extent, these activists were fulfilling a role often played by the social worker–as community organizer and builder (Itzhaky & York, 2002). Several individuals spoke at more than one hearing. Public hearings held by standing committees or ad hoc commissions have long been a method of gauging public sentiment on pressing issues from civil rights, to gun laws, to highway construction. As Hardcastle, Wenocur, and Powers wrote, "A public hearing epitomizes a situation where we typically face myriad desires, preferences, and perceived needs . . . After allowing interest groups to speak and make proposals at the hearing, a social worker must integrate this oral input with studies" (1997, p. 185).

Shortly after the hearings were completed, the Commission presented the Governor with an interim report which was to be used to guide legislation in the Spring 2001 legislative sessions. That interim report summarized the testimony and included quotes from both the proponents and opponents. It also contained attachments that were germane to the anti-discrimination bill. This included a report from the Government Accounting Office (GAO, 2000) that studied the impact on employers in other states where anti-discrimination bills have been passed. The Commission's Interim Report made one recommendation–that the same bill that passed the House in 1999 be resubmitted. This would amend Law 49B and add the words "sexual orientation" to race, religion, creed, sex, age, color, familial status, national origin, marital status, and physical or mental disability as protected classes.

In 2001, the resubmitted bill came to the Senate Committee a third time. The composition of the Committee had changed since the previous year and, after public testimony and lengthy debate, the bill passed and was ultimately approved by the legislature. Maryland became the twelfth state to pass an anti-discrimination bill that included protection for lesbians, gay men, and bi-sexuals (trans-sexuals were not mentioned in the bill).

Discrimination

The discrimination experienced by lesbian, gay, bi-sexual, and transgendered adults and youth in society is well-documented. Not only is it encountered in employment, housing, and public accommodations (the foci of the legislation in Maryland), it is also encountered in education, partnership benefits, court, prisons, and other areas where society and individuals intersect (see, e.g., Kulkin, Chauvin, & Percle, 2000, for an example of the toll discrimination can exact on youth, and Bepko & Johnson, 2000, for the toll on adult relationships). Some level of discrimination against homosexuals can exist even in a state that is considered one of the most liberal in the nation. A 2000 survey of Maryland residents indicated that while 60% favored a ban on discrimination against gay men and lesbians, 32% were opposed to such a ban (Waldron & Libit, 2000).

While homophobia is one reason people discriminate against homosexuals (Theodore & Basow, 2000), religious beliefs are also often at the root of discrimination (Hoffman, Hevesi, Lynch et al., 2000.) In a circular manner, beliefs drive legislation which, in turn, can affect the climate for homosexuals. According to Fassinger (1991), "The current legal status of gay people in the United States is largely dependent on local and state statutes, varying according to geographic location and the whims of employers, public officials, and the lower courts" (p. 161). Beliefs may also affect who gets elected. Herrick and Thomas (2001) asked research subjects to respond to hypothetical candidates for a non-partisan city council race. Candidates who were "out" as lesbian or gay were less apt to get elected.

Despite such circumstances, the situations of gay men and lesbians have improved in the workforce as well as generally. An increasing number of companies have non-discrimination policies and offer partner benefits (Human Rights Campaign Foundation, 2000). In addition, an increasing number of Americans oppose discrimination against gay men and lesbians in the workplace (Human Rights Campaign Foundation, 2000). Public opinion is also more favorable in housing and in approval of homosexual practices (Yang, 2000).

Clinical work is affected by what happens politically. A positive "climate" in a state or a significant political event can benefit those struggling with acceptance. Davidson (1995), a therapist specializing in LGBT issues, describes how the 1993 Gay Rights March on Washington aided both lesbian attendees and non-attendees in their own evolutions. She writes, "The impact of the march . . . propelled ambivalent clients into seeking psychotherapy . . . Political action and media coverage force a multitude of issues to the forefront" (Davidson, 1995:48-49). People struggling with their identities may be heartened by marching with or reading about others. The impact of the passage of the 2001 bill on Maryland's LGBT community as well as its straight community cannot be evaluated at this point. Anecdotally, though, gay men and lesbians are reporting less fear in their own lives.

METHODOLOGY

Our analysis is limited to the 113 testimonies from people who spoke at the five public hearings. Written testimonies which came to the Commission over a number of months are not included and are unlikely to be read by anyone other than a Commissioner. (They are available as part of the public record.)

These oral testimonies provide a picture of the atmosphere of the hearings which submitted written testimonies do not. We believe using oral testimony is especially important when considering that hearings on this topic were seminal events for some of the regions of the state where gay and lesbian issues were rarely discussed in an open forum.

The 113 testimonies were compiled from two sources: summaries written by a representative of the Governor's Office for use by the Commission and written testimonies that accompanied the oral testimonies. (Slightly more than half of the speakers submitted written testimonies.) In a few cases, the Governor's representative did not record the testimony, and we have relied on the written testimonies submitted by the oral presenters. In the cases where both the representative's summaries and written testimonies were available, the authors relied on the representative's summaries as more accurately reflecting the atmosphere of the hearings.

This follows Padgett's (1998) description of the method for analyzing documents and existing data to draw conclusions about a population or an event. She writes, "The least intrusive type of data, documents can provide valuable information on the lives of individuals, on the history of an important social agency or institution, or even on broad social trends" (p. 67). Once the data set was established, each author independently performed a content analysis of the data looking for common themes and then together formulated categories for the testimonies. Padgett (1998) also notes that direct observation is key in understanding phenomenon. At least one of the authors was present at all the hearings, and the other attended some of the hearings. Direct quotes are used from the testimonies to highlight the categories.

One weakness of the methodology is the reliance on a summary of the written testimony by the Governor's representative. A comparison of her summaries with the actual written testimonies shows that her summaries are highly reflective of the testimony presented. That leads us to conclude that people who only testified orally and did not turn in written testimony were accurately characterized by the representative. In addition, the first author chaired the Commission and verified that the content of the summaries coincided with his recollection of the testimonies.

Another weakness can be the nature of the sample. Public hearings tend to draw the most interested and most willing to speak in public. Members of advocacy groups (often part of listserve groups), both for and against an anti-discrimination bill, were most apt to testify. This tends to make the testimony skewed about discrimination. Many gay men and lesbians may have been unwilling to speak publicly or even to write confidentially for fear of retribution. In addition, many opponents may not have strong enough objections to a proposed bill to travel to where the hearings were being held. Finally, as at any public hearing, there is no independent verification of what is said. A speaker could claim he or she had been fired or that all people were treated equally at a job without substantiating evidence being presented. Yet, the sample is exactly representative of the kind of people who appear at hearings. In this way, their testimonies can help future advocates prepare.

FINDINGS

Of the 113 oral testimonies, 87 were in favor of passage of the proposed bill and 26 were opposed. Some people testified at more than one hearing. Analysis of the 87 oral testimonies in favor of the bill (proponents) can be classified into three groups: (1) those speaking on behalf of themselves or others about being the target of discrimination; (2) those speaking on behalf of organizations (e.g., unions, large employers, religious groups); and (3) those offering information and legal opinions about the impact of the law in other states and the implementation of the law in Maryland. The personal stories (the first group) fell into four general categories: employment discrimination (the most prevalent), housing discrimination, public accommodations discrimination (including schools), and victimization akin to hate crimes.

The testimonies in opposition fell into two primary groups: (1) those believing homosexuality is immoral and invoking religious teachings for their beliefs (the most common) and (2) those arguing legal protection of LGBT will open up a floodgate of litigation. Those opposed to the bill because they believe homosexuality is immoral made four arguments: it is against the teaching of the Bible, it is a behavior, not an orientation; it will lead to pedophilia; and it will lead to same sex marriage. Related to these arguments was the belief that gay men and lesbians should not be afforded the same type of special protections that people receive on the basis of race, religion, and disability.

Proponents' Testimony

The majority of those testifying related personal stories or the personal stories of others who had experienced discrimination. The most common complaint dealt with employment discrimination. Those testifying discussed fearing that someone at work would discover they were gay, and they would lose their job. For a number of those testifying, this had happened. They had been "let go" because their employers thought "they would be happier somewhere else." One man, who had achieved partner in his law firm, was told it was time to "move-on, no one here wants to work with a faggot." Others believed they had been hired at lower salaries or had not received raises because they were gay. Several people testified about the lack of domestic partner benefits, which in effect meant that they worked for less compensation than work colleagues with legally recognized spouses. Some had lost jobs that were very meaningful to them as well as financially successful. Others remained on the job but were consumed with fear about what would happen if someone found out they were not heterosexual. The net effect for those in this category was that their work lives were seriously compromised.

The second most numerous group of proponents were those who stated that they and/or the organization they represented thought that the bill was a good idea. Some of these speakers were gay or lesbian themselves or represented LGBT organizations. Others were heterosexual and wanted to go on record as being supportive. This group included a union representative, a speaker from the ACLU, a local mayor, and a number of parents of LGBT persons. One minister of a Baltimore church with almost 40 members who were "out" talked of his parishioners' fears, "As long as discrimination is legal, the fear of it is also hurtful. Some members of my congregation feel they must remain 'in the closet' except in church. They live dual lives, in fear that if their employers discover they are gay, they will lose their jobs."

One woman, who identified herself as a heterosexual psychologist with gay friends, family, and clients, presented herself as an expert and testified that in the past ten years public opinion toward gays had changed, and a majority now favor protecting homosexuals from discrimination and abuse. She stated that scientific research concludes that laws to prevent discrimination against lesbians and gay men can reduce prejudice. She further stated that empirical research consistently demonstrates that having personal contact with an openly gay person is one of the most powerful influences on heterosexuals' tolerance and acceptance of gay people. Anti-gay attitudes are significantly less common among the one-third of the population who has a friend, relative, or acquaintance who is known by the person to be gay, she said. Of all the types of prejudice studied, interaction with homosexuals produced the greatest reductions in prejudice. Passing the anti-discrimination bill in Maryland, she concluded, could significantly reduce the discrimination and prejudice against lesbians and gay men, and this could improve the psychological, economic, and social lives of lesbians and gay men. Another proponent expressed her belief that fear was the basic problem of opponents. Objections to renting to or employing someone whose sexuality is different from one's own may be explained as based on religion or morals or lifestyle differences, she said, though ultimately the root cause is fear of someone different from oneself.

Some supporters merely requested "a level playing field." In the second group of proponents, those speaking on behalf of organizations, many of the individuals pointed out benefits they thought would accrue if nondiscrimination legislation were to become law. The representative from the local Service Employees International Union stated that though they changed their by-laws in 1996 to prohibit discrimination on the basis of sexual orientation, "standing with gay, lesbian, and bisexual employees has not dissuaded workers from joining our union." He further stated that discrimination protections, including those for sexual orientation in collective bargaining agreements, reduce the potential for arbitrary acts and provide employees with a greater sense of job security.

One business owner stated that he had adopted a non-discrimination policy for his business and that such a policy "fosters a work environment in which all employees focus not on their co-workers' sexual orientation, but on productivity and the bottom line." He felt that the proposed legislation would benefit the small business community by "removing arbitrary barriers to employment." Building on this testimony, another man advocated for the proposed policy stating that it would be good for economic development in the state. Non-discrimination legislation is an important factor in creating a climate where diversity is respected and celebrated, and consequently, where high-tech industries thrive, he said. If the State of Maryland wishes to provide a hospitable environment for this sector of the economy, it should provide legal protections for sexual minorities, he stated. Finally a faculty physician with the University of Maryland School of Medicine advocated for domestic partner benefits, stating that "providing domestic partner benefits is an inexpensive way to make the institution more competitive by having a positive impact on recruiting and retaining employees."

The third group testifying in favor of the proposed legislation offered information and legal opinions about the impact of the law in other states and the implementation of the law in Maryland (which sometimes overlapped with the second group). The managing attorney of the ACLU of Maryland testified that though four jurisdictions in Maryland currently prohibit discrimination on the basis of sexual orientation, there have been few complaints filed. He felt, though, that statewide protection is still needed because the majority of complaints come from parts of the state where there are no protections against sexual orientation discrimination. Some businesses in jurisdictions without such protections may currently feel free to discriminate on that basis. If a statewide statute were adopted, the vast majority of the businesses in Maryland would choose to comply with the law, just as the vast majority of businesses in Baltimore, Montgomery County, Prince George's County, and Howard County now follow the law, he believed.

A representative from Johns Hopkins University (JHU) spoke against the belief that passing non-discrimination legislation would "open the floodgates" to claims and expensive litigation. He stated that JHU (with 8,400 employees) has had a nondiscrimination policy in relation to sexual orientation in place since 1988, and there have been no claims on that basis filed in the last twelve years.

Opponents' Testimony

By far the most common opposition to the nondiscrimination legislation came from people who believe that homosexuality is immoral and invoked their religious beliefs to support their position. A representative of the Roman Catholic Diocese of Wilmington testified, "The teaching of the Catholic Church and societal tradition does not accept homosexuality as a legitimate lifestyle. The sexual act should be reserved for the union of a man and woman within the context of marriage." An individual, testifying on his own behalf, stated that he is a born again Christian and small business owner. He believes that, "Special rights' should not be given to people who are breaking the law (committing sodomy). God's law is supreme and God's law says it is a sin." Another individual testified, "We are in battle for the moral welfare of our children." One man who self-identified as a pastor and a father stated that, "When one makes a decision which is rejected by the community that person must accept the consequences. Persecution is self-inflicted."

Another representative of the Catholic Church who spoke to his belief that homosexuality is a behavior and not an orientation said, "My testimony concerns . . . a definition of 'homosexual orientation' that does not make expressly clear that orientation does not mean (and cannot fairly be interpreted as embracing) genital/sexual conduct. We believe that legislation to extend civil rights protections to persons whose orientation is homosexual must differentiate between the two, and make clear that its protections do not extend to conduct."

Among the opponents in the "homosexuality is immoral" group, there was a great deal of concern about pedophilia. Various speakers stated that if this legislation were approved it would open the door to legalizing all kinds of perverted acts including sex with children and animals. One opponent stated, "I'm not saying that all homosexuals are pedophiles, because there is certainly a fair share of heterosexual pedophiles too. What I am saying is that when we as a society start legitimizing sexual behaviors outside the normal, human beings will not be able to control or know the limits on their sexual behaviors and desires."

Others who opposed the anti-discrimination bill cited concerns that this legislation would "open the floodgates of litigation" (the second category) and add to health care costs due to the likely spread of HIV/AIDS that would occur as a result of giving gay men special protection. (Fears about the expense of litigation were also raised by legislators who opposed the bill.)

There was no evidence that during the hearings any of the proponents or opponents of the legislation convinced the other to change their way of thinking.

Most speakers were firmly entrenched in their views. But one minister did offer some hope from his perspective as a proponent when he said, "Injustices occur daily. Ultimately, a cure for them will be a change in the human heart–changes that will come about when all men and women learn that all of God's children are people of worth and value." It was, most tellingly, the change of heart of one legislator who sat on the Senate Committee, a former opponent that helped bring the bill to the Senate floor for eventual passage. The Commission's Interim Report and the proponents' advocacy may have swayed him.

IMPLICATIONS FOR SOCIAL WORK PRACTICE

Maryland is the twelfth state to include sexual orientation in its nondiscrimination statutes. This issue may arise in the near future in some of the other thirty-eight states. For members of the social work profession, the implications are clear. The social work profession has taken a strong stand on this issue.

> It is the position of NASW that same-gender sexual orientation should be afforded the same respect and rights as other-gender orientation. Discrimination and prejudice directed against any group are damaging to the social, emotional, and economic well-being of the affected group and of society as a whole. NASW is committed to advancing policies and practices that will improve the status and well-being of all lesbian, gay, and bisexual people . . . NASW is committed to working toward the elimination of prejudice and discrimination both inside and outside the profession. (Beebe, 1997)

Nondiscrimination laws are a step toward achieving the improved status and well-being of lesbians, gay men, and bisexual people. Achieving the passage of such legislation around the country may be approached in a variety of ways. Sometimes the approach is quiet and unobtrusive. In such cases, the best way for social workers to be supportive might be a simple letter, e-mail message or telephone call to one's legislators. But other times, as in the case of Maryland, quiet activism was not sufficient. Legislators and others needed to see the faces and hear the stories of those who have been discriminated against as well as those who are opposed to anti-discrimination legislation. The Commission's Interim Report helped put facts to paper and bring stories to the legislators. Various forms of nondiscrimination legislation came before the General Assembly of Maryland over a period of ten years before the anti-discrimination bill was finally passed in Spring, 2001 (though a referendum put its implementation on hold until November 21, 2001).

In other states social workers may need to consider advocating, as happened in Maryland, for a special commission to study sexual orientation discrimination. Such an approach puts discrimination into a context that legislators may be accustomed to. It is harder to ignore information presented in this format.

Proponents should anticipate the arguments against the legislation that were heard in Maryland. In the realm of human behavior, these arguments against passage are not atypical. Well-organized opponents share information nationally just as well-organized proponents do. Proponents should be wary of engaging in a debate about sexual orientation versus sexual behavior, i.e., whether someone can be homosexual but choose not to engage in homosexual behaviors. As a few proponents of the Maryland bill have stated, when asked about this, "Discrimination is discrimination." Proponents should also carefully consider how wide- ranging a bill to try and pass as a first step. The experience in Maryland was that a very narrowly defined bill had the best chance of passage. Had the bill advocated, for example, for protection for trans-gendered people, it is highly doubtful it would have passed. At the time the bill was passed in Maryland, the four local jurisdictions where there was protection for gay men, lesbians, and bi-sexuals, did not include protections for trans-gendered people.

The discrimination that some of those who testified have encountered should alert clinicians as to what their homosexual clients may experience. While discrimination is not universal, according to some of the testimony, it does exist. Clinicians should support clients that are on the receiving end of discrimination, attempt to normalize their reactions to it, and discuss with them ways of coping with it. An awareness of the legal rights of employees, in particular (as well as housing and public accommodations) can affect the actions the victim of discrimination may wish to pursue.

CONCLUSIONS

Social workers need to speak out about their opposition to discrimination. Clinicians should be open to hearing about discrimination their clients have experienced and be willing to explore such issues in-depth. Social work faculty members, when teaching about oppression (as is required by the Council on Social Work Education), need to connect their lectures to current examples of discrimination in their communities and states. Thirty-eight states in 2002 did not have specific statewide statutes protecting lesbians, gays, and bi-sexuals on the basis of their sexual orientation. This fact can be used to inform education. In addition, individuals should be prepared to attend public forums and speak up on behalf of themselves, their clients and the profession; that is part of the advocacy role that makes social work different from other professions. It is also part of the policy-practice continuum that underpins social change (Pearlmutter, 2002). Being present at hearings as either a supportive audience member or a speaker imparts the message that this is an important issue and one that citizens care about.

REFERENCES

Beebe, L. 1997. *Social Work Speaks*. Washington, DC: NASW Press.

Bepko, C., & Johnson, T. 2000. Gay and lesbian couples in therapy: Perspectives for the contemporary therapist. *Journal of Marriage & the Family, 26*, 409-420.

Davidson, N. S. 1995. Psychotherapy with women and political action. *Journal of Gay & Lesbian Psychotherapy, 2*(3), 39-50.

Executive Order. 2000. State of Maryland: 01.01.2000.22.

Fassinger, P. 1991. The hidden minority: Issues and challenges in working with lesbian women and gay men. *The Counseling Psychologist, 19*, 157-176.

Government Accounting Office. 2000. Sexual-Orientation-Based Employment Discrimination: States' Experience With Statutory Prohibitions Since 1997, a report prepared for The Honorable James M. Jeffords Chairman, Committee on Health, Education, Labor and Pensions, United States Senate.

Hardcastle, D., Wenocur, S., & Powers, P. 1997. *Community Practice: Theories and skills for social workers*. New York: Oxford University Press.

Herrick, R., & Thomas, S. 2001. "Gays and lesbians in local races: A study of electoral viability," *Journal of Homosexuality, 42*, 103-126.

Hoffman, L. G., Hevesi, A. G., Gomes, P. J., Chodorow, N. J., Roughton, R. E., Frank, B., & Vaughan, S. 2000. "Homophobia: Analysis of a 'permissible' prejudice: A public forum of the American Psychoanalytic Association and the American Psychoanalytic Foundation," *Journal of Gay & Lesbian Psychotherapy, 4*, 5-53.

Human Rights Campaign Foundation. 2000. *The State of the Workplace for Lesbian, Gay, Bisexual, and Transgendered Americans*. Washington, DC: Human Rights Campaign.

Itzhaky, H., & York, A. S. 2002. Showing result in community organization. *Social Work, 47*, 125-131.

Kulkin, H. S., Chauvin, E. A., & Percle, G. A. 2000. "Suicide among gay and lesbian adolescents and young adults: A review of the literature," *Journal of Homosexuality, 40*, 1-29.

Padgett, D. K. 1998. *Qualitative methods in social work research: Challenges and rewards*. Thousand Oaks, CA: Sage Publications.

Pearlmutter, S. 2002. "Achieving political practice: Integrating individual need and social action," *Journal of Progressive Human Services, 13*, 31-51.

Theodore, P. S., & Basow, S. A. 2000. Heterosexual masculinity and homophobia: A reaction to the self? *Journal of Homosexuality, 40*, 31-48.

Waldron, T. W., & Libit, H. 2001. Answers put state among progressives. *The Baltimore Sun*, January 10, pp. A1 & A14.

Yang, A. 2000. *From wrongs to rights: 1973 to 1999. Public opinion on gay and lesbian Americans moves toward equality*. Washington, DC: The Policy Institute of the National Gay and Lesbian Task Force.

Conceptions
of Gay Male Life-Span Development:
Past and Present

David Roseborough

SUMMARY. Four of Erikson's eight psychosocial crises were used in this qualitative, exploratory study as an organizing framework. Using a semi-structured questionnaire, seven men were interviewed with the goal of understanding how they have navigated Erikson's life stages. Significant results included: an early sense of being different and a period of time between "coming out to self" and "coming out to another person," both complicating Erikson's sense of "social trust." The men also described finding non-biological ways of achieving generativity as well as the development of a strong internal sense of authority or locus of control. Other strengths gained included: achieving a broad base of social support or a "family of choice," and becoming role models themselves in response to a clear absence of positive role models during their own adolescence, which many identified as delaying their coming out. Finally, AIDS was discussed by many as a critical factor affecting how these men navigate each of Erikson's stages. Implications of these tenta-

David Roseborough, LICSW, is affiliated with the School of Social Work, University of Minnesota, 105 Peters Hall, 1404 Gortner Avenue, St. Paul, MN 55108 (E-mail: rose0455@umn.edu).

[Haworth co-indexing entry note]: "Conceptions of Gay Male Life-Span Development: Past and Present." Roseborough. David. Co-published simultaneously in *Journal of Human Behavior in the Social Environment* (The Haworth Social Work Practice Press, an imprint of The Haworth Press, Inc.) Vol. 8, No. 2/3, 2003, pp. 29-53; and: *Sexual Minorities: Discrimination, Challenges, and Development in America* (ed: Michael K. Sullivan) The Haworth Social Work Practice Press, an imprint of The Haworth Press, Inc., 2003, pp. 29-53. Single or multiple copies of this article are available for a fee from The Haworth Document Delivery Service [1-800-HAWORTH, 9:00 a.m. - 5:00 p.m. (EST). E-mail address: docdelivery@haworthpress.com].

Journal of Human Behavior in the Social Environment, Vol. 8(2/3) 2003
http://www.haworthpress.com/web/JHBSE
Digital Object Identifier: 10.1300/J137v8n02_03

tive findings are suggested for research, teaching, practice, and for psychosocial theory itself.*[Article copies available for a fee from The Haworth Document Delivery Service: 1-800-HAWORTH. E-mail address: <docdelivery@haworthpress.com> Website: <http://www.HaworthPress.com> © 2003 by The Haworth Press, Inc. All rights reserved.]*

KEYWORDS. Life span, Gay, coming out, social development

INTRODUCTION

While the study of adult development is rather new (Merriam, 1984), the study of what life-span development looks like for gay and lesbian people is almost untouched. Strong historical reasons exist for both of these realities, the two most central of which include: (1) Freud's assumption that development ended at puberty, with the onset of the genital stage, and (2) the assumption of both Freud and subsequent theorists (i.e., Adler, Erikson, Jung, etc.) that heterosexuality constituted normative development, culminating in the heterosexual union. Freud's emphasis on early childhood as formative left adult development largely unexamined, except in so much as an adult played out unresolved childhood conflicts. Later theorists' belief that adult development meant *heterosexual* development resulted in homosexuality being labeled as a deviation from that norm, versus a normal developmental path in its own right.

Since these assumptions are only now being challenged (most powerfully in the 1973 declassification of homosexuality from the DSM-III), it is important as practitioners and teachers to know what the unique developmental paths are of gay and lesbian people. What does development look like for people whose lives are often not characterized by the traditional heterosexual "marriage and kids," for people "whose lives have departed from heterosexual socialization patterns" (D'Augelli, 1994, p. 120)? What are the developmental tasks faced? What are the milestones and ritual markers? Who are the supports and what are the strengths gained? These questions are important in gaining an overall conceptual framework of what adult development looks like for gays and lesbians. For as D'Augelli (1994) points out, "earlier frameworks, which view lesbian and gay men as psychiatrically impaired and which dictate a focus on etiology have yet to be replaced with frameworks that effectively suggest different fundamental issues for analysis . . . theory building and empirical research on lesbian and gay lives that is consistent with a human development point of view simply has not been done" (p. 120, 130).

LITERATURE REVIEW

Section 1:
Historical Developmental Perspectives on Homosexuality–
Locating the Problem Within the Individual

In many ways psychologists and psychodynamically oriented clinical social workers have claimed Freud as the first developmental theorist. Freud postulated five stages of psychosexual development, beginning in infancy and ending around age twelve with the onset of puberty and ideally–sexual maturity (Freiberg, 1987). According to Freud, however, few made it to this point. Many got "stuck" at earlier developmental stages; most notable among this group were homosexuals. Freud postulated that gay men were victims of incomplete psychosexual development, unable to resolve the oedipal conflict, and arrested at an earlier stage of development (Beard & Glickauf-Hughes, 1994). Although he hedged on this view toward the end of his life, as in his 1935 "Letter to an American Mother" (in Isay, 1989), it is his earlier perspective that won favor and was adopted by most of Freud's successors. It is this earlier view that can be seen in object relations theory, with Klein repeating Freud, positing homosexuality as an issue of an infant boy's frustrated attempts to separate from his mother (Klein, 1932, in Beard & Glickauf-Hughes, 1994).

The implications of this thought have been far-reaching; it would be a mistake to see this premise as academic or removed. Isay (1989), a clinical professor of psychiatry at Cornell, explains, "traditional psychoanalytic theory asserts that unimpeded normal development leads to the mature expression of heterosexuality. Homosexuality, the theory holds, is caused by severe early developmental disturbances" (p. 4). He writes about the significance of this view, showing how it set the stage for later developmental theorists, and how its effects are still felt in training schools for analysts excluding gay practitioners, remaining "committed to the conviction that homosexuality is always pathological" (Isay, 1989, p. 14). Echoing D'Augelli, he shows how it has also "interfered with our being able to conceptualize a developmental pathway for gay men and thus has seriously impeded our ability to provide a psychotherapy that is neutral and unbiased by cultural expectations" (Friedman, in Isay, 1989, p. 5).

This belief that homosexuality is "stunted growth" is also still voiced by several renowned psychoanalytic theorists today. In 1981 Basch published what has become a "classic" instructional test for therapists in training called *Doing Psychotherapy*. It is a work which has achieved broad distribution and is used in many training programs for therapists. Writing this book eight years after the official declassification of homosexuality from the DSM-III, Basch (1981) describes a session with a client in which he told the latter of his nephew, "the possibility of Bobby's becoming homosexual is much greater if he continues to be deprived of reasonable affection, including physical affection, from a male" (p. 49). Here Basch is simply reiterating the long-standing belief that homosexuality is the natural consequence of a distant father and a domineering mother, where the son fails to identify with his same-gender parent: his father. He remains "trapped" in a feminine identification and unable to sexually differentiate.

The influence of this early theory is enormous, and remnants of it can be heard from other contemporary authors. In *Social Work Treatment*, Strean (1986) contributes a chapter on current application of psychoanalytic theory by social workers. In this chapter, he writes that the social worker acts, in therapy, as a "benign superego in the treatment situation and [to] encourage the client to explore and verbalize id wishes to . . . homosexually seduce [so that] anxiety is reduced and the ego becomes stronger–strong enough to enjoy a more mature sexual relationship with someone of the opposite sex" (p. 22). He goes on to describe gay men as "defending against an oedipal conflict . . . identifying with an oral mother so that by feeding his sexual partner, he is vicariously ministering to his own oral hunger" (p. 28). Each of these above views echo Freud in asserting that it is heterosexuality that is normative. Homosexuality is a deviation. It is "stunted growth": a normal aim directed against the "wrong object": another male.

Contemporary Developmental Perspectives on Homosexuality– Locating the "Problem" Within the Gene

In contrast to the above paradigm, a number of contemporary efforts have emerged which have sought to transcend this assumption of heterosexuality. Both Friedman (1988) and Isay (1989) have attempted to synthesize current scientific evidence that sexual orientation likely has a genetic component (Hamer, 1993; Pillard, 1993; Bailey, 1992; LeVay, 1993; Ellis & Ames, 1987; Money, 1987) with a revision of psychoanalytic theory. D'Augelli (1994) criticizes these neo-analytic efforts as "prescientific" and "not subject to formal disproof" (p. 119) on the one hand, while critiquing "scientism" (p. 119) on the other as ignoring the environmental, historical, and political contexts in which gay men develop.

Beginning efforts have been made in this direction, however, and include those of Kegan (1982) as well as of Driggs and Finn (1990). Kegan uses psychodynamic concepts, particularly object relations, to talk about the developmental processes of internalizing truth and being more active in determining one's own meaning-system based on experiences with dissonance. He writes particularly about how minorities are uniquely engaged in this process due to many early experiences of dissonance. He illustrates this with the example of a young man questioning his sexual identity in *The Evolving Self* (1982) where the primary threat perceived by the man, Kegan says, is what being gay would represent: how it would put him at odds with the culture to which he belongs. Kegan connects the young man's struggle to the question "who really determines my identity?" Similarly, Driggs and Finn (1990) have shown how gay men appropriate and experience "births" of their own in artistic and creative expressions, beyond biological childbirth. These creative life-giving acts are all subsumed under the broader labels of spirituality and "generativity" (p. 120).

Some of the most thorough treatment of gay identity development from a developmental perspective (as opposed to Kegan and other psychodynamic theorists), has been done by Coleman (1982). Coleman focuses on the stages of the coming-out process, dividing it into five stages. These stages begin with a sense of being different, often as a child and with varying levels of denial, an end with "integration": a stage characterized by having integrated one's sense of self in gay and heterosexual communities. The final stage is one in which the individual is "out," and where the person can be oneself without hiding or bifurcating parts of his or her life. Coleman builds his model on the foundation of a similar model by Cass (1979), who proposed a six-stage model outlining various degrees of gay identity formation, including: confusion, comparison, tolerance, acceptance, pride, and finally synthesis.

Each of these models stresses the important point that assuming a gay identity happens in the context of taking on a socially stigmatized label and role (Bozett, 1981; Cain, 1991; Coleman, 1981; Paradis, 1992; Reiter, 1989). Paradis (1992) discusses how this is compounded by AIDS, in terms of the public's historic perception of AIDS as a "gay disease." He also points to the "lack of an opportunity to explore gay identity during adolescence" (p. 263). He echoes Kegan in pointing to a lack of public role models as one of the consequences of internalizing a socially stigmatized label. Lastly, Reiter (1989) suggests seeing this difficulty in achieving congruence between sexual orientation and sexual identity as the logical consequence of living in a heterosexist culture, and "as part of a normative stage of gay identity development" (p. 149). Like Kegan, she argues that "identity, not orientation, is open to choice" (p. 138).

These are examples of directions that are only beginning to be taken in applying developmental theory specifically to the experiences of gay and lesbian people. They are positive steps in that they shift the focus from etiology to life span development. They counter the notion of homosexuality as sin, crime, sickness, or deviation, and turn attention to gay identity as a normal developmental path in its own right. As Reiter (1989) points out, while sexual orientation is likely early and fixed, the process of internalizing a gay identity is a long and difficult one. What this process looks like at certain ages, though, or with more detail than a five- or six-point progression, has not yet been done. As D'Augelli writes, it is now necessary to fill in some of the gays, focusing on what development looks like at different ages and life stages.

CONCEPTUAL FRAMEWORK

Erikson's Psychosocial Model as a Direction for Future Developmental Perspectives on Homosexuality–Locating the Problem Within the Person-Environment Transaction

Erikson, like Freud, saw adult development in largely heterosexual terms. Erikson did, however, depart from Freud in some significant ways which make his psychosocial approach potentially useful in understanding gay identity development. He departed dramatically in the importance he ascribed to social influences in shaping human development, a primacy equivalent to that which Freud gave to sexuality as a motivating force. Whereas Freud saw society as predominantly a limiting force which regulated the unbridled desires of the individual id, Erikson saw society as having at least a potentially positive, growthful role to play in supporting individual development. Secondly, Erikson was more optimistic than Freud about the potential for human growth. Erikson did not share Freud's "cut your losses" mentality. According to Erikson, there is always room for healthy personality development, providing social support exists to foster it. In this way, Erikson's approach to development could be said to involve a more open energy system than Freud's. That is, the individual is driven by social forces outside of his or her internal sexual and aggressive drives. In these ways, Erikson provides a strong and relevant conceptual framework by which to understand gay men's development.

METHOD

This study employed a qualitative and exploratory methodology. I interviewed seven self-identified gay men, ages 40-55, in the greater Twin Cities area. To give some parameters to the study, I chose to limit it to a sample of men. I did this to acknowledge that my results may not be easily generalized to the experiences of middle aged lesbians. I would anticipate many parallels, but

I see these women as comprising a population meriting its own research. This study used purposive sampling. Participation consisted of an hour and a half semi-structured interview administered in person either at their home or a site of their choice. Questions were used which corresponded to and tried to draw out each of Erikson's eight psychosocial stages and how they might play out uniquely for these men. This article will speak to four of those stages. The interviews were audio taped and then coded for "recurring themes" or "conceptual clusters" (Berg, 1989) using analytic induction (i.e., seeing how well these men's experiences matched with Erikson's psychosocial crises).

Some basic demographic information was collected as well. The sample consisted of seven mostly non-Native Minnesotan men of varied ethnic, racial, and economic backgrounds, who live in urban or suburban areas near a large gay community and who identify themselves as gay. Respondents varied in age from 40 to 52 (mean 46.57, SD = 4.39). Five of the seven respondents (71%) are Caucasian, while the remaining two (29%) are African American. All respondents are male. A wide range of occupations are represented, including: a law professor, counseling psychologist, computer consultant, police officer, public administrator, administrative assistant, and a research lab technician. Religious representation varied, with three of the men (43%) having been raised Baptist, two Roman Catholic (29%), and the others: Episcopal (14%), and Methodist (14%). Only one of the men described any current religious involvement. Only one respondent was born in Minnesota. The others were from the East Coast, the Midwest, and the South–all represented almost equally in thirds. One half were raised in urban settings and one-half in rural settings. As a trend, most intentionally sought out and moved to a larger urban area; 43% are currently partnered (between 18-29 years) and the remainder are single.

Despite this diversity, this sample represents a small group of gay men who came of age prior to the advent of Stonewall and even before the word "gay" was applied to homosexual men. A second crucial variable affects these respondents' perspectives: these men were in the age-bracket most devastated by AIDS in the 1980s. Their experiences therefore likely differ significantly from gay men born after Stonewall, who will age in a very different social context. This change, however, also points to the importance of hearing from a time-bound group whose experiences may otherwise be left unheard. These men give voice to a very different social reality, to a grief and "silent war" of which many younger gay men are unaware.

Lastly, as a qualitative study, this project involved a non-probability sample and relied exclusively on self-reporting. I conducted and transcribed all of the interviews myself. Field notes were taken after each interview regarding initial themes emerging, tentative hypotheses, and remaining questions. I also wrote up a composite ecomap after each interview, to give me a spatial picture of what each man's social support system looks like. The resultant themes are tentative and in many ways time and culture bound. They come from a group of Midwestern, urban-based, "out," ego syntonic gay men who grew up in a very particular context. However, tentative hypotheses emerged from this data, suggesting directions for future research, both quantitative and qualitative.

RESULTS

In order to be included, a theme had to have been discussed by several people. More common themes emerged than I would have anticipated. Important themes which emerged will be discussed below according to how they cluster around Erikson's four of Erikson's eight psychosocial stages.

Trust vs. Mistrust

Although most of the men interviewed identified first coming out to another person between the ages of 15 and 24 (mean age 24, SD = 8.6), the majority (N = 5) pointed to a sense of being different that went back much further: most often to childhood or to mid-adolescence (by age 16). This sense of being different goes back to early schooling (by age seven for several), and it is only later in life that it is named "gay" (mean age = 18) and shared with another (mean age 23). A few examples of this early sense of being different include:

> [I came out] around age 30 . . . I knew long before then that I was different . . . In retrospect, all the indications were there that I was a gay little boy . . . I remember in retrospect I know I had crushes in junior high on male friends. I was intensely more into male friendships than they were and developed jealousies and had excuses for sleepovers or for going over to their houses or having them over to my house. And particularly was attracted to them physically . . . and then I remember sublimating it for religious reasons more than anything else . . . praying that I would grow up normal.

> I knew I was gay when I was thirteen years old . . . but when I actually came out was when I went to school at the university. I was eighteen years old. And I met a guy in the dorm the first week or so and within a month, I came out to him . . . well, I actually fell in love.

> I never applied the word 'gay' to myself; I was always bisexual or had 'a sinful thought': never gay or homosexual. I'd never apply that [label] to myself.

Note that several years pass between when the boy "realizes" and when he discloses as a man. This realization that one is different is most often kept to oneself, and it is one which causes dissonance, or conflict. The child realizes early on that his desires are in conflict with what the social world "other there" expects of him. In Erikson's language, the period of trust vs. mistrust is characterized by a continual testing of this "fit" between the outside world and one's internal sense of reality. At this stage, one seeks a sense of "social trust," whereby the world is seen as safe and predictable, where there is a sense of consistency or continuity and a sameness between the world outside as it is presented and the world as one experiences it internally.

Significantly, most men in this group learned early that the world is not a "safe place" outside to tell their secret. They experienced a great gulf between who society and families told them they were and who they knew themselves internally to be. This sense of "dissonance" led to a great deal of internal conflict for these men.

One man said:

> I remember very vividly at the age of sixteen having a conversation with myself: saying 'you know exactly who you are, and what you are. And what you're going to do is you're going to forget about it. And you're going to get married. And you're going to have a family and do exactly what society tells you to do because it's going to be way less hassle.' That was a conscious decision I made at the age of 16.

Another man said succinctly:

> You didn't come out back then.

And another:

> I became sexually active at seven, with some heterosexual boys. I really didn't see anything wrong with what I was doing . . . but I noticed that no one else seemed to talk about it or do it. I guess I was just feeling so bad about having to hide my entire life that I went to my parents and said, 'I think I'm queer.'

His family reinforced strongly society's negative image of what it meant to be gay when his parents sent him to a doctor, who "believe it or not gave me male hormones, which back then was one of the possible cures." Another respondent pointed to this dissonance he sensed, but could not name at the time:

I think traveling . . . one reason I chose to travel a lot when I was younger was a sense that somehow I was looking for something and things didn't all fit together right. I couldn't put my finger on it at the time, but I think that was part of it, and then I started to come out. Traveling was a way of placing myself remotely from the community I lived in, so I could go out and meet new people and there was no risk associated with it.

Finally, one man spoke to how this tension pulled him apart and how he became depressed as a result:

I look at this as one of the most intense periods of growth I've ever gone through; it's appropriate to be depressed when the premises you've had about life are being cracked–and that's exactly what it was. It was realizing that if I continued down this track, I would not be living for myself; I would not be accomplishing whatever it is I'm supposed to do.

For these men to achieve a positive sense of self-acceptance, they had to learn to trust themselves, and to deprioritize the messages from the outside which devalued them. Several men described quite powerfully his process of gaining an internal locus of control and of learning to define themselves. When asked what they have learned from being gay, several men said:

I learned that I'm o.k. Number one, I learned that I don't have to live for anyone else, especially any group. I don't have to fit into what society says these are norms to be happy; I don't need that. I am o.k. I'm fine.

The only thing I'm thinking is that you damn well better be true to yourself and you better tell yourself the truth about who you are. That's why teenagers are killing themselves is because they're afraid of telling even themselves about who they are. Because if you can tell yourself the truth about who you are–telling someone else is a joke.

You've got to give yourself permission to be loved by yourself and to like yourself.

It is important to feel inside honestly and learn to communicate that inside feeling outside.

And sometimes the pressures to follow that norm are overwhelming. So the individual has to find a voice and within that voice they learn to speak the truth of what they want in their life and that just makes people go through a tremendous amount of angst and agony . . . it is not always the mold that is presented to us that is the standard for success and being gay has challenged that.

It's a wonderful thing to know that I'm o.k. I don't think anyone can actually take that from me. You could tell me the rest of my life, "being gay is an abomination" and I'd laugh at you–'yeah, next. . . . '

A lot of people say that when they come out it's like a symphony: hearing symphonic music–when you realize that there's such a drastic difference between what society telling you you're supposed to have and what it is that you want. So that force, just pure life force for me–that was the strongest thing I had. This being true to myself is exactly what that said to me: and what you're dealing with has nothing to do with you are–all this stuff coming from other people is just something you have to deal with.

Powerfully, in this last example, the respondent is able to externalize society's negative messages about being gay. Like Erikson, he locates the problem not in himself, but in the person-environment fit. However, this internalizing of a positive self-image is a gradual one, and it takes work: often in the form of countering negative messages taken in, as we will see under "initiative vs. guilt."

We grow as a dependent child with parents or care-givers giving us rules in the form of 'do's' and 'don'ts.' As we grow forward and develop, we have to look into ourselves and decipher which parts we'll keep and which parts we'll throw away.

Initiative vs. Guilt

It is during this stage of "initiative vs. guilt" that Erikson says people become more themselves. It is a time, by his time-line, when parental voices are taken in and a stage in which social messages continue to be taken in, in the form of a super ego, experienced as a conscience. The self, he says, is divided for all people at this stage, and this crisis is an extension of the previous one (autonomy vs. shame and doubt). However, gay men struggle especially here by being acutely aware of "guilt over goals contemplated" (i.e., sexual fantasies, imagined identities). A danger is that these men might continue simply to identify with the outside messages that gay is bad. In relation to becoming more oneself: Two stories in particular serve as metaphors for the process by which these men saw themselves grow in relation to being able to "put back out" or to relativize negative messages they had taken in about being gay. The first is offered by a couple, who in speaking about ritual, reflected on how their anniversary cards changed in content over the years:

> We drug out all the cards one-day and you could see a progression. I guess our acceptance of ourselves and society's acceptance of us had changed . . . our first anniversary cards would be things like, 'L, Brian (not real name),' or 'L, Bill (not real name).' We wouldn't put the word love down on paper . . . there were times we'd just say 'love,' and no name on it. Not that we really felt bad about ourselves, but we always had this fear that someone was going to pick it up.

In reviewing the progression of becoming more open about their relationship, this couple points to the relationship between their own self-acceptance and that of society's. They speak to how they absorbed or "took in" society's negation of their relationship, and how it was only over time that they were able to overcome these fears about how those "outside" might view their relationship. They point also to Erikson's person-environment fit, where their relationship suffers from the hostile environment in which it is embedded.

Another man spoke powerfully to how he concretely internalized his mother's message that "gay is bad" and the resultant trust of self and sense of self-authorship he gradually learned:

> I can remember vividly a letter I got from my mother after coming out, you know, 'God did not make you a gay child and I pray that when you are lying with a man that God will nag you until you realize how wrong you are' and that did a major mind fuck on me for six months . . . it really truly is mind control, because making a suggestion like that to somebody forces them to do that. It just makes you realize how powerful people can be on each other, how much force they can apply . . . Against that much force, I actually did what she said: I would hear her voice and I actually examined my feelings deep down and realized there never was any change . . . I ended up being that much more sure of myself. In the end she did me a favor. It built such incredible strength . . . I know who I am, no matter how much society says I should be like them, this is who I am.

This is a vivid example of outer messages being taken in, critically examined, and let go of, with the conscious decision to listen to one's own voice over the opinions of many "outside." This same man later said regarding relativizing these outer voices and learning to trust his own: "I've rearranged where my family lives in my mind." He relativizes the importance of his family's perspectives and successfully becomes, in Erikson's language, more himself.

Generativity vs. Stagnation

All of my sample falls into the age group facing Erikson's normative crisis "generativity vs. stagnation" (ages 34-60). Erikson characterizes this as a stage in which attention turns to taking care of others. As argued earlier, this stage has been especially defined by the heterosexual markers of "marriage and kids." However, Erikson himself argued that this task got carried out through other avenues (i.e., as a mentor, teacher, or leader). He described it as a spiritual time in which people sought to "give back" to their culture what they had internalized and uniquely made their own. All of this happens, Erikson argues, particularly in relation to teaching and giving to the succeeding generation. It is a care for those who come after oneself.

While two of the respondents had been married, most had not. To find out how each of these seven men achieved generativity, I asked each how he saw himself "giving back" or "giving life," either to the gay community or to society at large. I would usually introduce it as a question when a respondent was discussing some creative project or volunteer work. I asked, "What (other) ways do you see yourself giving beyond yourself or trying to create life after your death? Do you have a desire to leave a 'mark' behind?" I found that these men have been very creative in finding ways to give and to "parent." This giving took many forms and included: taking care of friends with AIDS, sponsoring people in Alcoholics Anonymous (AA), doing volunteer work for an AIDS organization, traveling with nephews and nieces, leaving money in one's will to a gay organization, as well as teaching and mentoring college students in one's profession.

Additionally, two men spoke of being "out" at work as a professor or police officer and therefore a role model for both gay and heterosexual students and colleagues. Another spoke of writing a play. For one, it was as simple as listening to a friend at a coffee shop who was having a hard time and "knowing in that hour that I made a difference." For another, it was his very choice of profession: becoming a therapist, someone who would tend to other people's psychological and spiritual growth.

One couple began answering this question by making the distinction Erikson did between biological and metaphorical "parenting." This couple said of biologically bringing life into the world: "Anybody can connect and egg and a sperm. That's not productivity; that's reproduction." That is, I think, a succinct and helpful distinction. Although these two men have no biological children of their own, they definitely see themselves as having a parenting role, which they carry out largely by sponsoring newly sober men (mostly heterosexual) and by caring for gay and heterosexual people with AIDS. By intentionally seeking out formative roles with heterosexual men, they also echoed two other men who said they sought to be role models, the kind they identified missing in their youth:

> One time there was this counselor who said, 'I really appreciate what you are doing with all these gay guys who are coming through this house.' 'But they aren't gay.' The first assumption is that we are there helping the gays get started in their sobriety. But they're not gay. It's a lot of comfort to be able to demonstrate to heterosexual kids and their families, cause we do get involved in their families, that this is a gay person who is helping you out here; this is not one of your straight buddies who kept you stoned all the time. There's a lot of comfort in that: a lot of pride, gratification.

In reaching out to heterosexuals, they are in a sense transcending or "reaching beyond themselves"–going outside of their communities and in this way achieving generativity. Regarding their roles as sponsors in AA, on of the two said:

> We're very active in AA and we sponsor some young men coming into the program; I consider them a part of my extended family. Because basically to us they are kids, because they are new in the program; you end up treating them like you would trying to raise your own kids. So they really are a part of the extended family.

The two also see themselves having something of a corrective role in terms of "re-parenting" other men who have lacked care from their own biological families: "I think we're more productive than many [heterosexuals] out there . . . the ones creating these kids with the problems to start with" or "one said, 'you're not my father.' 'No, but would you rather have me treat you like he did?' 'No.' 'Anything else?'"

> We helped–when he was in the process of coming out, the one who calls us dad and dad; we get a father's day card from him.

This couple also spoke to a sense of connection true to Erikson with those who came before and a responsibility to those who will come after:

> I had a real close friend in AA; he died. He helped me through a lot of struggling times. He was also gay. And I remember one time I asked, 'what on earth can I do to repay you for all of this?' And he said, 'just do it for someone else.'

Another man carries this out with a particular commitment to gay youth who will come of age in the years to come, with the hope it will be easier for them:

> I used to work with the gay and lesbian youth task force; I was one of the founding members of that group. We set up a student scholarship that still exists.

Other men spoke of a desire to be a role model:

> I like being visible at school in terms of being a competent teacher and being known as being gay. So I think that's valuable not only for the gay folk but also for the heterosexual students to realize that there are professional gay people. It's good for them to know that.

> I think my big thing is sharing with people and being there for people.

Caring for friends with AIDS also turned out to be a big way in which these men give. Many of them are involved in AIDS-related service organizations, and several (n = 3) had been in direct care giving roles for friends with AIDS. One man mentioned how it relativized for him the importance of his own life and his own need to be individually remembered.

Related to this, it is striking to me that in all of these responses, not one of the men expressed a desire to be remembered *personally* for his contributions. Not one of them felt an urge to leave behind the legacy of his name:

> If things go as planned, after I retire . . . there will be enough to leave some to a gay organization. So there will be a little bit of a trust fund. But it'll be just a tiny little thing. But it'll be a little bit of a legacy. In terms of replicating myself, I have no interest in that–it's mostly just to be helpful. I don't even care about having my name attached to my own gifts. That's not important.

> That's an ego trip I'm not on yet. I'm leaving two daughters behind. I'm leaving friends behind. I've made my mark on a lot of people; individually I've made my mark on numerous people; when I was at work with the patrol, I met people and they were surprised that I was who I was and nice and caring . . . my mark has been made.

> When I got married I said, we will have two kids; we will replace ourselves and nothing more. Period. I mean I was firm on that.

One man understood the reason for this to be:

> Because as a gay person there have been several times when the spotlight
> is shining on you so huge.

Many men spoke to the sense that "there's some contribution to make here"
and one man identified it as becoming pressing in his forties. A few men spoke
to the impulse to give, or to make a contribution, and even to an intuitive sense
of when they had done so. However, none of these men described a desire to be
remembered personally–by name. I am not sure what to make of this, other
than to speculate that gay men have often by this time in their lives come to
peace with the idea of not leaving behind biological offspring (though many
do), and therefore do not think in those categories or terms. This may also be
another interesting area for future research. The men have, however, found
many ways to give.

Ego Integrity vs. Despair

Erikson (1963) believed that this last crisis in life involves religious and
spiritual questions. He argued that only people who have truly given, by taking
care of other people or by generating new "products and ideas" (p. 268) (i.e.,
successfully resolving the previous stage: achieving generativity), can truly
face death. The man who successfully resolves this stage accepts his own limitations and looks back at his life with contentment and a general acceptance.
He does not wish for it to have been otherwise. He feels a connection with
those who have lived before and those who will come after. The risk here is to
despair, which Erikson frames as a loss of faith–to despair at one's own life. To
get at these questions with gay men, I asked (1) what events do you look forward to or fear in the future, and (2) what losses have you already faced and
how have you coped with them or changed as a result? Do you have any re-
grets?

In terms of my first question, gay men spoke to looking forward to retirement, potential future relationships, retiring with, and living with friends. One
man discussed fearing a social backlash against gays and lesbians in the future
and several fear "losing other friends to AIDS." Several mentioned looking
forward to traveling with their partners and friends. Traveling was a big topic,
with four of the seven respondents (57%) seeing it in their futures. Again,
friends are central. One man has already named his friends (as well as gay organizations) as "primary beneficiaries and as executors" of his estate.

Two men spoke to the gradual realization that they are aging and to the acceptance that this requires: "you have to realize that you're getting older. It's
different: to really be o.k. with being old." Again here I saw this internal sense
of authority re-surface:

It's like my hair and piercing my ear. If I live to be as old as my father, I have twenty odd years left, and these are some things I want to do. I'm not hurting anyone by doing them, so if you don't like me for doing them, I'll find somebody who does. And that's sort of a bad attitude maybe, but hey—my time on this planet is winding up and I want to do what I want to do.

This man knows that time is limited and is sure enough of himself to be the one who determines how he spends it. In the language of Kegan, it is a move toward self-authorship. At the same time, in the language of Erikson, these men seem to be gradually letting go of individual power and are reaching beyond themselves. This can be seen in the ways they have achieved generativity, evidenced in the above section. Each of the men gives in an individual way, but most do so anonymously, and none expressed a desire to have personal recognition for what they will leave behind (countering the notion of gay men as narcissistic). One couple discussed fears of one dying first and a desire for their ashes to be spread together. His partner discussed a regret at not having kids, but both agreed they had parented sufficiently through their roles as sponsors in AA.

One man echoed Erikson with particular clarity and practically defined this stage by describing his struggle to remain open to life and to new experiences without despairing:

I imagine my future with challenge and passion. And hopefully a lot of judgment as I grow older . . . the challenge to keep looking, questioning, examining my motives, my thinking, the paradigms I use, the models that I play off of. Challenging in the sense that I want to have some task, some direction, some project that will shake me up, make me uneasy to the point of pushing me forward. And so I want to have compassion so I can be open rather than sarcastic or what's that word I always forget? Jaded. Cause I think you really can. It's the old spinster stereotype: the lonely old lady who gets cynical about the world. I don't want to get there. And I struggle with that sometimes, when my heart gets hurt. I struggle with feeling like nothing's going to work . . . I'm too old . . . the window gets smaller . . . I think the window of opportunity gets smaller as age increases, and I just . . . I'm hopeful that I can jump through that window before it's too small to get my big butt through (laughs).

In relation to my second question, "what losses have you faced, and how have you coped or changed as a result of them?", the responses overwhelmingly focused on AIDS:

> The greatest loss is the loss of AIDS . . . first because of the dynamic that
> it is so large. And second because it is so invisible.

This man points to two recurring themes: the sense that AIDS has affected
everyone in his community , and secondly the dynamic that this grief is neither recognized nor legitimized by much of broader society. Many described
the sense that they are in the midst of a war, viewing the lists of the dead,
while the rest of society walks by, ignorant that the war is even going on. Regarding the first dynamic of the sheer magnitude of the loss:

> It's a hell of a thing when people come up to you and say, "well you
> know . . . so and so is dead." . . . It's not like you wonder how they're do-
> ing or how their job is; you wonder if they're dead or alive.

Regarding the second dynamic of an invisible pandemic and of "silent grief":

> It's like screaming in a silent room; nobody hears you.

> And it happens silently in this society. In the heads of many people it
> happens to a population of people who deserve this death. They have
> broken God's law or some spiritual law and so there is no mourning for
> the people who died. There is no understanding of their lives. There is no
> appreciation for their goodness. There is nothing but contempt and these
> are real people. I think that's one of the saddest things I have experi-
> enced.

It is a loss so encompassing, that many of the men said that they were not even
fully aware of or yet able to take in its significance:

> Very innocently, we were going through some photo albums and he
> asked, well, where are all these people? And we kind of went through,
> and I would say, this is so and so and he died last year, and this is so an so
> and he's sick, not doing very well. This person's sick . . . this person's
> dead. He died five years ago and all of a sudden it was he who said to me,
> 'my God, all your friends . . .' and it did not dawn on me until he actually
> said that to me.

The men said that the losses had become so commonplace that they felt "normal." One man said simply, "you assimilate this into your life." One man
spoke to the anticipatory grief that came with learning friends are HIV posi-

tive, saying that the real grief begins then, "and the rest of it is just being with the person while they complete their life, however much time they have."

A recurring theme, however, seemed to be the awareness that they are facing mortality prematurely. Many identified with their parents, but felt sadness and anger that they were facing what felt like a "normal" life-task for their parents at seventy or eighty, but not for them at forty to fifty-five:

> We're facing the exact same issues that our parents are now.

> There's a certain feeling that you're not old enough yet to be losing friends. You hear your parents talk about how they lose . . . my parents, my dad's approaching eighty and my mom is in her early seventies and they're talking about how their friends are dying and somehow that seems more understandable or more normal just because of the age, but you don't expect to lose a lot of your friends of your own age I'm at, and it started ten years ago.

Men also spoke to the related losses that went with AIDS:

> Society has been incredibly ugly and cruel to people who are HIV positive. Insurance companies delete and shun; school systems expel and suspend; neighborhoods reject; neighbors turn away; friends leave; lovers depart. In our society today, there are few situations which provide such isolation as when you're HIV positive.

> If you have full-blown AIDS, one of the greatest losses you feel is that people won't touch you. They no longer feel like you are a viable entity to be held. That's an awful thing. Human beings, in their very nature, are instinctually toucher-beings. We need to be held as infants; we need to be held as children. We need to be held as adults. And what happens if you have AIDS is that no one wants to touch you.

And lastly, two men spoke to the impact of losing a large percentage of men in their age group on their friendships and on the formation of romantic relationships:

> I don't know how to verbalize what that loss is. It's like this, David. People tease me about liking younger men, o.k. But the flip side is 'if all these people who died premature deaths were here, what would dating be like today?' I can't even begin to imagine. Just because I'm so used to the fact that in my age group, there's been . . . a lot of people gone. When I go out, the number of people I'll see in the forty-year age group; it's a tougher crowd. I don't know how much that affects me. It affects me, though.

In terms of how these men have coped with and what they have learned from facing the losses associated with AIDS, most of the men (n = 5) spoke to learning that life involves loss. AIDS relativizes the importance of other things, and reminds them of the importance of friendships as sustaining:

> I've lost a lot of good friends to AIDS. How has that affected me? It's made me realize how valuable close friendships can be and how much you miss people when they're gone.

Two men spoke to the struggle not to quit feeling or caring for people:

> It's like a bad train ride you can't get off. People keep dying and you keep going to funerals and you get somewhat numb and you're resistant to going to funerals because there have been so many, and I think there's a tendency to kind of ahhh . . . protect oneself. And that's what I think I've done.

> And you cope by sharing. This [the interview] is a coping in itself.

Finally, most of the men also spoke of losses in addition to AIDS, which included the loss of (and rebuilding of) self-esteem at different points in their lives as well as the loss of their own relationships–losses which are also often not validated or understood as "real losses" (i.e., disenfranchised grief). People also discussed the heavy losses of identity and of the security that went with being connected to one's biological family and religion of origin:

> The ones that really get you are family, the loss of affection, or of understanding even–that's a true loss.

And finally, the loss of the ability to be affectionate in public:

> One of the things that is tragic, I think, about being gay, is the loss of public expression. If you're heterosexual you can walk down the street holding hand in hand, have your arm around somebody's waist. You can kiss in public; you can sit and be touching in movies and things like that; about the only thing we don't do is we don't do intercourse in public. If you're gay, your world is very different.

These men spoke to multiple losses which are invisible to much of broader society and to their biological families. They thus spoke to learning to cope by turning to gay friends, which again become family, and to turning inward to find spiritual resources outside of their religions of origin. These men are successfully facing a task in middle age that Erikson reserved for the end of life. It is one which has made these men strong, or given them what Zuhl (1995) calls "crisis competency" (i.e., a strong internal capacity to handle difficult situations, often prematurely). One man summed this up by saying he had been reading that one characteristic of people who live long or achieve "longevity" is that they successfully face and learn to cope with losses early in their lives. Regarding losing friends to AIDS, he said:

> It's helped me to adapt the skill, I mean it's a terrible way to have to do it, but those who are going to do well have realized that you're going to suffer losses.

And finally,

> I've got to think that with all these testings that we've had, I mean I think gay people ought to live to be 120 years old. (laughs)

DISCUSSION

I will attempt to suggest a few implications of the above for research, teaching, theory, and practice by drawing some broad strokes. To get at this, I asked respondents "what supports weren't there that you wish had been? What was missing that would have helped you in your coming out?" I asked these questions to get ideas for future supports and resources that can aid gay men in their development and which many or most found lacking. I will trust the rest to the reader: that you will have had your own ideas sparked in reading the above.

Let me say first, however, more generally that gay men can be helped most by society: by friends, family, and care givers alike coming to see gay men and women not as deviates, stunted in their psychosexual growth, but as human beings, developing in their own way. These men saw many of the problems they faced as human problems, not so different from what their heterosexual friends and peers are facing, albeit sometimes at different ages, often prematurely—before they would have planned to do so. They too sought meaningful social, familial, and romantic relationships. The social, political, and religious context in which they have developed, however, has presented some unique struggles and in Erikson's language: an often "non-nutritive" environment in which to develop.

These men's struggles in achieving social trust and their experience of learning to trust their own sense of self over and against negative external messages may have implications for positively framing what it means to be gay. Gay men might learn that there is a positive pay-off for all of that difficult work they do. Their ability to think critically and to trust themselves can be framed as strengths. These men can be helped too by externalizing the negative messages about being gay, and by understanding them not as "conscience," "guilt," or as "proof that gay is bad," but as social prejudices that have been taken in, and now need to be consciously evaluated and "put back out." By locating the problem in the person-environment transaction, and not in the person, victim blaming is avoided and empowerment is possible. It demonstrates also that service providers need to appeal to internal more than external sources of authority when working with gay clients.

The fact that the majority of these men have left organized religion points also to the need for churches and religious bodies to be accountable for the messages they are sending and for the effects these messages have. It points to the need for gay men to have gay-affirming environments in which to worship if they are going to be a part of such religious communities. It should also "red-flag" ministers and therapists that this is potentially a source of emotional injury for many gay men.

It points, too, I think, to the need gay men have for non-church related rituals and for spiritual "tools," especially in facing their multiple losses. Gay men can benefit from creating their own rituals which are meaningful to them and by finding ways that they can "join with something greater" outside of a church context (i.e., rituals among friends), as so many in this study have successfully done. Gay men can be helped to frame their individual faith narrative, and can be referred to authors such as Fortunato (1982) who have used both psychodynamic and narrative approaches in helping gay men to compose their own faith narrative, and thus to put themselves "back into the story" (i.e., to reappropriate the symbols, and to make their faith "their own").

"Initiative vs. guilt" seemed to be most characterized by the conscious process of re-externalizing negative messages about what it means to be gay. Supports identified as most relevant here focused on having positive images out there to take in about what it means to be gay. Respondents stressed the importance of "visibility": that gay pride parades, "libraries full of books," "activities with people who are out and supportive of it," and society in general "talking about it" are all important.

In terms of achieving generativity, these men can be helped simply to see the ways they already do give life and "give back." Gay men can be helped to frame the ways they already parent and contribute, for what I found was that these men are all already doing so. Gay men in general can be helped by society granting them a place in the family, and by not equating "family" with "nuclear, child-bearing, and heterosexual." Gay men are as much a part of their families as are their siblings who marry and bear children.

Finally, the themes that emerged in relation to ego integrity vs. despair focused largely on AIDS. This portion of my interviews points to the reality of how many of these men are in direct-care positions for people with AIDS.

These men need to be supported emotionally and institutionally in their natural care-giving networks. They face enormous grief, which is often unseen, invalidated, and disenfranchised. The men can be helped by having their care-giving roles appreciated, their relationships validated and their grief heard. This grief is not far under the surface. Few men brought up AIDS in the interview, but when I asked, a few cried or got teary. AIDS and its related losses are important topics to raise in an assessment, or to consider in therapy.

It is finally a testament to the strength of these men who have not only survived but thrived in the face of social oppression. Contrary to the myth of the gay man as narcissistic, self-absorbed, and youth conscious, these men have transcended their own concerns, begun to accept the reality of their aging with comfort, have cared for their sick, served as role models, and as one summed up:

> That's where I think our gay friends are our strongest help . . . we build each other back up, better than anyone else can.

Where are the implications of the above for Erikson's psychosocial theory itself? Though my goal was not to rework Erikson, my data do suggest a few implications for psychosocial theory as it is understood and taught in social work curriculum. I would say that my results lend support to Erikson's contention that people do navigate certain life stages, that attention does turn to different concerns with age. I saw this evidenced by these men deprioritizing the gay label and reprioritizing a desire for intimacy with age. However, these men's experiences also challenge Erikson's notion that such tasks are carried out in a uniform order or within the strict age-delineations Erikson identified. This is evidenced by many of the men in my sample feeling that a lack of role models and of social supports delayed their coming out and thus their subsequent solidification of identity, initial dating, and achievement of intimacy. Erikson did allow for such variations, however, arguing that humans cross-culturally navigate these eight "universal" crises, but that the content of each stage, or the way it is resolved depends as much on the cultural side of the equation as on individual ego strength.

I would say my research also supports the emphasis Erikson gives to development as something life-long and as something socially informed. Development for the men in my sample seems to have been influenced by society as much as by sexuality. Though my research does questions the "uniformity" and "universality" with which theorists such as Erikson speak about human development, it is a reminder of the importance of examining the impact of culture on identity development, as opposed to seeing development as strictly an intrapsychic unfolding.

This last point demonstrates the need for more explicit treatment in social work theory courses (i.e., Human Behavior and the Social Environment) as to how identity development varies across variables such as race, class, gender, sexual orientation, and society's understanding of each. The above research points, I hope, to the need for psychosocial theory to take account of more groups' experiences as they challenge, complement, and eventually change existing categories of what constitutes "normative" development.

REFERENCES

Basch, M. (1981). *Doing Psychotherapy*. NY: Basic Books.

Beard, J., & Glickauf-Hughes, C. (1994). Gay identity and sense of self: Rethinking male homosexuality. *Journal of Gay & Lesbian Psychotherapy, Vol. 2*(2), 21-37.

Berg, B. (1989). *Qualitative Research Methods for the Social Sciences*, 2nd Ed. Boston: Allyn and Bacon.

Bozett, F. (1991). Gay fathers: Evolution of the gay-father identity. *American Journal of Orthopsychiatry, 51*(3) July, 552-59.

Cain, R. (1991). Stigma management and gay identity development. *Social Work, 36*(1), 67-73.

Cass, V. (1979). Homosexual identity formation: A theoretical model. *Journal of Homosexuality, 4*, 219-35.

Coleman, E. (1982). Developmental stages of the coming out process. *Homosexuality and Psychotherapy*. NY: The Haworth Press, Inc.

D'Augelli, A. (1994). Lesbian and gay male development. In Greene, B., & Herek, G. (Eds.), *Lesbian and Gay Psychology: Theory, Research, and Clinical Applications*. Thousand Oaks: Sage.

Driggs, J., & Finn, S. (1991). *Intimacy Between Men*. NY: Plume.

Ellis, L., & Aimes, M. (1987). Neurohormonal functioning and sexual orientation: A theory of homosexuality-heterosexuality. *Psychology Bulletin, 101*, 233-58.

Erikson, E. (1963). *Childhood and Society*. NY: Norton.

Frieberg, K. (1987). *Human Development: A Life Span Approach, 3rd Ed*. Boston: Jones and Bartlett Publishers, Inc.

Hamer, D. (1993). Towards a genetic basis of homosexuality. Lecture delivered at the Harvard Medical School Symposium on the Biological Nature of Homosexuality and the Psychological Development of Homosexual Men and Women. March 6.

Isay, R. (1989). *Being Homosexual: Gay Men and their Development*. NY: Avon Books.

Kegan, R. (1982). *The Evolving Self: Problem and Process in Human Development*. Cambridge: Harvard University Press.

Levay, S. (1993). The Brain and sexual orientation. Lecture delivered at the Harvard Medical School Symposium on the Biological Nature of Homosexuality and the Psychological Development of Homosexual men and Women. March 6.

Merriam, S. (1984). *The Nature of Adult Development*. Information series no. 282. Columbus, OH: ERIC Clearinghouse on Adult, Career, and Vocational Education. The National Center for Research in Vocational Education.

Money, J. (1987). Sin, sickness, or status? Homosexual gender identity and psycho-neuroendocrinology. *American Psychologist, 42*, 384-99.

Paradis, B. (1992). Seeking intimacy and integration: Gay men in the era of AIDS. *Smith College Studies in Social Work, 61*(3), 260-74.

Pillard, R. (1993). Is sexual orientation genetic? Data from twins, siblings, and adoptees. Lecture delivered at the Harvard Medical School Symposium on the Biological Nature of Homosexuality and the Psychological Development of Homosexual Men and Women. March 6.

Reiter, L. (1989). Sexual orientation, sexual identity, and the question of choice. *Clinical Social Work Journal, 17*(2), summer, 138-50.

Strean, H. (1986). Psychoanalytic theory. In Turner, F. (Ed.). *Social Work Treatment, 3rd Ed.* NY: The Free Press.

Zuhl, T. (1995). Lecture at the Minnesota Social Service Association. Spring. Bloomington, MN.

Getting a Piece of the Pie:
Cultural Competence for GLBT Employees at the Workplace

Nan Van Den Bergh

SUMMARY. This article outlines challenges facing gay, lesbian, bisexual, and transgendered employees at the workplace because of a lack of federal legislation prohibiting discrimination based on sexual orientation. A conceptual framework, PIE, is offered which addresses the protection, inclusion and equity issues which must be considered in order to create a safe and productive working environment for gay, lesbian, bisexual, and transgendered employees. Additionally, attitudes, knowledge and skills are described which a practitioner would need to acquire, so as to become culturally competent in working with sexual minority employees. *[Article copies available for a fee from The Haworth Document Delivery Service: 1-800-HAWORTH. E-mail address: <docdelivery@haworthpress. com> Website: <http://www.HaworthPress.com> © 2003 by The Haworth Press, Inc. All rights reserved.]*

KEYWORDS. Cultural competence, GLBT employees, workplace issues, gay and lesbian workers

---

Nan Van Den Bergh, PhD, LCSW, is Associate Professor, School of Social Work, Florida International University (E-mail: vandenan@fiu.edu).

[Haworth co-indexing entry note]: "Getting a Piece of the Pie: Cultural Competence for GLBT Employees at the Workplace." Van Den Bergh, Nan. Co-published simultaneously in *Journal of Human Behavior in the Social Environment* (The Haworth Social Work Practice Press, an imprint of The Haworth Press, Inc.) Vol. 8. No. 2/3, 2003, pp. 55-73; and: *Sexual Minorities: Discrimination, Challenges, and Development in America* (ed: Michael K. Sullivan) The Haworth Social Work Practice Press, an imprint of The Haworth Press, Inc., 2003, pp. 55-73. Single or multiple copies of this article are available for a fee from The Haworth Document Delivery Service [1-800-HAWORTH, 9:00 a.m. - 5:00 p.m. (EST). E-mail address: docdelivery@ haworthpress.com].

Journal of Human Behavior in the Social Environment, Vol. 8(2/3) 2003
http://www.haworthpress.com/web/JHBSE
© 2003 by The Haworth Press, Inc. All rights reserved.
Digital Object Identifier: 10.1300/J137v8n02_04

OVERVIEW OF WORKPLACE ISSUES FOR GLBT EMPLOYEES

The Bureau of Labor Statistics estimated that in 1990 there were over 147 million Americans within the labor force. If the assumption is true that 10% of the population comprises persons identifying as gay, lesbian, bisexual, or transgendered (GLBT), that means there are approximately 14,700,000 sexual minority employees within the United States. Since the overwhelming majority of GLBT individuals are within the paid labor force, this means that a very large segment of the American populace is vulnerable to employment discrimination, as they are not protected from adverse employment practices as are other minority status persons. Title VII of the 1964 Civil Rights Act precludes employment discrimination based on race, ethnicity, national origin, religion, and sex. Federal law also precludes discrimination based on age and disability status. The question becomes, are there any protections from job discrimination for GLBT employees?

Executive Order 11478 signed by President Clinton in May 1998 prohibits discrimination based on sexual orientation within the federal civilian workforce; however, it did not create a vehicle for enforcement. At present, there is no omnibus federal law that prohibits adverse employment actions against GLBT persons, and as such, sexual minority employees cannot file employment grievances with the EEOC for workplace-based inequities. The only protections against employment discrimination for GLBT individuals exists through a patchwork of state and local laws, as well as private sector company policies. Eleven states, the District of Columbia, plus 122 cities and counties ban anti-gay discrimination in private workplaces as well as in public-sector jobs. An additional 10 states and 106 city or county governments protect their own employees from sexual orientation discrimination (HRC WorkNet, 2001). Because they explicitly ban employment discrimination based on sexual orientation, state and local ordinances represent the greatest potential source of legal protection for GLBT employees. However, local regulation of employment discrimination against GLBT persons is limited in several respects. First, executive orders are subject to rescission by referendum or judicial invalidation. Second, local anti-discrimination ordinances may be unenforceable when they conflict with federal interests or constitutional rights. Since public policy has failed to comprehensively preclude employment discrimination against GLBT persons, are there any other mechanisms for preventing adverse employment actions based on sexual orientation?

There has been momentum building within the private sector to prevent job discrimination against sexual minority persons. For example, as of 2001, 59% of Fortune 500 companies have included sexual orientation in their non-discrimination policies, including 88% of the top fifty companies. Additionally,

1217 other private companies, nonprofits, and unions have crafted specific policies prohibiting sexual orientation discrimination. Furthermore, 336 colleges and universities include sexual orientation in their non-discrimination policies, including 45 of the nation's top universities and 33 of the best liberal arts colleges (2002 U.S. News and World Report on college rankings noted in HRC WorkNet, 2001, p. 17). Despite the increasing number of governmental entities, businesses and institutions of higher education prohibiting discrimination based on sexual orientation, the vast majority of gay, lesbian, bisexual, and transgendered employees are still in jeopardy, as it is legal to discriminate against them in 39 of the 50 states.

Discrimination based on sexual orientation does exist. Research quoted in *Harvard Law Review* (Editors, Harvard Law Review, 1989) noted that one third of all gay males surveyed reported discrimination. Seventeen percent had lost jobs or were denied employment because of their homosexuality. Similarly, nearly 25% of lesbians respondents reported having been discriminated against in the workplace. A review of literature on sexual minority workplace discrimination (Croteau, 1996), which examined studies between 1980 and 1990, found that 25%-66% of respondents had reported discrimination based on their sexual orientation. The more "out" an employee, the greater the likelihood they had experienced adverse employment actions.

Even if a GLBT employee has not experienced discrimination, research has indicated that the fear of such is a pervasive concern among sexual minority employees (Croteau, 1996; Levine and Leonard, 1984). A national study conducted for Out and Equal Workplace Advocates which surveyed 2000 straight and gay employees found that: (a) one out of four GLBT employees was harassed on the job by coworkers, (b) 12% were denied promotions or advancement, (c) 9% were fired or dismissed unfairly, and (d) 8% were pressured to quit a job because of harassment or hostility against them in their workplace (Out and Equal Workplace Advocates, 2002). Within the same study, 73% of respondents noted GLBT employees as vulnerable to discrimination and harassment at the workplace.

There are two types of discrimination that GLBT employees face: de facto and de jure. The former means failing to hire, firing, denying a promotion or raises. The latter covers more subtle discrimination such as failure to allow benefits' coverage for an employee's domestic partner, noninclusion within dependent care policies, omission of GLBT employees' partners from work-related social events, and failure to include content about gay, lesbian, bisexual, and transgendered issues within organizational diversity training. A survey of employment discrimination practices in state and local government found that unequal access to benefit programs for domestic partners and dependents was a major and unique form of sexual orientation discrimination (Riccucci and Gossett, 1996).

Gay employment discrimination exists within both the public and private spheres. The former would include military employment, employment in jobs that require a security clearance and in the civil service. For example, gays were deemed unfit for military service during WWII. The Department of Defense has argued that gay and lesbian applicants constitute security risks. Furthermore, from 1947 to 1950, the federal government denied 1700 individuals employment because of alleged homosexuality. During this same time period, which coincided with the McCarthy era, homosexuality was grouped with communism as a grave evil to be rooted out of the federal government. It was during this time that President Eisenhower issued Executive Order 10450 excluding from government employment "persons guilty of sexual perversion" (Poverny, 2000). Similarly, the FBI as well as CIA have been known to establish a ban on employing gay men or lesbians (Editors, Harvard Law Review, 1989).

Sexual orientation discrimination is most pervasive in military employment, the nation's largest employer. For example, within a ten-year period, the U.S. armed forces discharged 15,000 persons because of allegations of homosexuality (Editors, Harvard Law Review, 1989). President Clinton's 1993 "Don't Ask, Don't Tell" policy, although ostensibly a panacea for discrimination against GLBT military personnel, has actually resulted in more military separations. For example, a 1997 Pentagon statistic noted a 67% increase in military discharges or firings, based on "Don't Ask, Don't Tell" which bore an estimated cost exceeding 29 million dollars (Electronic Gay Community Magazine, 1998, in Poverny, 2000). The Servicemembers Legal Defense Network reported a record number of discharges and complaints during 2001 (SLDN, 2002). According to Department of Defense figures, the Pentagon fired 1250 women and men, approximately three to four service members each day, for being gay, lesbian, or bisexual. This was the highest number of gay discharges since 1987. In 2001, there were 1075 incidents, an increase of 23% from 2000. The SLDF report for 2001 notes that each branch of the armed forces has virtually ignored a July 2000 Pentagon "Anti-Harassment Action Plan" which called for prevention training of all military personnel (SLDF, 2002).

Although most public attention seems to have focused on gay males within the military, it is presumed that there may be a higher percentage of lesbians, and they have been discharged at a rate ten times that of their male counterparts. Women continue to be discharged at a rate nearly twice their presence in the service. While females comprise 14% of the total armed forces' strength, 30% of gay discharges were lesbians. Within the Air Force, during 2001, 43%

of gay discharges were female (SLDF, 2002). It has been suggested that the military campaign against lesbians reflects the generally low level of respect with which women in the military are treated (Moore, 1988; Salholz et al., 1993).

Despite the bleak situation for gays and lesbians in the military, there is somewhat more protection for sexual minority persons employed by public agencies. This is based on constitutional requirements of due process and equal protection, which precludes the government's ability to hire and fire at will. However, there are no such protections for employees of private companies. Employment-at-will continues to provide the basis for private employers' ability to fire employees without cause. No court has held that dismissals based on an employee's sexual orientation have violated federal public policy (Editors, Harvard Law Review, 1989).

The above data have clarified many risks confronting GLBT employees. Clearly, the lack of sexual orientation civil rights has created second-class employment status for GLBT individuals. Since work is such an important aspect of one's life and is deemed a bellwether for psychological health and well-being, much needs to be done to help empower GLBT employees. Within the next section of this article, a framework will be offered which can inform how to create a work environment which could optimize the strengths and capabilities of sexual minorities, hence allowing them to be optimally productive.

CREATING A PRODUCTIVE WORK ENVIRONMENT FOR GLBT EMPLOYEES

Despite the workplace being a potentially stressful venue for a GLBT employee, paradoxically, it could also be a place where one could operate from her strengths, and experience empowerment. What, then, would be the components of an organizational context that would allow sexual minority employees to be optimally productive?

The answer to that question is that GLBT employees want a piece of the *PIE*. As an acronym, *PIE* stands for *protection, inclusion,* and *equity*. Protection includes policies and programs that prohibit discrimination and prevent harassment. Inclusion relates to creating an organizational culture whereby GLBT employees are acknowledged and appreciated. Equity entails providing equal access to dependent care benefits and domestic partner eligibility for health insurance coverage. Each of these areas will be elaborated below, with remedies suggested.

Protection

The Issues. As was noted earlier, there is no federal legislation that protects GLBT persons from employment discrimination; and as such, they may not file a complaint with the Equal Employment Opportunity Commission. In order to redress this problem, Senator Edward Kennedy has introduced into every session of Congress since 1994, the Employment Nondiscrimination Act (ENDA). This policy would affect employers with 15 or more employees, prohibiting them from using an individual's sexual orientation in making employment decisions. In addition, the bill specifies remedies, including reinstatement and punitive damages. In essence, this extends civil rights' protections to sexual minority employees. However, ENDA would exempt religious organizations and the Armed Forces.

ENDA has received broad support from political, business, labor, and civil rights groups. Joining Senator Kennedy are 30 senators, 194 congressional representatives, Fortune 500 firms, numerous small companies and organized labor. There are good economic reasons to outlaw discrimination based on sexual orientation. First, because of greater competition for qualified workers, talented GLBT employees will gravitate to those employers prohibiting sexual orientation discrimination. Second, discrimination bears costs to taxpayers, consumers, and corporations. It is estimated that 42,000 gay workers are dismissed each year due to sexual orientation, which translates into a $47 million loss. Third, within a hostile work environment, GLBT employees' productivity declines, which results in an additional $1.4 billion yearly loss (Poverny, 2000). Fourth, research has shown that employees working for organizations having sexual orientation antidiscrimination policies experience enhanced job satisfaction (Ellis and Riggle, 1995; Day and Schoenrade, 2000). It would be safe to assume that more satisfied employees will be more productive.

In addition to freedom from discrimination, GLBT employees also need to be protected from sexual orientation harassment. Hate crimes are a reality, and gay bashing is prevalent. For example, there were approximately 1900 hate crimes against gays and lesbians in 1992, within only *five* major U.S. cities (Van Den Bergh, 1994). Data from FBI Uniform Crime Reports, 1991-1997, note that hate crimes against lesbians and gays are ranked third, constituting 14% of such incidents. The majority of these crimes are perpetrated on gay males, as can be evidenced by EEOC reported harassments tripling from 481 in 1991, to 1500 in 1994 (Pride at Work, AFL-CIO, 1999). It may be that attacks against lesbians are noted as sexual assault.

It is assumed that attacks on gay employees may represent 10% of all workplace harassments (Mims and Kleiner, 1998, homosexuals harassment in workplace article). A randomized telephone poll conducted by Louis Harris and Associates in 1994 found that of 782 workers polled, 7% of gay male workers claimed harassment at work, and 62% took no action against the perpetrator (Out and Equal, 2002). Examples of harassment include: (a) sexually demeaning statements, questions or jokes, (b) remarks about sexual activity or speculations about sexual experiences, (c) remarks of a sexual nature about a person's body or clothing, and (d) display of sexually explicit materials in the workplace.

To deal more pointedly with the elimination of harassment based on sexual orientation, including within the workplace, a Hate Crimes Prevention Act has been proposed to Congress, that has been renamed as the Local Law Enforcement Enhancement Act (LLEEA). This bill would add sexual orientation and gender identity to protected classes under federal hate crimes law. There is bipartisan congressional support for this policy, having been passed in the Senate; however, it has never been voted upon in the House (HRC, 1/10/03).

An emerging issue related to protection is ensuring that gender identity is also safeguarded within antidiscrimination policies. Although one may think this exclusively applies to persons who are transgendered, it also relates to discrimination based on gender nonconformity. For example, a lesbian preferring short hair and masculine clothing could be discriminated against based upon her nontraditional gender identity.

To date, two states, the District of Columbia, and 32 local governments have passed laws prohibiting employment discrimination against transgendered persons. Three other states have extended some legal protections and about 20 private employers (including five Fortune 500 companies) include gender identity in their nondiscrimination policies.

The Solutions. First and foremost, every organization should create a specific antidiscrimination policy, plus procedures, for addressing sexual orientation and gender identity discrimination. Such a policy must be distributed to all employees, included within employment orientation materials, and prominently displayed at the workplace.

Furthermore, organizations must explicitly prohibit harassment based on sexual orientation by ensuring it is covered within workplace harassment policies and procedures. Information about this must be disseminated to all employees, and it needs to be included within supervisor training.

Additionally, it is important to respect employees' rights to bargain collectively for sexual orientation antidiscrimination protections. In some locations, a collective bargaining agreement may be the only real source of protection for GLBT workers.

It is also very important to advocate for macro level policy initiatives that create local and state laws precluding discrimination based on sexual orientation.

Similarly, it is important to communicate with senators and congresspersons regarding support for ENDA and LLEEA.

Additionally, since knowledge is power, it is highly recommended that one become familiar with GLBT organizations that monitor workplace discrimination and harassment. Specifically, this means acquiring familiarity with the Human Rights Campaign WorkNet (*www.hrc.org/worknet*), National Gay and Lesbian Task Force Workplace Project (*www.ngltf.org*), Pride at Work, (*www.prideatwork.org*), Out and Equal (*www.outandequal.org*), and the National Center for Lesbian Rights (*www.nclr.org*).

Inclusion

The Issues. An inclusionary work environment would be one whereby employees feel free to be "out" at the workplace. They could be honest and forthcoming about aspects of their personal and family life, including sharing photos of their "loved ones." Additionally, a GLBT employee would have no hesitation about bringing his/her domestic partner or significant other to workplace-related social events. Also, there could be GLBT employee networking groups. Organizational communications would be free from heterosexist bias, including use of terms like partner instead of husband or wife. Workplace diversity initiatives would be inclusive of sexual orientation, and valuing of GLBT employees would be part of the organization's overall diversity agenda.

Research has substantiated that GLBT employees who feel free to be "out" have greater commitment to their organization (Ellis and Riggle, 1995). A strong predictor to greater commitment includes top management creating policies as well as procedures to manage sexual orientation harassment and discrimination (Day and Schoenrade, 2000). In a service, post-industrial economy where the demand for qualified employees exceeds the supply, firms are advantaged by creating a welcoming and inclusive workplace for sexual minority employees. This is because GLBT employees may tend to have higher education than the population as a whole; hence, they are desirable employees (Van Den Bergh, 1994).

What percent of the GLBT workforce is actually "out?" This is challenging to ascertain because of the difficulty in obtaining probability samples when seeking GLBT respondents. Information suggests that a significant percentage of sexual minority employees are "closeted." For example, a national survey revealed that only 33% of lesbians and 62% of gay men had "come out" at work (Seck et al., 1993). In a related vein, other national research found that 15% of gay men and 19% of lesbians selected their job or profession because of their sexual orientation (Badgett, 1996). So, what does that mean? Perhaps sexual minorities perceive certain kinds of jobs, or careers, as safer in that they do not have to conform to traditional gender roles.

In terms of trends related to disclosure, some research has found an inverse relationship between income and level of "outness" (Van Den Bergh, 1999). Perhaps GLBT employees with higher incomes or professional occupations fear they have more to lose by being honest about their sexual orientation. It is also interesting that lesbians are only half as likely as men to be "out," and black GLBT employees were less likely than either whites or Hispanics to disclose their sexual orientation (Badgett, 1996). These data may suggest concern with the effect of interlocking oppressions in predicting discrimination. That is, sexism and racism, in combination with heterosexism, could make "coming out" even more of a risk.

Additional manifestations of "outness" include acknowledging one's same sex partner. In research comparing straight and gay employees, only 24% of GLBT respondents were comfortable displaying a photo of their significant other, compared to 47% of heterosexuals. Additionally, while 51% of heterosexuals would feel comfortable introducing their partner at a work-related social event, only 32% of GLBT employees felt the same way (Out and Equal Workplace Advocates, 2002).

A significant amount of literature has recounted the positive benefits of being "out" for a GLBT individual's mental, physical, and spiritual health (Nissen, 1993; Sussman, 1996). Hence, it can only be in the best interest of organizations to promote an organizational climate that allows GLBT employees to feel safe in being honest about whom they are and their "family of choice."

The Solutions. What are steps that can be taken to create an inclusionary work environment for GLBT employees? The most critical is establishing policies and procedures that forbid sexual orientation discrimination and harassment. Having ensured policy protection, below is an articulation of other actions that can promote a sense of inclusivity for GLBT employees:

1. Top management articulating the need to build a safe working environment for GLBT employees.
2. Organizational mission statements that articulate accepting diversity in sexual orientation of employees and clients.
3. Diversity awareness training for all employees, including supervisors and managers that address sexual orientation and gender identity.
4. Development of "safe zones" whereby GLBT employees feel accepted for their sexual orientation. As an example, placing the pink lambda triangle or rainbow flag on an office door sends the message, "you can be who you are here."
5. Establishment of GLBT employee networks. Most Fortune 500 companies, as well as professional associations such as NASW, CSWE, BPD,

APA, and AMA have such affiliation groups. At present there are at least 270 employers with a GLBT employee group (HRC WorkNet, 2001).

6. Creation of corporate social responsibility endeavors within the sexual minority community, including charitable support for GLBT organizations. Corporations may be particularly amenable to consider sponsorship of youth programs, since young GLBT individuals are in need of support and mentoring.
7. Engagement in assertive outreach and appropriate marketing to GLBT clients and constituents. This can encourage GLBT clients to utilize services.
8. Affirmative interviews for job candidates, letting them know the organization supports diversity including sexual orientation.
9. Extension of invitations to, and welcoming of same sex partners at company events.
10. Discouragement of homophobic jokes and heterosexist statements in workplace banter.
11. Inclusivity in terminology within organizational communications and forms by use of terms such as "partner" rather than spouse.
12. Awareness that not all employees or clients are heterosexual!

Equity

The Issues. Equity for GLBT employees entails being able to use dependent care leave and to have health insurance coverage for domestic partners. Benefits fall under the rubric of compensation, which includes salary plus health insurance costs and governmental tithes for Social Security, Medicare, etc. Typically it is assumed that an employer pays about 30% on top of an employee's salary, to offer benefits. Hence, benefits are part of one's "earnings."

Related to dependent care, the issue for GLBT employees is having time off from work, without threat of job loss, in order to care for whomever they deem to be a "dependent." Dependent care benefits are provided by employers in recognition of employees' roles in caretaking responsibilities. Because of the ever-increasing presence of women in the workforce, no one is "at home" to care for an ill child, partner/spouse, aging parent, etc. The Family and Medical Leave Act of 1993 allows an employee up to 12 weeks of *unpaid* leave from the workplace, without threat of job loss. However, it is questionable as to whether a GLBT employee could avail herself of this opportunity since family has been construed as those bonded by blood or marriage. With the burgeoning of multiple family forms within the GLBT community as evidenced through lesbian births, adoption by gay men as well as lesbians, plus caretaking stressors related to AIDS-affected partners, sexual minority employees need equal access to dependent care benefits.

The equity issue surrounding domestic partner health care benefits is equal pay for equal work. GLBT people are not allowed to marry, and most benefit plans are written to include one's spouse and children. Hence, this systematically excludes domestic partnerships, plus families where children are being raised and the biological parent is not the covered employee.

The percentage of households consisting of persons cohabitating who are not legally married is increasing. Data from the 2000 census indicated that the number of Americans living in "unmarried partner households" rose from 3.2 million in 1990 to 5.5 million. This means that unmarried partner households are growing at a faster rate than married partner households. Furthermore, same-sex partner households are present in 99.3 percent of all counties within the United States (HRC WorkNet, 2001).

Domestic partner benefits are not an "extra." They are essential for GLBT employees who cannot get married, are in committed domestic partnerships and whose partner is not covered by her/his own benefit plan. In an age of high employment as well as increasing use of part-time rather than full-time employees, persons not having access to health care benefits may become more of a norm than an anomaly.

Even when provided with the option of domestic partner benefits, a GLBT employee is disadvantaged by the way monies for those benefits are extracted from his/her pay. Unlike health care insurance for one's legal spouse, domestic partner benefits are taxable, and premiums must be paid from the worker's after tax dollars (not pretax as they are for married workers). In addition domestic partners are not treated equally under COBRA that provides continuation of benefits to spouses and offspring in the event of an employee's death, divorce, reduction in hours, or termination of employment (HRC FamilyNet, 2002). Furthermore, medical savings accounts cannot be used to reimburse a domestic partner's medical expenses nor can a domestic partner automatically receive pension benefits in the event of her/his partner's death.

One might wonder how expensive it would be for an organization to offer DP benefits. Research orchestrated by Apple Computer of technology firms providing DP benefits found that average cost increases were from 0.4% to 0.7%. Study undertaken by Stanford University also found that costs associated with covering domestic partners to be less than a 1.0% increase. One reason for this minimal increase would be that members of same-sex couples are typically both employed; hence, not needing DP coverage (Spielman and Winfield, 1996).

Another reason why offering DP benefits may not be costly is that to prove a domestic partnership requires significant verification. For example, Columbia University defines domestic partners as " . . . two individuals of the same gender who live together in a long term relationship of infinite duration, with an exclusive mutual commitment similar to that of marriage, in which the partners agree to be financially responsible for each other's welfare and share financial obligations" (Columbia University, 1993, in Spielman and Winfield, 1996). Typically domestic partners must prove:

1. Co-habitation for at least six months with the intent to do so indefinitely
2. Joint responsibility for each other's common welfare and shared financial obligations as demonstrated by the following:
    a. Registration as domestic partners in locales where that is possible. Currently, two states and 56 cities or counties have established domestic partner registries
    b. A joint mortgage or lease
    c. Designation of one's partner as a beneficiary on life insurance, a will or retirement benefits
    d. Assignment of durable power of attorney or health care proxy to one's domestic partner
    e. Joint ownership of a car, bank account, or joint credit account (Spielman and Winfield, 1996)

Given its relative inexpensiveness, how prevalent is domestic partnership benefits' coverage? The number of employers that provide DP health insurance benefits has increased at a rapid pace in the last several years. A national survey released in 2001 of 570 large U.S. employers found that the number of companies offering DP benefits has doubled since 1997. Data garnered by the Human Rights Campaign demonstrated similar trends with a 50% increase in the number of firms offering DP benefits from 2856 in 1999, to 4285 in 2001. Employers that offer domestic partner health benefits operate in all 50 states with California, Illinois, Massachusetts, New York, and Washington leading the way. The total numbers of employers that offer this coverage as of 2002 include:

1. 181 Fortune 500 companies, including 54% of the top fifty firms
2. 5209 other private companies, non profit organizations and unions
3. 179 colleges and universities, including 34 of the nation's top 50 universities and 29 of the best liberal arts colleges
4. 10 state governments
5. 142 local governments and quasi-governmental agencies (HRC Work Net, 2001)

The Solutions. It is important to organize at the workplace so that personnel administrators include DP coverage within the overall employee compensation package. Additionally, DP benefits should be negotiated within collective bargaining agreements. Proposals can be placed before municipalities (counties, towns, and cities) to create domestic partnership registries. State government and congressional representatives can be lobbied for passage of legislation allowing for DP registry (as well as coverage of government employees for DP benefits). As policy examples, the Domestic Partnership Benefits and Obligations Act of 2001 (sponsored by Rep. Barney Fran, D-Mass) would provide DP benefits to all federal employees. In a related vein, a bill introduced by Rep. Carolyn Maloney (D-NY) in 2001 would broaden the Family and Medical Leave Act to allow time off from work to care for a domestic partner with a serious illness.

Within the foregoing discussion a conceptual framework, *PIE*, has been elaborated to address protection, inclusion and equity issues for GLBT employees. This coverage has stressed macro and mezzo level interventions. In the next section, principles of culturally competent practice will be used to suggest micro level practice approaches with GLBT employees.

CULTURALLY COMPETENT INTERVENTIONS WITH GLBT EMPLOYEES AT THE WORKPLACE

It is fair to say that most practitioners working with GLBT employees on a micro level would be offering employee assistance program services. Or, a pracitioner could be working with an employee utilizing her mental health benefits. Both EAP and managed care services are time-limited in approach and require the practitioner to understand employment laws and policies, as well as health care benefit programs. In other words, workplace-related practice is a specialty and one should not venture forth into this realm without proper training.

The best framework for informing practice with GLBT employees at the workplace is cultural competence. As the latest iteration in paradigms suggesting how to deal with multicultural clients, cultural competence addresses attitudes, knowledge, and skills a practitioner must acquire to be effective with culturally diverse clients (Crisp and Van Den Bergh, 2002; Lum, 1999; Leigh, 1998; Weaver, 1999; Fong and Furuto, 2001). NASW has published standards for cultural competence (NASW, 2001), which includes sexual minorities, and GLBT clients are also mentioned in a *Social Work Speaks* position paper on cultural competence within the profession (NASW, 1996).

Principles of gay affirmative practice (GAP) offer a good starting point in developing a culturally competent approach with sexual minorities. GAP is a philosophical approach that considers a gay, lesbian, or bisexual identity as equally valid to heterosexuality. Clients are supported in their coming out process, and their relationships are validated. It can be applied to many different treatment modalities including individual, couple, and family treatment (Appleby and Anastas, 1998).

Attitudes

Any discussion of culturally competent practice always begins with a discussion of attitudes, since they will play a significant role in the extent to which a practitioner is motivated to be more effective with culturally diverse clients. As this pertains to sexual minority clients, the first step would be self-awareness as to how one feels about gay, lesbian, bisexual, and transgendered persons. This self-perusal should include reflection on the development of one's own sexual orientation as well as reflection on experiences with GLBT individuals. If a practitioner experiences heterosexist or homophobic biases in her or his thinking then s/he should: (1) not accept referrals of GLBT clients or (2) engage in personal and professional development so as to acquire more exposure to gay and lesbian people and sexual minority issues.

As an example, below are some beliefs that would be important for an occupational practitioner to hold if s/he was to demonstrate cultural competence with GLBT clients:

1. It is important to assess sexual orientation during an intake
2. Sexual orientation should not be assumed as the primary problem
3. Services should be offered to domestic partners of GLBT employees
4. Same-sex couple interventions should be provided
5. Domestic partners should have access to health insurance benefits
6. GLBT employees should be able to utilize dependent care benefits for their "family"
7. There should be specific workplace policies protecting GLBT employees from discrimination or harassment based on sexual orientation
8. Content related to GLBT issues should always be included within diversity training agendas

Knowledge

Practice with any culturally distinct group should encompass information about history, traditions, terminology and language, celebrations and symbols, as well as challenges and unmet needs. Related to working with GLBT employees, important knowledge is awareness of the significant diversity within the GLBT community related to race, ethnicity, religious/spiritual orientation, income, occupational type and profession, relationship status, and age. Hence, practitioners need to honor the individuality of their GLBT clients, so as to not operate from stereotypes.

Specific to the workplace, occupational practitioners need to have knowledge about: (a) organizational nondiscrimination as well as antiharassment policies and how they apply to GLBT employees, (b) procedures which a GLBT employee should follow to pursue a discrimination or harassment claim, (c) GLBT organizational support groups or networks, (d) availability of domestic partner or dependent care coverage, and (e) ways to access reasonable accommodation for a health-related disability.

Additional critical knowledge that an occupational practitioner must acquire concerns resources specific to the GLBT community. This includes health care clinics, mental health agencies, substance abuse treatment providers, and other social service agencies that are affirming and welcoming of sexual minority clients. Information about gay affirming resources within one's geographic locale could be acquired from any of the following groups: (a) National Association of Gay and Lesbian Alcoholism Professionals (*www.naglap.org*), (b) Gay and Lesbian Medical Association (*www.glma.org*) and (c) National Coalition for Lesbian, Gay, Bisexual, and Transgender Health (*www.nclgbth.org*).

Additional areas a practitioner would need to acquire knowledge about would include the following: (a) GLBT faith organizations, (b) business or professional associations, (c) mutual aid and peer support groups such as Parents, Families, and Friends of Lesbians and Gays (PFLAG), (d) gay parenting groups, (e) local GLBT advocacy organizations or affiliates of national organizations such as GLSEN (Gay, Lesbian, Straight Educators Network), (f) state and local sexual orientation antidiscrimination policies, (g) opportunities to register as domestic partners, (h) financial as well as legal professionals who address GLBT issues, and (i) 12 Step meetings specific for GLBT persons.

Finally, to be of greatest service to GLBT employees, an occupational practitioner should have information on GLBT "family" law. This would include GLBT custody and adoption rights, as well as second parent adoption options.

Skills

This dimension of culturally competent practice requires one place attitudes and knowledge into action. The foremost skill that a practitioner should acquire is the ability to create a "gay-safe" treatment milieu. Previously, attention has been given to mezzo and macro interventions that would engender a safe workplace for GLBT employees. On the micro level, safety would be imparted by: (a) assessing sexual orientation while being gay affirming, (b) sensitivity in use of terms like partner as opposed to spouse, (c) querying for relationship as opposed to marital status, (d) having materials within one's office which imparted awareness of GLBT resources as well as literature, (e) having symbols such as the rainbow flag or lambda triangle prominently displayed.

Related to assessment skills, it would be important to determine the extent to which a client's challenge could be due to heterosexism or homophobia. Similarly, it would be valuable to determine if internalized homophobia lay at the root of any anxiety, fear, or self-deprecatory tendencies. Ascertaining a client's level of "outness" is also important, as it will guide the appropriateness of certain intervention alternatives.

Of additional importance is probing, acknowledging, and validating a client's strengths as a sexual minority. Hence, it would be important to ascertain how sexual orientation may have affected a client's coping strategies. Those that are healthy should be validated, and others may have to be retooled or eliminated. Clients who may be struggling with their sexual orientation should be supported, and their discomfort should be reframed as a normal response to a period of uncertainty and questioning. It may be useful to describe the "coming out" process as investigative research, whereby one has to obtain data in order to know what is true or valid for oneself. Hence, someone "coming out" would need to explore aspects of sexual minority culture and meet gay, lesbian, bisexual, or transgendered persons in order to define his or her own identity.

Cultural competence with GLBT clients requires including within treatment whomever a client considers to be "family." This will be particularly important within addiction and mental health programs. In those contexts it is necessary to ensure safety for GLBT clients and their significant others, should other clients have a heterosexist or homophobic bias.

It is critically important to offer and continually update gay affirming referrals. The areas in which these need to be developed were elaborated previously within the knowledge section.

Finally, it is the wise, accountable, and ethical practitioner who knows when it is time to acquire supervision as well as professional development to improve one's work with GLBT clients. If a practitioner has an impasse in work with a sexual minority employee and does not have the benefit of agency supervision, it would be a good idea to gain peer supervision. Additionally one could seek consultation through GLBT caucuses within NASW, CSWE, or BPD. It would also be possible to make contact with one of the GLBT national health and mental health organizations previously mentioned.

CONCLUSION

Gay, lesbian, bisexual and transgendered employees are an integral component of the national workforce. They are everywhere, and represent all occupational strata and professions. In order to make maximum use of this population's talents, skills, abilities and energy, they need a piece of the workplace *PIE*, related to protection, inclusion and equity. And, as clients of occupational practitioners, GLBT employees need to feel safe and culturally validated, having confidence that their worker is capable of referring them to gay affirming community resources and services.

As the last bastion of civil rights advocacy, ensuring a safe work environment for sexual minorities allows for a more productive workplace, an empowered workforce, and the potential for unlimited personal empowerment.

REFERENCES

Appleby, G. & Anastas, J. (Eds.). (1998). *Not just a passing phase: Social work with gay, lesbian, and bisexual people*. New York: Columbia University Press.

Badgett, M.V. Lee (1996). Employment and sexual orientation: Disclosure and discrimination in the workplace. *Journal of Gay and Lesbian Social Services, 4*(4), 29-51.

CCH Editorial Staff (1997, July). Homosexuals. *Human Resources Management: Equal Employment Opportunity in Two Volumes*. Chicago: IL, 343-345.

Crisp, C. & Van Den Bergh, N. (2002). Challenges in defining and measuring cultural competency with sexual minorities. Paper presented at the Council on Social Work Education Annual Program Meeting, Nashville, TN, February 26, 2002.

Croteau, J. (1996). Research on the work experiences of lesbian, gay, and bisexual people: An integrative review of methodology and findings. *Journal of Vocational Behavior, 48*, 195-209.

Day, N. & Schoenrade, P. (2000). The relationship among reported disclosure of sexual orientation, anti-discrimination policies, top management support, and work attitudes of gay and lesbian employees. *Personnel Review, 29*(3), 346-363.

Editors, Harvard Law Review. (1989). Employment issues affecting gay men and lesbians. *Developments in the Law-Sexual Orientation and the Law, Harvard Law Review, 102*, 1511-1584.

Ellis, A. (1996). Sexual identity issues in the workplace: Past and present. *Journal of Gay and Lesbian Social Services, 4*(4), 1-16.

Ellis, A. & Riggle, E. (1995). The relation of job satisfaction and degree of openness about one's sexual orientation for lesbians and gay men. *Journal of Homosexuality, 30*(2), 75-85.

Fong, R. & Furuto, S. (Eds.) (2001). *Culturally Competent Practice: Skills, Interventions, and Evaluations*. Boston: Allyn & Bacon.

Gonsiorek, J. (1993). Threat, stress and adjustment: Mental health and the workplace for gay and lesbian individuals. In L. Diamant (Ed.) *Homosexual Issues in the Workplace*. Washington, D.C.: Taylor and Francis Publishers.

Hedgepeth, J. (1980). Employment discrimination law and the rights of gay persons. *Journal of Homosexuality, 5*, 67-78.

Hollywood Supports (1993, Fall). Group health coverage for employees' same sex partners. Los Angeles, Ca: GLAAD/LA.

Human Rights Campaign (12/7/02). Gay, lesbian, bisexual and transgender workplace issues. [on-line] Available: *www.hrc.org/issues/workplace/index.asp.*

Human Rights Campaign (12/16/02). Congressional Legislation Employment Non-discrimination Act (ENDA). [on-line]. Available: *www.capwiz.com/hrc/issues/bills/?bill=46908.*

Human Rights Campaign (1/10/03). GLBT Issues in the 107th Congress-2nd Session [on-line]. Available: *www.hrc.org/congress/107/index.asp.*

Human Rights Campaign FamilyNet (2002) Tax costs of domestic partner benefits. [on-line] Available: *www.hrc.org/familynet/cchapter.asp?article=700.*

Human Rights Campaign WorkNet (2001). The state of the workplace for lesbian, gay, bisexual and transgendered Americans, 2001. Washington, D.C.: HRC Foundation.

Human Rights Campaign WorkNet (1/10/03). Employers with nondiscrimination policies that include sexual orientation. [on-line]. Available: *www.hrc.org/worknet/asp_search/detail_search.asp.*

Human Rights Campaign WorkNet (1/24/03). The invisible minority: Making sure gay workers do not get stigmatized. [on-line]. Available: *www.hrc.org/worknet/wworkalert/2003/0601/article08.asp.*

Kovach, K. (1995). Proposal would expand civil rights legislation. *Employment Relations Today*, 22(3), 9-15.

Leigh, J. (1998). *Communicating for Cultural Competence.* Boston: Allyn & Bacon.

Levine, M. (1979). Employment discrimination against gay men. *International Review of Modern Sociology*, 9(July-Dec), 151-163.

Levine, M. & Leonard, R. (1984). Discrimination against lesbians in the workforce. *Signs: Journal of Women in Culture and Society, 9*, 700-710.

Lum, D. (1999). *Culturally Competent Practice: A Framework for Growth and Action.* Pacific Grove, CA: Brooks/Cole Publishing Co.

Mims, C. & Kleiner, B. (1998). Homosexual harassment in the workplace. *Equal Opportunities International, 17*(7), 16-20.

Moore (10/2/88). Military found to further limit women. *Washington Post,* AA113, col 1.

NASW Delegate Assembly (1996). Cultural competence in the social work profession. *Social Work Speaks*, 59-62.

NASW National Committee on racial and Ethnic Diversity (2001). *NASW Standards for Cultural Competence in the Practice of Social Work.* Washington, D.C.: NASW Press.

Nissen, J. (1993). Healing from cultural victimization: Recovery from shame due to heterosexism. *Journal of Gay and Lesbian Psychotherapy, 2*(1), 49-63.

Obear, K. (2000). Best practices that address homophobia and heterosexism in corporations. *Diversity Factor, 9*(1), 26-30.

Out and Equal Workplace Advocates (2002). Survey finds lesbians and gay men face persistent discrimination and hostility in corporate America. *Out and Equal, 4*(4), 7-8.

Poverny, L & Finch, W. (1988). Integrating work-related issues on gay and lesbian employees into occupational social work practice. *Employee Assistance Quarterly, 4*(2), 15-29.

Poverny, L. (2000). Employee assistance practice with sexual minorities. *Administration in Social Work, 23*(3/4), 69-91.

Powers, B. (1996). The impact of gay, lesbian, and bisexual workplace issues on productivity. *Journal of Gay and Lesbian Social Services, 4*(4), 79-90.

Pride at Work AFL-CIO (1999). Hate Crimes and the Hate Crimes Prevention Act. Washington: D.C.: Pride at Work *www.igc.org/prideatwork.*

Riccucci, N. & Gossett, C. (1996). Employment discrimination in state and local government: The lesbian and gay male experience. *American Review of Public Administration, 26*(2), 175-200.

Salholz, E., Glick, D. Beachy, L., Monserrate, C., King, P., Gordon, J. & Barrett, T. (1993, June 21). *Newsweek*, 54-60.

Seck, E., Finch, W., Mor-Barak, M. & Poverny, L. (1993). Managing a diverse workforce. *Administration in Social Work, 17*(2), 67-79.

Servicemembers Legal Defense Network (SLDN) (3/14/02). Conduct unbecoming: The 8th Annual Report on "Don't Ask, Don't Tell." [on-line]. Available: *www.sldn.org/templates/law/record.html?section=22&record=473.*

Spielman, S. & Winfield, L. (1996). Domestic partner benefits: A bottom line discussion. *Journal of Gay and Lesbian Social Services, 4*(4), 53-77.

Susser, P. (1986). Sexual preference discrimination: Limited protection for gay workers. *Employment Relations Today, 13*, 54-65.

Sussman, T. (1996). Gay men in the workplace: Issues for mental health counselors. *Journal of Gay, Lesbian, and Bisexual Identity, 1*(3), 193-211.

Van Den Bergh, N. (1994). From invisibility to voice: Providing EAP assistance to lesbians at the workplace. *Employee Assistance Quarterly, 9*(3/4), 166-177.

Van Den Bergh, N. (1999). Workplace problems and needs for lesbian and gay male employees: Implications for EAPS. *Employee Assistance Quarterly, 15*(1), 21-60.

Weaver, H. (1999). Indigenous people and the social work profession: Defining culturally competent services. *Social Work, 44*(3), 217-225.

Winfield, L. & Spielman, S. (2001). *Straight Talk About Gays in the Workplace.* New York: Harrington Park Press.

Heterosexism and Social Work: An Ethical Issue

Maryann Krieglstein

SUMMARY. This study examined heterosexism among 409 Illinois school social workers. Heterosexism was found to be negatively corre-lated with "education about" and "positive contacts with" gay and les-bian individuals and positively correlated with "religiosity." Most respondents showed some level of heterosexism with a few having very high levels. Only 15% were non-heterosexist. Respondents reported re-ceiving little or no education about sexual minorities in their social work training. Most indicated that the training received was not adequate prep-aration for working with gay and lesbian individuals. Amount of educa-tion received increased with each of CSWE's educational mandates about sexual minorities but had no significant effect on heterosexism. *[Article copies available for a fee from The Haworth Document Delivery Service: 1-800-HAWORTH. E-mail address: <docdelivery@haworthpress.com> Website: <http://www.HaworthPress.com> © 2003 by The Haworth Press, Inc. All rights reserved.]*

KEYWORDS. Ethics, gay and lesbian, and hetho sexism, social work

---

Maryann Krieglstein, PhD, is Assistant Professor, George Williams College of So-cial Work, Aurora University, Aurora, IL 60506-4892.

[Haworth co-indexing entry note]: "Heterosexism and Social Work: An Ethical Issue." Krieglstein, Maryann. Co-published simultaneously in *Journal of Human Behavior in the Social Environment* (The Haworth Social Work Practice Press, an imprint of The Haworth Press, Inc.) Vol. 8, No. 2/3, 2003, pp. 75-91; and: *Sexual Minorities: Discrimination, Challenges, and Development in America* (ed: Michael K. Sullivan) The Haworth Social Work Practice Press, an imprint of The Haworth Press, Inc., 2003, pp. 75-91. Single or multiple copies of this article are available for a fee from The Haworth Document Delivery Service [1-800-HAWORTH, 9:00 a.m. - 5:00 p.m. (EST). E-mail address: docdelivery@haworthpress.com].

Journal of Human Behavior in the Social Environment, Vol. 8(2/3) 2003
http://www.haworthpress.com/web/JHBSE
© 2003 by The Haworth Press, Inc. All rights reserved.
Digital Object Identifier: 10.1300/J137v8n02_05

INTRODUCTION

Gay and lesbian (GL) students are at tremendous risk in the nation's schools (Human Rights Watch, 2001; Lipkin, 1999). They are at high risk for substance abuse, suicide, low self-esteem, HIV/AIDS, prostitution, running away, violence and various school problems (Grossman & Kerner, 1998; Remafedi, French, Story, Resnick, & Blum, 1998; Russell & Joyner, 2001). Heterosexism not only causes many of these stressors but also serves as a barrier to lesbian and gay youth accessing services that could help them cope with these stressors (American Academy of Pediatrics, 1993; Lipkin, 1999; Lock & Kleis, 1998). All too often those working with these students have heterosexist attitudes which compromise the services they should be providing and add to the level of stress of this at-risk population (American Academy of Pediatrics, 1993; Brown, 1996).

Appleby and Anastas (1998) aptly point out that since social workers make up the largest professional group in the social service and mental health systems, it is vitally important that they be aware of their own issues concerning GL individuals, and be prepared to work with this population around the multiple stressors society places on them. Cramer's (1997) research shows that the failure to identify and deal with the heterosexism of social workers does an injustice to social work's GL clients.

There is a perception that since the Council on Social Work Education began requiring content on homosexuality in the curriculum of schools of social work, the "problem" of heterosexism among social workers has been adequately addressed. Many have expressed concern, however, that this is not the case because too little attention is given to these issues in social work education. Social work graduates can enter the field of social work with their heterosexism intact (Berkman & Zinberg, 1997; Cramer, 1997; Mallon, 1998; Morrow, 1996; O'Hare, Williams, & Ezoviski, 1996).

School social workers have the potential for extensive contact with sexual minority youth, yet an extensive search of the literature revealed no study that examined heterosexism among this population. This silence in the social work literature is part of the ethical issue that Hartman and Laird (1998) say needs to be addressed if social work is to fulfill its mandate to service this at-risk population in an ethical manner.

REVIEW OF THE LITERATURE

Heterosexism

The term "heterosexism" was first used in the early 1970s to describe negative attitudes toward lesbians and gay males in terms of an ideology similar to racism and sexism (Herek, 2000). It addresses the sexist aspect of prejudice toward GL individuals. The term has been used to broaden the discussion of oppression of sexual minorities to include an analysis of societal behaviors and the impact these have on attitudes and beliefs (Appleby & Anastas, 1998), as well as actions (Neisen, 1990). Herek (1990) explains heterosexism as " . . . an ideological system that denies, denigrates, and stigmatizes any non-heterosexual form of behavior, identity, relationship, or community" (p. 361), and that views homosexuality as inferior to heterosexuality (2000). He notes that heterosexism has both cultural aspects and individual, psychological aspects which erupt into anti-gay prejudice (Herek, 1990, 1995). The hegemony of heterosexism in our society promotes and condones the individual expression of anti-gay prejudice (Herek, 1988; Murphy, 2002; Perry, 1998; Pharr, 1988).

Social Work and Heterosexism

Since issuing its first policy statement of commitment toward gay males and lesbians in 1977, NASW has reinforced and elaborated on it several times (National Association of Social Work (NASW), 1980, 1991, 1992, 1996, 1997a, 1997b, 2000). The 1997 policy statement states that "It is the position of NASW that same-gender sexual orientation should be afforded the same respect and rights as opposite gender orientations . . . NASW is committed to advancing policies and practices that will improve the status and well-being of all lesbian, gay, and bisexual people" (NASW, 1997b , p. 202).

In 1996 NASW revised its Code of Ethics to clarify and strengthen its ban on discrimination based on sexual orientation. "Social workers should act to prevent and eliminate discrimination against any person or group on the basis of . . . sexual orientation" (NASW, 1996, VI, 1, p. 9).

The Council on Social Work Education (CSWE) has also come out strongly against heterosexism. In 1992 it revised its Accreditation Standards to require all Bachelor of Social Work (BSW) and Master of Social Work (MSW) programs to include course content, in their core curriculum, that relates to the needs and practice concerns of sexual minority persons. This content was to be both theoretical and practical, including the impact of discrimination and oppression on the life chances of GL individuals. In 1995 CSWE issued a more specific policy in regards to gay and lesbian content (Appleby & Anastas, 1997). The new Education Policy and Accreditation Standards (EPAS) that went into effect in June of 2002 states that social work programs are to make "specific and continuous efforts to provide a learning context in which respect for all persons and understanding of diversity (including . . . sexual orientation) are practiced" (CSWE, 2002, accreditation standard 6). These new standards, however, are weaker than the previous mandates concerning education about

GL individuals in schools of social work (Elizabeth Cramer, personal communication, 1-29-02).

These various statements from NASW and CSWE give a resounding message that there is no place for heterosexism in social work. Any discrimination or prejudice toward lesbians or gay males is in violation of the NASW Code of Ethics. In spite of these strong statements, many social work authors have expressed concern that in practice, negative attitudes toward sexual minorities persist among some social workers and social work students (Appleby, 1998; Beckman & Zinberg, 1997; Black, Oles, Cramer, & Bennett, 1999; Black, Oles, & Moore, 1996, 1998; Cain, 1996; Cramer, 1997; Cramer, Oles, & Black, 1997; Hartman & Laird, 1999; Mackelprang, Ray, & Hernandeaz-Peck, 1996; Mallon, 1998; Morrow, 1996; O'Hare, Williams, & Exoviski, 1996; Parr & Jones, 1996; Van Soest, 1996; van Wormer, Wells, & Boes, 2000).

Morrow (1996) examined the course content of 27 textbooks used in the core curriculum of one master's level social work program and found that more than 50 percent of the texts did not adequately address GL issues. Mallon (in review) examined four major social work journals for topic content between 1964 and 1993 and found that of a total of 5,907 articles only 38 (1%) gave any coverage to GL issues (Mallon, 1998). The author of this study examined the topic index of the three main school social work textbooks used throughout the country. Two of the three (Constable, Flynn, & McDonald, 1999; and Freeman, Franklin, Fong, Shaffer, & Timberlake, 1998) contain no reference to sexual minority populations. The third (Allen-Meares, Washington, & Welsh, 2000) gives good coverage to GL issues, pointing out the risk factors for this population within the schools and the need for school social workers to be prepared to work with sexual minority students.

Morrow (1996) argues that the " . . . central component in the limitation of gay and lesbian content in social work education is a lack of knowledge about the subject by social work educators" (p. 10). This lack of knowledge is perpetuated by a historic failure of colleges and universities to actively support GL research. Many faculty refrain from scholarship in GL studies due to an implied fear that it is too controversial and might be detrimental to their future careers. This is an example of institutionalized heterosexism (Appleby & Anastas, 1997; Epstein & Zak, 1993, as cited in Appleby & Anastas, 1997; Mallon, 1998; Tierney & Rhoads, 1993; Morrow, 1996). Humphreys (1983) and Aronson (1995) state that heterosexism also keeps the early contributions of lesbians out of social work history thus denying students a chance to see the key roles they played in the beginnings of the profession.

Jones (1996) criticizes the profession for its compromise of social work's ethical standards in accrediting social work programs within host settings that consider homosexuality a sin. He sees this as validating heterosexism and adding to the oppression of sexual minority individuals. Mallon (1998) sees that "such moves signal a reluctance on the part of the professional from allowing gay and lesbian persons full and equal access to being included in the curriculum" (p. 8). Jones notes that such discrimination against any other minority group would not be tolerated. Appleby and Anastas (1997) report that the 1995 CSWE revision of evaluative standard 3, seeking to strengthen the requirement of course content on sexual minority issues, was " . . . vigorously resisted by a vocal and well-organized few" (384). Mallon (1998) points out that " . . . social work has generally lagged behind other helping professionals in putting resources behind its commitment" (p. 7).

Previous Studies of Social Workers' Attitudes Toward Sexual Minority Individuals

Though the literature shows no other study of school social workers' attitudes toward sexual minority individuals, three studies were identified that looked at such attitudes in social workers in general. Only one of these, however, took place after the 1992 implementation of CSWE's standards. De Crescenzo (1984) found that social workers in her non-random sample (N = 140) of mental health professionals were more homophobic than psychologists or psychiatrists. Wisnieswki and Toomey (1987), using a non random sample (N = 77) of clinical social workers, found that almost a third had negative attitudes toward gay and lesbian individuals. Berkman and Zinberg (1997), using a national probability sample of NASW (National Association of Social Workers) members having an MSW (N = 202), found that a majority of the sample had some heterosexist attitudes. Several studies have found heterosexism to be a problem among social work students (Black et al., 1996; Cramer, 1997; Black et al., 1999; Oles, Black, & Cramer, 1999).

METHODS

Purpose

The purpose of this study was to examine a random sample of Illinois school social workers' attitudes toward gay and lesbian individuals. Three correlates to attitudes about GL persons were observed: amount of education about this population, number of positive relationships with GL individuals, and religiosity. These variables were chosen because the literature indicates that they are three of the most salient predictors of heterosexism (Fisher, Derison, Polley, & Cadman, 1994; Herek, 1984, 1993, 1994, 1995; Sears, 1997;

Wells, 1991). They also represent aspects of social work education or the field in general which can be taken into consideration in ways that increase the cultural competency of social workers, thus allowing them to better meet the needs of sexual minorities. The impact of CSWE's educational standards on education about sexual minorities and heterosexism was also examined.

Sample

The sample consisted of School Social Workers in the State of Illinois who hold a Type 73 certificate (school social worker) and are listed in the *Membership Directory of the Illinois Association of School Social Workers*. Questionnaires were sent to a systematic random sample of 650 names from the membership directory. Responses were completely anonymous. The response rate was 70% with a total of 453 questionnaires returned. Of these, 409 met the criteria for inclusion in the study. Those eliminated did not have enough data to be useful or came from respondents who did not fit the parameters of the study.

Demographics

The average respondent was a Caucasian (84%, n = 343) female (77%, n = 315), with a mean age of 41 years (SD = 11.7), who did not have a BSW degree (69%, n = 283) and identifies as Christian (68%, n = 282). She has approximately 10 years of experience as a school social worker (SD = 8.2), and practices on multiple levels (47%, n = 193) in a predominately suburban environment (56%, n = 229). All respondents had an MSW degree. The mean year for having received this was 1988 (SD = 10.2).

Variables

Heterosexism was measured using the short version of Herick's (1988) "Attitudes toward lesbians and gay men scale" (ATLG-S). The items were coded from 1 to 5, with negative items reverse scored. The scale had a range from 10 to 50 with a higher score reflecting a more heterosexist attitude. The ATLG-S showed very good internal consistency for this study with a Cronbach's alpha of .94.

Number of hours of education about gay males and lesbians was measured by asking a serious of six questions. These included hours received in BSW and MSW programs, other academic degree programs, professional development and job training, supervision and case consultation, and self-directed learning. The hours were summed to arrive at a total score. *Number of positive relationships with GL individuals* was measured by asking respondents to self report any such relationships. *Religiosity* was measured by asking individuals to indicate how important traditional religious beliefs are in their life. The rating was on a five point scale from 1 (they have no importance at all in my life) to 5 (they are an extremely important part of all aspects of my life). *Usefulness of information received in BSW and MSW programs* for preparing respondents to work with GL individuals was also asked. A four point scale was used from "I received no education" to "It prepared me very well."

Data Analysis

Spearman's rho (r_s) was computed to describe the relationship of variables to heterosexism. The "heterosexism," "education about," and "positive relationships" scores are interval level but skewed. "Religiosity" is ordinal level. Spearman's rho is an appropriate measure for the ordinal level data. It was also deemed more suitable than Pearson's r for the interval/ratio data because it provides a more conservative measure of association for this skewed data by treating the variables as ordinal. Using the same measure for all three independent variables provides a common statistic for comparison of their relationship to the dependent variable. One-tailed tests of significance were used since all the hypotheses were directional. All tests used the raw scores. T-tests were used to examine differences in heterosexism and hours of education based on year of MSW degree and CSWE's two mandates to include content on GL individuals in social work programs (1992, 1995).

FINDINGS

Heterosexism

A majority of social workers in this study showed low levels of heterosexism. Sixteen individuals (4%) scored the maximum of 50 (the higher the score the greater the level of heterosexism). Sixty respondents (15%) scored 30 or more, putting them in the upper half of the heterosexism scale. Only sixty respondents (15%) scored 10, non-heterosexist (see Table 1). T-tests showed no significant difference in heterosexism scores based on year of MSW degree in relation to CSWE's educational mandates about GL education in schools of social work.

Hours of Education Received About GL Individuals

The mean for total hours of education received about GL individuals in the six categories listed was 18 (*SD* = 28) but due to a heavy skew the median of 9

TABLE 1. Total Heterosexism Score[a]

Mean	Median	Mode	SD	Range	
				Minimum	Maximum
19	15	10	10	10	50

[a]N = 409

is a more useful statistic. Respondents reported receiving little education about GL individuals in their formal social work preparation. Thirteen percent (n = 54) of those who indicated a BSW degree and 39% (n = 159) of MSWs reported receiving no education about this population in their respective programs. Fifteen percent of the sample (n = 60) indicated receiving no education at all about GL individuals. Most of the education about GL individuals reported by respondents was acquired on their own, but the average for this was only 3 hours. A few, reporting large numbers, skewed this statistic.

Hours of education was negatively correlated with heterosexism. All 16 school social workers who scored 50 on the heterosexism scale reported no education about GL individuals. Of the 28 who scored 40 or greater on this scale, 23 reported no such education. This finding is different from that of Berkman and Zinberg's (1997) study that found no correlation between negative attitudes and amount of education about GL individuals. DeCrescenzo (1984) and Wisnieswki and Toomey (1987) did not include this variable in their studies.

Of the respondents who reported having a BSW degree (n = 126), 80 percent (n = 101) had no education about GL individuals in their program or felt that the education they did receive did not prepare them very well to work with this population. Very good or sufficient preparation was reported by 25 respondents (20%). A majority (78%, n = 318) reported receiving no education about GL individuals in their MSW program or felt the education they did receive was not adequate preparation for working with this population. Very good or sufficient preparation was reported by 88 (22%) respondents.

Fifty-three percent of the sample (n = 217) received their MSW in or before CSWE's first educational mandate in 1992. Sixty-eight percent (n = 278) received theirs on or before 1995 when CSWE issued a stronger statement. T-tests showed the mean hours of MSW education regarding GL individuals for those who received their MSW in 1993 or later (M = 5.2, SD = 7.8) was significantly higher than the mean of those who received their MSW in 1992 or earlier (M = 2.7, SD = 9.3), t (398) = −3.5, p < .05, two tailed (see Table 2). This significant difference held true for those who received their MSW after CSWE's later policy. The mean hours of MSW education regarding GL individuals for those who received their MSW in 1996 or later (M = 6.1, SD = 8.6)

TABLE 2. BSW and MSW Education as Preparation for Working with GL Individuals

Response	BSW[a]		MSW[b]	
	Frequency	Percent	Frequency	Percent
No education in program	42	33.3	129	31.5
Prepared very little	59	46.8	189	46.2
Sufficient preparation	20	15.9	78	19.1
Prepared very well	5	4.0	10	2.4
Left blank	0	0.0	3	.7

[a]N = 126
[b]N = 409

was significantly higher than the mean of those who received their MSW in 1995 or earlier (M = 2.9, SD = 8.6), t (398) = −3.5, p < .05, two tailed. This question was unanswered by five individuals.

Number of Positive Relationships With GI Individuals

Most of the sample (91%, n = 374) reported having some positive contacts with GL individuals, with 38 percent (n = 154) indication 10 or more. The mean number of positive relationships was 11 (SD = 23), but because of the degree of skew, the median of 6 is a better indication of central tendency. Number of positive relationships with GL individuals was negatively correlated with heterosexism. Only 39 (10%) respondents reported no positive contacts. All 16 respondents who scored 50 on the heterosexism scale, however, indicated having no positive contacts with GL individuals. Twenty-three of the 28 school social workers who scored 40 or above indicated no positive relationships. Berkman and Zinberg (1997) and De Crescenzo (1984) found the same result in their studies. Wisnieswki and Toomey (1987) did not include this variable.

Religiosity

A majority of respondents stated that traditional religious beliefs are extremely important or important in their life (65%, n = 265), while 17 percent (n = 68) found them to have little or no importance. The remaining 18 percent (n = 73) indicated indifference to traditional religious beliefs. Religiosity was positively correlated with heterosexism. All of the 16 school social workers with a heterosexism score of 50 reported that traditional religious beliefs were extremely important to them. Of the 28 respondents who scored 40 or higher on heterosexism, all but one indicated that they were extremely important, with one indicating they were important. Of the 62 school social workers who scored 10 on the heterosexism scale (non-heterosexist), only two indicated that traditional religious beliefs were extremely important to them (see Table 3). Berkman and Zinberg (1997) and DeCrescenzo (1984) found a similar correlation in their studies. Wisnieswki and Toomey (1987) did not include this variable.

LIMITATIONS

Self selection for participation could have eliminated some individuals holding more negative attitudes toward sexual minorities. Generalizability of findings is maximized, however, because of the large probability sample and high response rate (63%). Several questions relied on memory which is not an exact metric. This was not reported as a problem in a pilot test of the questionnaire, and these measures are useful indications of the constructs measured.

The scale measuring heterosexism, while having extensive use and good reliability and validity (Herek, 1994, 1998), was constructed in 1988 and can be seen as somewhat dated in the language used in some of the questions. This can be considered a limitation in that some respondents reacted to the wording and thus left questions blank. Thirteen questionnaires were eliminated due to incomplete answers on this scale. Some questions were worded in a reverse fashion which could have been confusing. Many respondents crossed out their initial answer to these questions and then marked them at the opposite point on the scale.

The religiosity measure was very subjective. The term "traditional religious beliefs" may have different meaning for different respondents. This measure has been shown to have good reliability and validity (Sheeran, Spears, & Abraham, 1996), however, and it is the very subjectivity of the answer that is useful in the research looking at the relationship between religiosity and attitudes about sexual minorities.

TABLE 3. Spearman's Rho Correlation Matrix

	Heterosexism	Hours of Education	Positive Relationships	Religiosity
Heterosexism	1.000	−.323**	−.428**	.476**
Hours of education		1.000	.484**	−.151**
Positive relationships			1.000	−.192**
Religiosity				1.000

**p < .01 (1-tailed)

Responses concerning the utility of social work education in working with GL individuals are very subjective. Due to the professional nature of the respondents and their "knowing the right answer" (social desirability), response bias could also be considered a limitation. This, however, has not been an issue in other research of this kind, which tested for social desirability (Berkman & Zinberg, 1997).

IMPLICATIONS FOR SOCIAL WORK PRACTICE, POLICY, AND RESEARCH

A majority of the school social workers in this study had some heterosexist attitudes, and these were correlated to education about and contact with GL persons, and religiosity. Due to the paucity of studies on this topic, more research needs to be done to see if these findings hold true with other populations of social workers. Researchers also need to assess the impact of a social workers' heterosexism on services for gay and lesbian individuals. Black et al. (1999) have been researching this with social work students and found that attitudes do impact what they refer to as *anticipated professional behavior*. The field needs to understand what this means for the at-risk population of gay and lesbian students in the schools and GL clients in general that heterosexist social workers interact with. The field of multiculturalism is challenging the idea that one's personal attitudes can be kept in check so as not to interfere with the social work process (Green, 1999). Social work needs to encourage and support more research on this topic, with a variety of practitioners in the field, especially in light of NASW's and CSWE's strong statements against heterosexism.

Schools of social work need to provide students with more and better education about sexual minorities, education that provides the necessary skills for responding to the needs of this at-risk population. Social work associations need to offer more educational opportunities for those in the field who are not culturally competent in working with GL individuals. The profession needs to encourage more research to determine the best teaching methods for providing this training to students and practitioners. Schools of social work also need to provide training regarding sexual minorities for their faculty and staff. According to Morrow (1996) lack of education about sexual minorities by the very social work educators who are supposed to provide such education to students is a main reason that sufficient education about this population is not provided in social work education. Faculty cannot teach to others that which they are not familiar with themselves.

Increasing education about GL persons is also the responsibility of each individual social worker, including assessing ones' attitudes toward sexual minorities. The code of ethics states that "social workers should obtain education about and seek to understand the nature of social diversity and oppression with respect to . . . sexual orientation" (NASW, 1996, 1.05c). Social workers in the field need to take it upon themselves to seek out educational opportunities in order to increase their cultural competency with this population if they wish to abide by the code of ethics. Elia (1993) points out that those working in schools cannot begin to assist sexual minority students until they have addressed their own attitudes toward this population.

To the knowledge of this researcher, no other study has examined the impact of CSWE's mandates to include information about sexual minorities in the social work curriculum. Mackelprang et al.'s 1996 study on GL content in social work programs prior to the implementation of the present standards showed that little was being offered. Their study provides some baseline information for comparative studies, but the weakened standards of the new EPASS add another dimension to research in this area.

The fact that "education about sexual minorities" was significantly correlated to the year of MSW degree in relation to CSWE's educational mandates but "heterosexism" was not needs to be further examined. Although education about sexual minorities increased after the mandates, and such education seems to contribute to lower levels of heterosexism, that was not the result for this sample. This indicates that the mandates alone, and the increased education about GL individuals, have not produced enough of an effect to reduce overall levels of heterosexism among social workers, at least as suggested by this sample. More research is needed on this.

In order to utilize the correlation between heterosexism and personal contact with sexual minority individuals, schools of social work can provide opportunities for students to interact with GL individuals. Personal stories can give students a sense of the strengths and stressors of this population and be a powerful learning tool for dispelling myths and providing factual information. Schools can support student clubs that are formed around GL issues and encourage students of all sexual orientations to participate. Schools of social work need to make an effort to recruit more GL faculty, staff, and students and make sure the school climate is a safe place for these individuals to grow and develop in their respective spheres. This needs to be a conscious effort with mechanisms in place to make sure that everyone in the school, including all faculty and staff, are educated about GL individuals and that classrooms are safe places for discussion about the topic of sexual orientation. Invisibility thrives when the climate is hostile or indifferent, and invisibility is a major barrier to overcoming heterosexism. A safe climate is mandated by CSWE's (2002) accreditation standard 6.

Another area for the profession to address is religiosity and its correlation to heterosexism. Though religious beliefs are protected in this country and each person has a right to his or her own, not every person has an automatic right to a social work education and degree. The profession is not value free and has a very specific set of ethical mandates to which social workers are supposed to adhere (Van Soest, 1996). CSWE's Schools of social work need to consider the policies issued by NASW and CSWE, regarding sexual minorities, when admitting students. Prospective students need to be made aware of these standards, including the statement in the code of ethics that "social workers should not practice, condone, facilitate, or collaborate with any form of discrimination on the basis of . . . sexual orientation" (NASW, 1996, 1.05 c). These need to be read and signed off on before individuals are admitted into schools of social work. This does not negate the very real fact that students learn and grow within social work programs, but they must at least be made aware of social work's expectations and agree to be open to this possibility of change, regarding their attitudes toward sexual minorities, before they enter the program. If students know up front about these policies and know their beliefs are in conflict with them, they can make the decision not to seek entrance into the program if they do not wish to question and challenge their beliefs. This is a common practice in the field where many agencies ask their prospective employees to agree to abide by the rules of the workplace. Asking prospective students to agree to abide by the values and ethics of the profession should not be seen as any different. It is no more an infringement on anyone's rights than signing off on non-discrimination and sexual harassment policies is in the workplace. As Jones (1996), van Wormer et al. (2000), and others in the field keep stating, discrimination against any other minority group would not be acceptable within the profession, even if it was based on religious beliefs. If, as a profession, we admit heterosexist students into our training programs and they pass through these programs without altering their heterosexist ideologies and graduate with a BSW or MSW, we collude in the perpetuation of heterosexism in the field.

The profession needs to research the implications of its decision to exempt religious host schools from non-discrimination policies toward GL individuals. How can social workers become culturally competent regarding sexual minorities within an institution that openly discriminates against this population? What does this discrimination do to the possibilities, within these programs, for education about and contact with this GL persons? What impact will the new, relaxed EPAS (CSWE, 2000) requirements concerning education about sexual minorities have on these exempted schools and others that do not want to provide such information? Just how much heterosexism is too much heterosexism when viewed from the perspective of the high risk population of GL adolescents? Research needs to address these and other questions.

As Van Soest (1996) notes, there are two competing ideologies about sexual minorities in the profession, one supports the professions' non-discrimination stance, and the other does not. One sees the exemption as a compromise of the profession's ethical standards; the others see it as religious freedom. This discord within the field and within individual schools of social work cannot be ignored as Van Soest and others indicate is the present situation. Research needs to be done about the impact of these contradictory policies on the profession, and ultimately on those who are the subject of the debate–sexual minority individuals.

CONCLUSIONS

This study indicates that heterosexism is still a problem that needs to be addressed within social work. There are many actions the profession can take, in its schools of social work, in the field, in policy and in research, to address the issue of heterosexism. Lack of attention to this socially acceptable form of discrimination is an example of institutionalized heterosexism and cannot be tolerated in a profession that prides itself on acceptance of diversity and non-discrimination. Heterosexism enforces a devastating invisibility on gay and lesbian individuals, especially GL youth. The 2001 Human Rights Watch study, *Hatred in the hallways*, found the situation to be so bad for sexual minority youth in the public schools that they deemed it a human rights violation.

The lack of research on this subject within social work adds to the silence about this population and is a major barrier to the fulfillment of social work's mandates about non-discrimination toward GL individuals. All social workers need the appropriate education and training that allows them to look beyond the stereotypes and myths about GL individuals in order to acquire the skills needed to become culturally competent practitioners. Often, especially in schools, a well-trained, culturally competent non-heterosexist social worker may be the only support sexual minority youth have. The words are there in the many non-discrimination statements issued by social work to truly make an impact toward eliminating heterosexism. Now the profession needs to walk the walk and understand that this is indeed an ethical issue. To do otherwise increases the vulnerability of an already at-risk population and makes a sham of the code of ethics.

REFERENCES

Allen-Meares, P., Washington, R. O., & Welsh, B. (2000). *Social work services in schools* (3rd ed.). Boston: Allyn and Bacon.
American Academy of Pediatrics. (1993). *Homosexuality and adolescence. Pediatrics, 92*, 631-634.
Appleby, G. A. (1998). Social work practice with gay men and lesbians within organizations. In G. P. Mallon (Ed.), *Foundations of social work practice with lesbian and gay persons* (pp. 249-269). New York: The Harrington Park Press.

Aronson, J. (1995). Lesbians in social work education: Processes and puzzles in claiming visibility. *Journal of Progressive Human Services, 6,* 5-26.

Berkman, C., & Zinberg, G. (1997). Homophobia and heterosexism in social workers. *Social Work, 42,* 319-332.

Black, B., Oles, T., Cramer, E. P., & Bennett, C. K. (1999). Attitudes and behaviors of social work students toward lesbian and gay male clients: Can panel presentations make a difference. *Journal of Gay & Lesbian Social Services, 9,* 47-68.

Black, B., Oles, T., & Moore, L. (1996). Homophobia among students in social work programs. *The Journal of Baccalaureate Social Work, 2,* 23-41.

Black, B., Oles, T., & Moore, L. (1998). The relationship between attitudes: Sexism and homophobia among social work students. *Affilia, 13,* 166-189.

Brown, L. S. (1996). Preventing heterosexism and bias in psychotherapy and counseling. In E. D. Rothblum, & L. A. Bond (Eds.), *Preventing heterosexism and homophobia* (pp. 36-57). Thousand Oaks, CA: Sage.

Cain, R. (1996). Heterosexism and self-disclosure in the social work classroom. *Journal of Social Work Education, 32,* 65-76.

Constable, R., Flynn, J. P., & McDonald, S. (1999). *School social work: Practice and Research Perspectives* (4th ed.). Chicago: Lyceum Books Inc.

Council on Social Work Education (CSWE). (1992). *Handbook of accreditation standards and procedures* (4th ed.). Alexandria, VA: CSWE.

Council on Social Work Education (CSWE). (1997). *Handbook of accreditation standards and procedures.* Alexandria, VA: CSWE.

Council on Social Work Education (CSWE). (2002). *Education policy and accreditation standards.* Alexandria, VA: CSWE.

Cramer, E. P. (1997). Effects of an educational unit about lesbian identity development and self-disclosure in a social work methods course. *Journal of Social Work Education, 33,* 461-472.

Cramer, E. P., Oles, T. P., & Black, B. (1997). Reducing social work students' homophobia: An evaluation of teaching strategies. *Arete, 21,* 36-49.

Elia, J. P. (1993/94). Homophobia in the high school: A problem in need of a resolution. *The High School Journal, 77,* 177-185.

Fisher, R. D., Derison, D., Polley, C. F., & Cadman, J. (1994). Religiousness, religious orientation, and attitudes towards gays and lesbians. *Journal of Applied Social Psychology, 24,* 614-630.

Freeman, E. M., Franklin, C. G., Fong, R., Shaffer, G. L., & Timberlake, E. M. (1998). *Multisystem skills and interventions in school social work practice.* Washington, DC: NASW Press.

Green, J. W. (1999). *Cultural awareness in the human services: A multi-ethnic approach* (3rd ed.). Boston: Allyn and Bacon.

Grossman, A., & Kerner, M. (1998). Self-esteem and supportiveness as predictors of emotional distress in gay male and lesbian youth. *Journal of Homosexuality, 35,* 25-36.

Hartman, A., & Laird, J. (1998). Moral and ethical issues in working with lesbians and gay men. *Families in Society: The Journal of Contemporary Human Services, 79,* 263-275.

Herek, G. (1984). Beyond "homophobia": A social psychological perspective on attitudes toward lesbians and gay men. *Journal of Homosexuality, 10,* 1-21.

Herek, G. (1988). Heterosexuals' attitudes toward lesbians and gay men: Correlates and differences. *The Journal of Sex Research, 25*, 451- 477.

Herek, G. (1990). The context of anti-gay violence: Notes on cultural and psychological heterosexism. *Journal of Interpersonal Violence, 5*, 316-333.

Herek, G. (1993). Interpersonal contact and heterosexuals' attitudes toward gay men: Results from a national survey. *The Journal of Sex Research, 30*, 239-244.

Herek, G. (1994). Assessing heterosexuals' attitudes toward lesbians and gay men: A review of empirical research with the ATLG scale. In B. Green, & G. M. Herek (Eds.), *Lesbian and gay psychology: Theory, research, and clinical applications.* (pp. 206-228). Thousand Oaks, CA: Sage.

Herek, G. (1995). Psychological heterosexism in the United States. In P. D'Augelli (Ed.), *Lesbian, gay, and bisexual identities over the lifespan* (pp. 321-346). New York: Oxford University Press.

Herek, G. (2000). The psychology of sexual prejudice. *Current Directions in Psychological Science, 9*, 19-22.

Human Rights Watch. (2001). *Hatred in the hallways: Violence and Discrimination against lesbian, gay, bisexual, and transgender students in U.S. schools.* Retrieved July 8, 2001, from *http://www.hrw.org/reports/2001/uslgbt/toc.htm.*

Humphreys, G. E. (1983). Inclusion of content on homosexuality in the social work curriculum. *Journal of Social Work Education, 19*, 55-60.

Jones, L. (1996). Should CSWE allow social work programs in religious institutions an exemption from the accreditation nondiscrimination standard related to sexual orientation? No. *Journal of Social Work Education, 32*, 304-310.

Lipkin, A. (1999). *Understanding homosexuality, changing schools.* Boulder, CO: West View Press.

Lock, J., & Kleis, B. (1998). A primer on homophobia for the child and adolescent psychiatrist. *Journal of the American Academy of Child & Adolescent Psychiatry, 37*, 671-673.

Mackelprang, R. W., Ray, J. A., & Hernandeaz-Peck, M. (1996). Social work education and sexual orientation: Faculty, students, and curriculum issues. *Journal of Gay and Lesbian Social Services, 5*, 17-32.

Mallon, G. (1998). Knowledge for practice with gay and lesbian persons. In G. P. Mallon (Ed.), *Foundations of social work practice with lesbian and gay persons* (pp. 1-30). New York: Harrington.

Morrow, D. (1996). Heterosexism: Hidden discrimination in social work education. *Journal of Gay & Lesbian Social Services, 5*, 1-16.

Murphy, B. C. (2002). Anti-gay/lesbian violence. In D. Christie, R. Wagner, & D. D. Winter (Eds.), *Peace, Conflict, and Violence*: Peace psychology and social justice perspectives. NY: Prentice Hall.

National Association of Social Workers (NASW). (1980). *Code of Ethics.* Washington, DC: NASW Press.

National Association of Social Workers (NASW). (1991). Lesbian and gay issues. *Social Work Speaks: NASW Policy Statements,* 147-151. Silver Spring, MD: NASW Press.

National Association of Social Workers (NASW). (1996). *Code of Ethics.* Washington, DC: NASW Press.

National Association of Social Workers (NASW). (1997a). Gender, ethnic, and race-based workplace discrimination. *Social Work Speaks: NASW Policy Statements,* 146-154. Washington, D.C.: NASW Press.

National Association of Social Workers (NASW). (1997b). Lesbian, gay, and bisexual issues. *Social Work Speaks: NASW Policy Statements*, 198-209. Washington, D.C.: NASW Press.

National Association of Social Workers (NASW), National Committee on Lesbian, Gay, and Bisexual Issues. (1992). *Position statement: "reparative" or "conversion" therapies for lesbians and gay men*. Washington, DC: NASW Press.

National Association of Social Workers (NASW), National Committee on Lesbian, Gay, and Bisexual Issues. (2000, January 21). *Position statement: "reparative" and "conversion" therapies for lesbians and gay men*. Washington, DC: NASW Press. Retrieved July 15, 2001 from *http://www.naswdc.org/NASW/Diversity/lgbt/reparative.htm*.

Neisen, J. H. (1990). Heterosexism: Redefining homophobia for the 1990's. *Journal of Gay & Lesbian Psychotherapy*, *1*, 21-35.

O'Hare, T., Williams, C. L., & Exoviski, A. (1996). Fear of AIDS and homophobia: Implications for direct practice and advocacy. *Social Work*, *41*, 51-58.

Oles, T. P., Black, B. M., & Cramer, E. P. (1999). From attitude change to effective practice: Exploring the relationship. *Journal of Social Work Education*, *35*, 87-100.

Parr, R. G., & Jones, L. E. (1996). Should CSWE allow social work programs in religious institutions an exemption from the accreditation nondiscrimination standard related to sexual orientation? *Journal of Social Work Education*, *32*, 297-313.

Perry, B. J. (1998). Defenders of the faith: Hate groups and ideologies of power in the United States. *Patterns of Prejudice*, *32*, 32-54.

Pharr, S. (1988). *Homophobia, a weapon of sexism*. Inverness, CA: Chardon Press.

Remafedi, G., French, S., Story, M., Resnick, M., & Blum, R. (1998). The relationship between suicide risk and sexual orientation: Results of a population-based study. *American Journal of Public Health*, *88*, 57-60.

Russell, S. T., & Joyner, K. (2001). Adolescent sexual orientation and suicide risk: Evidence from a national study. *American Journal of Public Health*, *91*, 1276-1281.

Sears, J. T. (1997). Thinking critically/intervening effectively about heterosexism and homophobia: A twenty-five year research retrospective. In J. T. Sears, & W. L. Williams (Eds.), *Overcoming heterosexism and homophobia: Strategies that work* (13-48). New York: Columbia University Press.

Sheeran, P., Spears, R., & Abraham, S.C.S. (1996). Religiosity, gender, and the double standard. *The Journal of Psychology*, *130*, p. 23-33.

Tierney, W. G., & Roads, R. A. (1993). Enhancing academic communities for lesbian, gay, and bisexual faculty. *New Directions for Teaching and Learning*, *53*, 43-50.

Van Soest, D. (1996). The influence of competing ideologies about homosexuality on nondiscrimination policy: Implications for social work education. *Journal of Social Work Education*, *32*, 53-64.

van Wormer, K., Wells, J., & Boes, M. (2000). *Social work with lesbians, gays, and bisexuals: A strengths perspective*. Boston: Allyn and Bacon.

Wells, J. W. (1991). What makes a difference? Various teaching strategies to reduce homophobia in university students. *Annals of Sex Research*, *3*, 229-238.

Coming Out as Lesbian or Gay:
A Potential Precipitant of Crisis
in Adolescence

Vanessa E. Ford

SUMMARY. The homosexual adolescent's decision to come out as gay or lesbian for the first time is a task which requires a certain level of inner and outer resources. Despite the fact that coming out is viewed by the literature as one of many necessary developmental steps in sexual identity formation and self-acceptance, coming out can be viewed as a unique stage in this developmental continuum. Coming out is an acknowledgment of one's orientation to another person. Thus, coming out is more than an intrapsychic process; it influences interpersonal relationships as well. A whole host of factors, including identity confusion, low self-esteem, depression, alienation, withdrawal, substance abuse, and indulgence in self-destructive behavior, may result if the adolescent has little or no support in this critical developmental stage process. Involvement in the gay community or other types of homosexual peer groups offers a unique sense of support that is especially needed during the coming out period. *[Article copies available for a fee from The Haworth Document Delivery Service: 1-800-HAWORTH. E-mail address: <docdelivery@haworthpress.com> Website: <http://www.HaworthPress.com> © 2003 by The Haworth Press, Inc. All rights reserved.]*

Vanessa E. Ford, MSW, 1521 West Farwell Avenue, Chicago, IL 60626.

[Haworth co-indexing entry note]: "Coming Out as Lesbian or Gay: A Potential Precipitant of Crisis in Adolescence." Ford, Vanessa E. Co-published simultaneously in *Journal of Human Behavior in the Social Environment* (The Haworth Social Work Practice Press, an imprint of The Haworth Press, Inc.) Vol. 8, No. 2/3, 2003, pp. 93-110; and: *Sexual Minorities: Discrimination, Challenges, and Development in America* (ed: Michael K. Sullivan) The Haworth Social Work Practice Press, an imprint of The Haworth Press, Inc., 2003, pp. 93-110. Single or multiple copies of this article are available for a fee from The Haworth Document Delivery Service [1-800-HAWORTH, 9:00 a.m. - 5:00 p.m. (EST). E-mail address: docdelivery@haworthpress.com].

Journal of Human Behavior in the Social Environment, Vol. 8(2/3) 2003
http://www.haworthpress.com/web/JHBSE
© 2003 by The Haworth Press, Inc. All rights reserved.
Digital Object Identifier: 10.1300/J137v8n02_06

KEYWORDS. Gay and lesbian, coming out, crisis, adolescent and teen-agers

INTRODUCTION

Erikson posited that identity formation is the most important task of adolescence. Gay and lesbian youth are burdened with the additional task of forming a positive self-image and identity with respect to their sexual orientation, despite society's pressure to be heterosexual (Magruder & Waldner, 1999). Several studies have noted the ill effects of hiding one's sexual orientation (Jordan & Deluty, 1998; Magruder & Waldner, 1999). Yet self-disclosure opens the individual up to greater criticism from society, which tends to be homophobic and rejecting of homosexual orientations (Hayes & Walters, 1998). For the purposes of this paper, "coming out" is defined as self-disclosure of a same-sex sexual orientation to another person, and "staying in the closet" is defined as an attempt to appear heterosexual and a failure to disclose one's true orientation. Initial coming out is seen as a part of the redefinition of one's sexual identity from society's imposed standard of heterosexual, to one's self- realized identity as homosexual (Coenen, 1998).

Certainly coming out is a process that is never-ending for the gay or lesbian individual; every time one makes a new friend, enters a new school or gets a new job, one is faced with the task of deciding whether or not one should disclose one's sexual orientation. Nonetheless, coming out for the first time, either to close friends or family, is probably the most important self-disclosing event, and is the event commonly referred to as self-disclosure in a developmental sense (Deluty & Jordan, 1998). Disclosing one's orientation is cited as a discrete component of an identity process. Coming out can improve psychological well-being in terms of identity expression and perceived resources (Magruder & Waldner, 1999). The process of self-disclosure of one's sexual identity assists a homosexual in establishing authentic interpersonal relationships, validating his or her lifestyle, and presenting an authentic self (Anderson & Mavis, 1996). Coming out is seen as a necessary step towards a positive identity formation with respect to sexual orientation.

The homosexual adolescent's decision to come out as gay or lesbian for the first time is a task which requires a certain level of inner and outer resources. Despite the fact that coming out is viewed by the literature as one of many necessary developmental steps in sexual identity formation and self-acceptance, coming out can be viewed as a unique stage in this developmental continuum. Coming out is an acknowledgment of one's orientation to another person. Thus, coming out is more than an intrapsychic process; it impacts interpersonal relationships as well. One study asserts that identity confusion can induce low self-esteem, depression, alienation, withdrawal, and indulgence in self-destructive behavior as a means of coping (Magruder & Waldner, 1999). Staying in the closet can also cause confusion, a sense of hypocrisy, negative affectivity, depression, and anxiety; but coming out can elicit negative responses such as rejection, even death (Deluty & Jordan, 1998). Recent research suggests that despite the fact that gay adolescents are becoming aware of their homosexual identity at a younger age and that the age of disclosure for adolescents is decreasing over time, some individuals, particularly lesbians, choose not to come out to parents because of the perceived risks of doing so (Magruder & Waldner, 1999). Although coming out is viewed by the literature as a necessary part of mental health and growing into a homosexual identity, this event can cause great strain for the homosexual adolescent.

Gay and lesbian teenagers are under greater strain than other adolescents. Gay and lesbian teenagers are more likely to abuse drugs and alcohol, and consider or attempt suicide (Grossman & Kerner, 1998; Peters, 1997). Homophobic reactions and a lack of support abound in the homosexual's peer group and in the social institutions s/he attends (Baker & Fishbein, 1998; Hayes & Walters, 1998). A family therapist who works with homosexual teenagers asserts that, in his clinical experience, coming out is a necessary prerequisite for forming a stable sexual identity, but that this process can result in negative feelings in the family (Coenen, 1998). One example by a group worker on an adolescent gay and lesbian project cites social and cognitive isolation as a common experience for homosexual adolescents (Peters, 1997). Grossman and Kerner (1998) cite a study that found the largest predictor of positive mental health in homosexuals was self-acceptance. Yet Deluty and Jordan (1998) cite a study which suggested correlations between difficult early experiences coming out as lesbian and poor adaptation, less involvement with the support network found in the lesbian community, and less positive attitudes toward being lesbian as an adult. Thus, coming out for the first time is not only an important developmental task for the homosexual adolescent, but is an event that can impact the individual's coping as a homosexual adult.

Coming out for the first time can be viewed as a potential precipitating event for a crisis state. The adolescent is struggling with the realization of their sexual identity prior to this developmental event. The crisis state may be induced in part, then, because the homosexual adolescent is in a hazardous situation prior to revealing their sexual identity to others. If one is to liken a coming out crisis to other types of crises, resolution of the crisis state has the potential to improve or negatively impact the homosexual adolescent's future coping. Thus, understanding current literature and research on coming out is critical to understanding why disclosure of sexual orientation may cause a crisis state, and the types of resources that are indicated for positive resolution of this sexual identity crisis. Nonetheless, a review of the literature reveals that little research has been focused specifically on the "coming out" event, nor has this event been explored in the literature as a potential precipitant to a crisis.

LITERATURE REVIEW

Coming out requires a certain level of inner and outer resources. Deluty and Jordan (1998) investigated the relationship between the coming out process and a lesbian's psychological adjustment through a questionnaire given to four hundred and ninety-nine participants. The study attempted to include closeted individuals by surveying women who did not regularly self-disclose their orientation, but had been in a same-sex relationship or encounter. The authors were interested in studying the causal relationship between self-disclosure and self-esteem, among other factors. The study's hypothesis that self-disclosing more often is correlated with lowered anxiety, heightened positive affectivity and greater self-esteem was substantiated by the quantified and correlated results of the questionnaire. The authors also found that being open about a homosexual orientation to friends was the best predictor of overall social support and satisfaction with that support, which suggests that isolation is reduced as the result of coming out. In addition, being out to one's family was the most important predictor of whether one received social support from one's family. This supports the assertion that lesbian women feel a more genuine interpersonal connection with people they feel they can be open with about their orientation. Involvement in the gay community was another predictor of self-disclosure. Indeed, being out to homosexual friends was the greatest predictor of whether one was satisfied with one's support network, suggesting that involvement in the homosexual community affords a type of support not found elsewhere (Deluty & Jordan, 1998).

Despite the strong correlations between self-disclosure and greater positive variables such as self-esteem, positive affectivity and a greater support network found in the research by Deluty and Jordan (1998), there are some limitations in the application of this study. It is difficult to state whether greater mental health and social supports allow one more comfort in coming out, or whether coming out enhances one's mental health and support network. Perhaps a bi-directional approach to this problem would serve as the best model. Although self-disclosure is a necessary prerequisite to receiving support for one's sexual orientation, the correlations between self-disclosure, and degree and satisfaction with the support group could be bi-directional as well. For example, one might come out to a wider group of friends if these friends are more accepting and supportive individuals to begin with (Deluty & Jordan, 1998).

Deluty and Jordan (1998) suggest that at least a minimal degree of self-disclosure is a prerequisite to receiving support. One cannot receive support for having a same-sex orientation unless one discloses this orientation to others. Disclosure was a requirement for receiving support from family for one's orientation, and receiving the unique support found in the homosexual community. In addition, satisfaction with one's support network was correlated with how "out" a lesbian was with her peers. However, initial and current reactions to disclosure were also correlated with a lesbian's perception of the quality of her social supports. Women who had negative coming out experiences were less likely to view themselves as having a positive support network. The findings of this study lead to the conclusion that intrapsychic and interpersonal benefits such as greater self-esteem, positive affectivity and a positive support network are correlated with coming out. Ironically, the findings suggest that a closeted lesbian adolescent may not have the inner and outer resources in place yet to feel comfortable with this event. However, the results support a notion that one's first coming out experience has lasting effects on one's intrapsychic and interpersonal resources, and that being out generally enhances one's functioning as a lesbian.

Grossman and Kerner (1998) examined self-esteem and satisfaction with supportiveness as predictors of emotional distress in a sample of ninety urban gay and lesbian youth. The participants were drawn from a teen gay, bi, and transgendered drop-in center, although only gay teenagers were used. The participants filled out three questionnaires, the *Sociodemographic and Risk Factor Questionnaire*, the *Support Network Survey*, and the *Rosenberg Self-Esteem Scale*, as well as the *Brief Symptom Inventory*. These authors posited that emotional distress such as isolation and self-hatred are risk factors of self-injurious behavior, such as suicidality. The results of this study revealed that gay and lesbian youth tend to experience high levels of stress and self-injurious behaviors. Over fifty percent of the sample reported using alcohol and drugs in the past month, as well as engaging in suicidal thoughts. High self-esteem was a predictor of moderate strength of low emotional distress for the total and male sample, and was a predictor of high strength in the female sample. Although the study did not support the hypothesis that satisfaction with supportiveness would be a predictor of low emotional distress, anecdotal evidence is to the contrary, suggesting that further studies need to be done in this area of research (Grossman & Kerner, 1998). Nonetheless, taken with the work by Deluty and Jordan (1998), this research is aligned with the notion that the coming out is an important event that may lead to lowered levels of emotional distress such as isolation, which in turn may reduce the risk factors for self-injurious behavior.

Anderson and Mavis (1996) studied the circumstantial and demographic variables related to coming out as lesbian. This exploratory study examined the connection between variables through the use of anonymous surveys that measured variables on the previously established *Self-Esteem Scale, Sexual Orientation Disclosure Scale, Multiple Affect Adjective Checklist-Revised,* and the *Likert Scale.* The survey was distributed to a sample of one hundred and thirty-four adult lesbians. The authors were attempting to utilize the theory of self-efficacy to understand which types of information serve as a source of strength in coming out as lesbian to others in part by developing a *Coming Out Self-Efficacy* scale that was developed for the purpose of this study. The authors outline self-efficacy theory while providing a specific application of the model to coming out self-efficacy. Four sources of self-efficacy were posed as potentially impacting a lesbian's confidence level in self-disclosure of sexual orientation. So-called "performance accomplishments (e.g., actually coming out to someone), vicarious experience (e.g., listening to the coming out experience of another lesbian), verbal persuasion (e.g., having a partner, friend, or sibling offer opinions about coming out), and emotional arousal, the affective and physiological cues associated with coming out and how they are interpreted (e.g., feeling overwhelmed, anxious, or proud in the face of coming out)" increase self-efficacy with respect to coming out (Anderson & Mavis, 1996, p. 39).

There was a significant relationship between coming out self-efficacy and each of the four sources of efficacy. This study refuted the theoretical model of efficacy, which posits that self-efficacy is correlated with mastery. Rather, the lesbians in this study attended to their own feelings and positive messages from others as the basis for self-efficacy in disclosure of sexual orientation. Interestingly enough, higher degrees of lifestyle satisfaction were not correlated with outness or self-disclosure of sexual orientation, but coming out self-efficacy was. This suggests that one's degree of confidence in the ability to be out rather than whether or not one *was* out was the significant factor is lifestyle satisfaction (Anderson & Mavis, 1996).

The results of this study suggest that self-disclosure is linked more with one's internal resources than in outcomes itself. This may be because the outcome of disclosure is unknown to the lesbian at the time of coming out. Thus, outcome *expectations* may be a greater predictor of coming out self-efficacy than past mastery, because a particular individual's reaction to disclosure is unknown until disclosure occurs. In addition, the author's stress that a lesbian can possess "coping efficacy," in which she may choose to declare her orientation even when she knows the message may be received badly (Anderson & Mavis, 1996, p. 49). This is the situation many adolescent homosexuals face in their families (Coenen, 1998). Coming out has more to do with a lesbian's feelings about herself as lesbian and about coming out than with previous experience. The study suggests that emotional arousal, vicarious experience, and experiences of verbal persuasion allows a lesbian to consider making a disclosure, and that this coming out self-efficacy in turn provides greater satisfaction with her life (Anderson & Mavis, 1996).

Magruder and Waldner (1999) surveyed one hundred seventy-two adolescents originating from a lesbian/gay support group. The survey explored the hypothesis that homosexual adolescents' perceptions of family relations, identity expression and perceived resources in the form of a connection to the lesbian/gay community are factors which influence the event of coming out to parents. The authors define coming out as disclosure of a homosexual identity, and define identity expression as a range of behaviors that express a gay identity, such as attending gay events, dating a same-sex person, etc. The authors posit that "developing a positive gay or lesbian self-image suggests . . . a healthy resolution of sexual identity issues," and that coming out is an indication that identity development has occurred (Magruder & Waldner, 1999, p. 84). In addition, the authors assert that identity confusion can induce low self-esteem, depression, alienation, withdrawal, and indulgence in self- destructive behavior as a means of coping. In contrast, coming out can improve psychological well-being in terms of identity expression and perceived resources.

Magruder and Waldner (1999) developed their hypothesis from a model that posits that identity disclosure is based upon perceived rewards and costs. The study found that homosexual "youth who perceived themselves as having positive resources, are already expressing their identity, and [those youth] who report weaker family relations are more likely to be 'out' to their parents" (Magruder & Waldner, 1999, p. 86). The authors speculated that strong family relations will inhibit seeking out a gay community and coming out because the majority of households will view homosexuality negatively. Similarly, the authors thought that adolescents whose families are very important to them would be less likely to overtly express their identity behaviorally, or come out to parents. Conversely, they theorized that a strong support network might encourage gay youth to come out. The findings of the study support the hypothesis that gay children with strong family relationships find it costly to express a gay identity and seek out gay resources, presumably due to a fear of rejection and reprisal. Ironically, a strong support network in the form of strong family relationships may actually inhibit a homosexual adolescent from coming out, because s/he may fear it would jeopardize these relationships. Although there was no direct connection between perceived family relationships and degree of disclosure, the findings concluded that strong (yet unsupportive/homophobic) family relations detracted from coming out to parents through the indirect means of identity expression and perceived resources. The lack of perceived resources and identity expression, in turn, inhibits coming out to parents. Strong outside supportive resources may "mediate the effects of family relations," making it more rewarding to come out to parents (Magruder & Waldner, 1999, p. 96). Gay adolescents who received supportive resources and who expressed their homosexual identity were more likely to come out to their parents as gay (Magruder & Waldner, 1999).

The authors of the study cited above developed their hypothesis from a model that posits that identity disclosure is based upon perceived rewards and costs (Magruder & Waldner, 1999, p. 85). This is a different approach from the coming out self-efficacy results of Anderson and Mavis (1998), who found that coming out occurs as the result of positive inner resources (e.g., feeling good about being gay and proud of coming out) and positive past experiences (e.g., being encouraged to come out by others and hearing about others' experience coming out). The perception that coming out is more rewarding than costly, which results in identity disclosure, could be based upon self-efficacy. In other words, this study showed that an adolescent might feel more empowered to come out as gay when they experience strong positive emotions toward that event, and feel supported through peers who have shared their experiences. This strong sense of coming out self-efficacy may lead to a perception that staying in the closet is too detrimental to the self, which is in keeping with the theories of Magruder and Waldner (1999).

Coenen (1998) presents a counseling model for working with homosexual adolescents and their parents. Coenen's model for dealing with the coming out process in adolescence that is based on problem-solving communication-training. He asserts that coming out is a necessary prerequisite for forming a stable sexual identity, but that this process can result in negative feelings in the family. These feelings can include denial, regret, and confusion. Coenen asserts that the initial disclosure of homosexuality is critical to stable identity formation and can impact self-esteem and the perception of the self and homosexual orientations in general. Thus, the role of the parent is significant to the stable formation of a sexual identity and strong self-esteem in the gay and lesbian adolescent. However, Coenen's review of the literature indicates that initial family reactions to self-disclosure tend to be overwhelmingly negative or ambivalent. Coming out causes great strain on the family system prior to acceptance of the teenager's orientation, if, indeed, acceptance is forthcoming.

Despite the risks of coming out, this event has a significant impact on the homosexual client. Greater self-esteem, positive affectivity and a positive support network have all been correlated with degree of outness (Deluty & Jordan, 1998). The culmination of findings of two studies suggest that coming out is associated with higher self-esteem, which in turn is associated with lower levels of emotional distress so common to homosexual teenagers. Lowered emotional distress may reduce the risk of maladaptive behaviors and coping mechanisms (Deluty & Jordan, 1998; Grossman & Kerner, 1998). One study showed that emotional arousal, vicarious experience and experiences of verbal persuasion allows lesbians to consider making a disclosure, and that this coming out self-efficacy in turn may provide greater satisfaction with lifestyle (Anderson & Mavis, 1996). Another study revealed the negative correlation between strong family relationships and the expression of a gay identity and involvement in the gay community. In spite of this finding, the authors felt that strong outside supportive resources may provide a buffer against the negative effects of family relations, making it more rewarding to come out to parents (Magruder & Waldner, 1999). Another author stresses that the role of the parent is significant to the stable formation of a sexual identity and strong self-esteem in the gay and lesbian adolescent. This is because the initial disclosure of homosexuality to parents and their subsequent reaction is critical to stable identity formation, and can impact self-esteem and the perception of the self and homosexual orientations in general (Coenen, 1998). The literature supports the notion that one's first coming out experience has lasting effects on one's intrapsychic and interpersonal resources, and that being out enhances functioning.

COMING OUT AS CRISIS

Teenagers can be extremely rejecting of their homosexual peers. Baker and Fishbein (1998) conducted a study that employed the *Homosexual Attitudes Scale-Revised* with two hundred seventy-six high school participants from several grades. This research confirmed and added to previous findings. Males were more prejudiced towards homosexuals than females, prejudice increased for both gender groups between the 7th and 9th grade, and same-sex prejudice is greater than opposite-sex prejudice. Although gay adolescents are realizing their orientation and coming out at younger age, a greater number of adolescents will come out as homosexual each successive year (Magruder & Waldner, 1999). Thus, homosexual adolescents are faced with less peer support, particularly same-sex peer support, at the same time that they struggle with sexual identity issues. On a positive note, female prejudice toward gays and lesbians decreased between grades 9 and 11, although it increased for males during this time. Nonetheless, in spite of variation in degrees of prejudice, homophobia was a common attitude in the participants sampled, regardless of grade level or gender (Baker & Fishbein, 1998). This may erode the homosexual adolescent's view of his or her own orientation.

Social institutions support peer rejection of homosexuality. Institutions such as schools often deny the existence of gay students, and therefore often refuse to implement policies that would protect and nurture these unrecognized students and faculty. Few schools provide support for their gay and lesbian students. Because teachers and policies fail to acknowledge their presence, they fail to educate teachers about how to provide for their homosexual students developmental and social needs, nor do they protect them from harassment. Despite recommendations for programs to address sexual orientation, Hayes and Walter (1998) found that few school districts were implementing these recommendations. Indeed, the authors found that many schools have policies that prohibit discussion of sexual orientation. Because of the additional strain placed on homosexual students and the lack of support of them, these authors suggest that homosexual and bisexual students are being denied "the educational opportunities accorded their straight peers" (Hayes & Walters, 1998, p. 14).

Coming out as homosexual can induce a crisis state. Disclosure of orientation can strain the family system because "[h]omosexuality is perceived as a major crisis because no rules exist in the family system to handle the disclosure, no roles relevant to homosexuality are present, no constructive language to describe the issue is utilized, and strong cultural biases against homosexuality are in place; family themes and structure become critical forces against adaptation" (Coenen, 1998, p. 77). For the homosexual adolescent him/herself, coming out can represent or cause rejection from peers and family. Coming out as gay is an acknowledgment of one's sexual orientation, thus it marks a critical period in sexual identity formation. If a homosexual adolescent does not have adequate resources, coming out can cause a crisis for the family system and for the individual.

One could assert that the discrete event of coming out for the first time has the potential to precipitate a crisis in the homosexual adolescent. Although all of the stages of sexual identity formation are stressful for the homosexual adolescent, coming out is unique in that it is an interpersonal acknowledgment of this developmental struggle. Unfortunately, the literature supports the assertion that a family's initial reaction to an adolescent member coming out as gay or lesbian is typically negative (Coenen, 1998). In addition, the homosexual adolescent is provided with less social support from peers and social institutions such as schools (Baker & Fishbein, 1998; Hayes & Walters, 1998). The event of coming out could be likened to the "homecoming" phenomenon in crisis intervention theory with traumatic stressors, in which the initial reaction of family and friends to the news is a predictor of how well the individual will handle the future stress of becoming a gay or lesbian individual.

In crisis intervention theory, several external factors are predictive of whether a stressful event will become a crisis for the individual. External factors such as a bad "homecoming," a loss of social support and a derisive view of the meaning of the precipitating event increase the probability that a difficult life event will induce a crisis state. Unfortunately, the homosexual adolescent will probably encounter these predictive factors. Coming out may constitute a precipitating event to a crisis state because it may have the pejorative meaning of a permanent loss of conformity, as well as a rejection from others (Baker & Fishbein, 1998). This event may result in a loss of several sources of social support as well. Homosexual adolescents also lack role models and are exposed to a pressure to conform to heterosexual expectations (Magruder & Waldner, 1999). Thus, homosexual adolescents are living in cognitive and social isolation (Peters, 1997).

The literature supports the notion that the probability of a poor response to homosexual adolescents' self-disclosure of their identity is high, and that homosexuals are, in addition, internally drained during adolescence. The process of sexual identity formation strains the homosexual adolescent's inner resources, resulting in maladaptive behaviors and coping mechanisms. S/he is in a hazardous condition prior to revealing his or her orientation to others, because s/he in the stressful middle stage of sexual identity formation (Magruder & Waldner, 1999). Research on adolescent gay and lesbian populations has found that they engage in more maladaptive coping mechanisms such as self-destructive activities than their heterosexual peers (Grossman & Kerner, 1998; Peters, 1997). Coming out for the first time has a heightened potential to be a precipitant of a crisis state for the adolescent. However, current research is aligned with the notion that coming out is an important developmental task for homosexual adolescents.

A crisis can be defined by several characteristics. A crisis must be preceded by a specific and identifiable stressful precipitating event. This event may pose a threat to life, security and/or interpersonal ties. Coming out or considering a disclosure meets these criteria because identifying oneself as gay or lesbian poses clear hazards to one's interpersonal relationships, and may elicit threats of bodily harm or even death (Deluty & Jordan, 1998). The perception of the event by the individual undergoing the stress must be meaningful and threatening as well, which the research suggests is the case in initial disclosure of homosexual orientations (Magruder & Waldner, 1999). Prior to entering a crisis state, the individual must also be in a preexisting hazardous condition. Once in a crisis state, the adolescent responds to the event by exhibiting a state of heightened anxiety that can be defined as disequilibrium of the individual's natural state. This disorganization of the adolescent's normal functioning is typically time-limited, usually from four to six weeks, as any organism cannot tolerate a heightened sense of tension and anxiety for any prolonged period. While in crisis, the client undergoes coping and intervention tasks that result in a termination of the crisis state. This resolution can be adaptive or maladaptive, and the individual's level of mental health functioning has the potential to improve, stay the same or worsen (Parad & Parad, 1990). Poor resolution of a crisis state, leading to deterioration of the homosexual adolescent's ability to handle future stressors, can negatively impact the individual's coping ability and self-image into adulthood.

Despite the importance of coming out, this event is unduly stressful. Gay and lesbian children with strong family relationships find it costly to express a homosexual identity and seek out gay resources. The lack of perceived resources and identity expression further inhibits coming out to parents (Magruder & Waldner, 1999). Homosexual adolescents are faced with less peer support, particularly same-sex peer support, at the same time that they struggle with sexual identity issues (Baker & Fishbein, 1998). Because of the additional strain placed on homosexual students and the lack of support of them, one article suggested that homosexual and bisexual students are being denied basic opportunities and support granted their straight peers (Hayes & Walters, 1998, p. 14). Thus, professional intervention to the homosexual adolescent during the coming out period is indicated. This intervention could be modeled after crisis intervention treatment, in which the therapist assists the adolescent client in regaining equilibrium despite the tensions inherent in coming out.

CLINICAL IMPLICATIONS

Once an adolescent is identified as struggling with sexual identity or making an initial disclosure, the client may be referred to crisis intervention treatment. While in a crisis state, a person may feel hopeless or helpless. Typically, an individual in a crisis state will have lowered defenses and may be more open to outside influence than normally. This provides a unique opportunity for growth, particularly with respect to strengthening existing or creating new coping mechanisms. Crisis intervention treatment should provide a response that is prompt and accessible, occurring as close as possible to the impact of the crisis event, in this case, initial disclosure of a homosexual orientation. The treatment should assist the client in decreasing their investment in the view of their homosexual identity as a loss, despite the inherent loss of the client's previously assumed identity as heterosexual that coming out represents. The treatment should seek to reconnect the client to their environment, despite the loss of this previously assumed identity. Lastly, the treatment should aim to connect the client to new social relationships. Crisis intervention treatment should seek to increase a client's coping, meaning, and support (Parad & Parad, 1990).

Brief treatment models are typically more focused and directive than longer-term therapy models. No set guidelines have been established for the frequency and duration of treatment, but weekly or bi-weekly sessions for four to six weeks could be utilized as a working recommendation. Although empathy, genuineness and warmth are preconditions to providing crisis intervention, they are not sufficient to assist the client in adapting. The crisis counselor should establish a clear-cut problem and related goals/tasks from the first session, in the case of the coming out adolescent, to adjust to their newly expressed identity as gay or lesbian. The clinician should evaluate the client's existing coping mechanisms and encourage adaptive behavior and the formation of new means of dealing with stress (Parad & Parad, 1990). This is of particular importance in work with homosexual adolescents, as the research indicates that they tend to engage in more self-destructive activities and maladaptive coping strategies than their straight peers (Grossman & Kerner, 1998; Magruder & Waldner, 1999; Peters, 1997). The therapist should be attuned to the client's perception of the precipitating event in crisis work. If the client views a homosexual orientation negatively, alternate meanings of the coming out event should be explored. The research suggests that one's confidence at being out (regardless of whether an initial disclosure has actually been made) has a positive impact on the ability to be out, even in the case of an expectation of negative reactions to the disclosure (Anderson & Mavis, 1996). Encouraging the client's use of community supports such as gay/lesbian support groups, etc., is indicated. Other homework assignments such as reading literature or poetry by leading gay and lesbian authors may be helpful also. By the end of the first session, a therapeutic plan, contract, and number of sessions should be defined.

The clinician can offer more direct advice and anticipatory guidance while a client is in a crisis state due to the client's lowered defenses. The client is in a unique position while in crisis to establish new resolutions to past crises and losses. Encouragement of adaptive behavior should take place, and the clinician should attend to the client's activities and tasks session-to-session. Mastery of new coping mechanisms and other positive movements towards successful resolution of the crisis state should be acknowledged and supported. The clinician should also listen for potential connections that the coming out event may have to previous losses, such as a previously experienced peer rejection or loss of parental support. The successful accomplishment of therapy tasks inside and outside of the session is key to increasing the client's sense of mastery over the coming out event, which in turn increases the client's self-esteem and ability to cope with future stressors adaptively (Parad & Parad, 1990). A therapist must also assist the adolescent in education about their orientation, as well as building self-esteem and healthy ways to move away from the family in order to form a cohesive, autonomous identity that includes a homosexual orientation (Peters, 1997).

The client's feeling regarding termination, the date of which has been tentatively established from the onset of treatment, should be addressed throughout treatment. Clients may have a tendency to want to continue treatment; this impulse should be dealt with in session by reviewing the client's increased coping mechanisms and by referring the client to community supports (Parad & Parad, 1990). A follow-up session may be indicated as a booster to the crisis intervention treatment. It may be helpful to include the family in this follow-up session, if the client feels comfortable with how the disclosure is being assimilated in the family system. Successful individual crisis intervention treatment should seek to improve the client's affective, cognitive, and behavioral response to the stressful event of coming out as gay or lesbian.

Based upon his own practice, one therapist asserts that the disclosure phase in which the adolescent comes out to his/her parent(s) is often met with by fear and guilt in the parents (Coenen, 1998). The family may seek counseling as the result of the adjustment phase. In this phase, family members initially rely on their own coping mechanisms, and often urge the homosexual child to remain in the closet to others. Therapy can have a positive impact on the final phases, resolution and integration. One therapist recommends that the clinician have knowledge of the models of the homosexual identity process; he states their common elements are concepts of confusion, awareness, acceptance, commitment, and disclosure. A positive attitude towards the disclosure is associated with better family adjustment overall (Coenen, 1998).

Crisis intervention treatment may be indicated for the family, if the family members appear to be in crisis over the disclosure, are amenable to treatment and are reasonably open to integrating the identified client back into the family system, despite the coming out disclosure. The clinician may want to further identify problem-solving techniques that are currently employed in the family system and point out those styles of coping and communicating that appear maladaptive. The clinician should identify the family's values, assess communication styles, and identify roles in the initial session (Parad & Parad, 1990). The counselor should pay close attention to values, especially with respect to the family's views of homosexual orientations. The mental health functioning of any one member, especially the coming out adolescent should be linked to family interactions. The family may be encouraged to re-define their perception of the precipitating event of the adolescent coming out from a negative meaning to a positive one. This shift in meaning could be conceptualized as a means of supporting the coming out adolescent, and may in addition be formulated to ameliorate residual guilt in parents, such as the fear that they "caused" the adolescent to be gay or lesbian.

As crisis intervention treatment progresses, the worker should continue to confront maladaptive thought patterns, communication, and activities in the family. Goals should be defined and reviewed session-to-session. The perceptual meaning of the adolescent's coming out should continue to be defined over time, while existing and new coping mechanisms and resources should be suggested, for instance a support group for friends and family members of gays and lesbians. Education regarding homosexual orientations is recommended. While remaining in the here-and-now of the session, the clinician should offer advice on more adaptive styles of interacting, with encouragement of compromises made between members. As new methods of communicating and coping are established, they should be reviewed and supported within the context of the day-to-day functioning of the family. The clinician should assist the family with a timely termination, including a possible follow-up session (Parad & Parad, 1990).

The role of the parent as well as peers and their reaction to a disclosure of homosexual identity is significant in the formation of positive sexual identity and a strong sense of self-esteem (Coenen, 1998). However, the research suggests that coming out as gay or lesbian will undoubtedly cause some level of rejection and isolation for the coming out adolescent, whether it stems from family or other social networks. The shock of coming out may be even greater for those adolescents who appear more "straight." Some families may be unwilling to work towards acceptance of a homosexual member. Resources external to the home are key, because the research has indicated that strong family relationships may inhibit coming out and other forms of identity expression, such as dating and attending gay events, presumably due to a fear of damaging close family relationships. External support systems may also mediate negative family reactions. Thus, the perceived cost of coming out may be ameliorated by a larger support network in the form of friends, a connection to the gay community, school counselors and the like, rather than strong family ties (Magruder & Waldner, 1999).

The process of forming a cohesive identity is harder for homosexual adolescents, who suffer from cognitive isolation, in which they are provided with little information about their orientation, as well as social isolation. The literature recommends peer support groups, which can assist the adolescent in decreasing their isolation and assist him/her in forming connections to the gay and lesbian community. This in turn may increase the client's coping mechanisms. Andrew J. Peters, a group worker on a lesbian and gay youth project, pinpointed several themes present in group work with this population. Peters (1997) identified isolation, coming out, learning/re-learning, and initiation into the community as the main tasks of group work (p. 51). Involvement in the gay community or other types of homosexual peer groups offers a unique sense of support that is especially needed during the coming out period.

Crisis intervention can be provided in group form. The clinician may decide to form an open-ended group for adolescents in the process of coming out. Each member would attend approximately six sessions. This format may allow clients to view other, similar adolescents in differing stages of crisis and coping. This format may also be useful to the clinician, as the likelihood of gaining referrals for a solid membership of clients coming out at the exact same time is small. The worker may want to consider the pros and cons of having various age groups and/or genders in the group. Although there may be some problems inherent in having too diverse of a membership, particularly with clients at different developmental stages, differences in the group may serve to highlight the similarities in the members' coming out difficulties.

The tasks of group crisis intervention work are similar to the suggestions cited above for work with individual and family crisis intervention. The clinician should assist the group members to define the coming out event and the meaning of this event should be re-framed in a positive light for the members. Current methods of coping should be explored as alternate coping methods are suggested, reviewed session-to-session and supported. Feelings regarding termination should be addressed and efforts at creating new coping mechanisms and a new meaning of being homosexual should be explored. Lastly, the clinician should refer the group's members to community resources (Parad & Parad, 1990).

There are several theories utilized in the literature that refer to coming out as a necessary developmental event in ongoing sexual identity development. The models incorporate positive identity formation, positive self-labeling, self-acceptance, disclosure, and pride in one's sexual orientation as tasks of a sexual identity process (Anderson & Mavis, 1996; Deluty & Jordan, 1998; Magruder & Waldner, 1999). Prior to coming out, the adolescent may not feel positive towards the self as a whole or the orientation specifically. Risk assessments, especially by those clinicians with frequent interactions with adolescent groups, such as school social workers, should be a routine precaution in preventing potential crises. Youths who appear to be engaging in self-destructive activities such as abusing substances, verbalizing suicidal ideation, self-isolating from peer groups, and the like should be considered at-risk in a general sense and should be referred for further assessment and brief or long-term treatment. Practitioners should be alert to the possibility that at-risk adolescents may be struggling with sexual identity issues. Assisting these clients in increasing their confidence and self-acceptance is key to averting a crisis state.

Another tool in preventing sexual identity crises includes routine education of parents, faculty and students about gay and lesbian issues within the school setting. Schools often fail to support their gay students (Hayes & Walters, 1998). Lesbian and gay students are at higher risk for poor coping mechanisms such as using drugs and alcohol than their heterosexual peers, and they have higher rates of suicide attempts (Grossman & Kerner, 1998; Peters, 1997). Therefore, school social workers have a particular responsibility to educate faculty about the risks to this student population and should act as advocates for referrals to supportive services outside of or within the schools. Although the focus of this paper has been on the potential crisis precipitated by coming out issues, an open-ended support group for gay and/or lesbian adolescents in general may provide additional peer support by providing newly coming out teenagers with role models, and may remind more confident or well-adjusted homosexual peers of how far they have come. If no existing resource is available, which maybe the case in more isolated rural areas, beginning an open-ended homosexual adolescent support group or crisis intervention group focused specifically on coming out issues may be indicated.

Education regarding a myriad of sexual identities should guide homosexual adolescents and others towards a more positive view of homosexual identities, and should seek to reconcile clients' perceptions that coming out is a pejorative loss of a heterosexual identity. Groups for adolescents who are questioning their sexual identity may be useful as well. Outcome expectations appear to be a greater predictor of coming out self-efficacy than past mastery (Anderson & Mavis, 1996). One's feelings of confidence or pride in a homosexual orientation may increase the likelihood that coming out will seem less of a loss to the individual. Again, brief treatment may be recommended if a particular adolescent appears to be coping poorly overall or actively in a crisis state. Those adolescents who lack confidence in their sexual identity in general or disclosing a homosexual orientation in particular may benefit from these services. By increasing a client's coping, positive view of coming out and support systems through treatment, the client's self-esteem, confidence, and successful resolution of sexual identity should likewise be increased, while coming out with a lesbian or gay identity will appear to be less of a threat.

Although coming out is a normal part of growing up homosexual, the initial disclosure of one's orientation, coupled with a preexisting hazardous situation, can constitute the requisite precipitating event which can result in a crisis state. Assisting the gay or lesbian adolescent with the coming out process is indicated, because this event is critical for the formation of the self and because this event is so stressful. Work with the homosexual adolescent can be modeled after crisis intervention treatment, in which the clinician seeks to improve the client's coping and positive meaning of the coming out event. The crisis intervention approach to the coming-out adolescent would endorse increasing the client's support network as well. Providing the homosexual adolescent with positive information about their orientation changes the meaning of coming out from a shameful event to one filled with pride. Once the initial self-disclosure is made, isolation from some relationships is to be expected. However, the adolescent may feel a more genuine interpersonal connection to others, as a new or newly defined relationship will be based upon a genuine representation of the self. Adequate resolution of the crisis period may not only avert the development of more long-term disorders, but will also assist the homosexual adolescent in forming a cohesive sexual identity. Furthermore, the research repeatedly cites the long-term benefits of experiencing the coming out process in a positive manner.

REFERENCES

Anderson, M. K., & Mavis, B. E. (1996). Sources of coming out self-efficacy for lesbians. *Journal of Homosexuality, 32*(2), 37-51.

Baker, J. G., & Fishbein, H. D. (1998). The development of prejudice towards gay and lesbian adolescents. *Journal of Homosexuality, 36*(1), 89-98.

Coenen, M. E. (1998). Helping families with homosexual children: A model for counseling. *Journal of Homosexuality, 36*(2), 73-83.

Deluty, R. H., & Jordan, K. M. (1998). Coming out for lesbian women: Its relation to anxiety, positive affectivity, self-esteem, and social support. *Journal of Homosexuality, 35*(2), 41-60.

Grossman, A. H., & Kerner, M. S. (1998). Self-esteem and supportiveness as predictors of emotional distress in gay male and lesbian youth. *Journal of Homosexuality, 35*(2), 25-37.

Hayes, D. M., & Walters, A. S. (1998). Homophobia within schools: Challenging the culturally sanctioned dismissal of gay students and colleagues. *Journal of Homosexuality, 35*(2), 1-15.

Magruder, B., & Waldner, L. K. (1999). Coming out to parents: Perceptions of family relations, perceived resources, and identity expression as predictors of identity disclosure for gay and lesbian adolescents. *Journal of Homosexuality, 37*(2), 83-98.

Parad, H. J., & Parad, L. G. (Eds.). (1990). *Crisis intervention book 2: The practitioner's sourcebook for brief therapy.* Milwaukee: Family Service America.

Peters, A. J. (1997). Themes in group work with lesbian and gay adolescents. *Social Work with Groups, 20*(2), 51-68.

Risk Factors of Gay, Lesbian, and Bisexual Adolescents: Review of Empirical Literature and Practice Implications

Sanna J. Thompson
Lon Johnston

SUMMARY. Many researchers of gay, lesbian, and bisexual adolescents describe them as an "invisible" minority. These youth are also one of the most "at risk" youth populations, as they often experience a range of problems related to society's stigmatization of same-sex orientation. Although sexual orientation is not necessarily related to heightened difficulties, lack of social support, infrequent positive interactions, and chronic stress may lead to increased problem behaviors for these youth. To further understand the risk and protective factors experienced by sexual minority adolescents, this article explores a number of these factors and reviews the current empirical research on specific topics, including: family, peer and school, substance use, suicide, and HIV/AIDS issues.

Sanna J. Thompson, PhD, and Lon Johnston, PhD, are affiliated with the University of Texas at Arlington, School of Social Work.

Address correspondence to: Lon Johnston, PhD, University of Texas at Austin, School of Social Work, Box 19129, Arlington, TX 76019-0129.

[Haworth co-indexing entry note]: "Risk Factors of Gay, Lesbian, and Bisexual Adolescents: Review of Empirical Literature and Practice Implications." Thompson, Sanna J., and Lon Johnston. Co-published simultaneously in *Journal of Human Behavior in the Social Environment* (The Haworth Social Work Practice Press, an imprint of The Haworth Press, Inc.) Vol. 8, No. 2/3, 2003, pp. 111-128; and: *Sexual Minorities: Discrimination, Challenges, and Development in America* (ed: Michael K. Sullivan) The Haworth Social Work Practice Press, an imprint of The Haworth Press, Inc., 2003, pp. 111-128. Single or multiple copies of this article are available for a fee from The Haworth Document Delivery Service [1-800-HAWORTH, 9:00 a.m. - 5:00 p.m. (EST). E-mail address: docdelivery@haworthpress.com].

Journal of Human Behavior in the Social Environment, Vol. 8(2/3) 2003
http://www.haworthpress.com/web/JHBSE
Digital Object Identifier: 10.1300/J137v8n02_07

Finally, practice implications are discussed to guide clinicians in working more effectively with this youth population. *[Article copies available for a fee from The Haworth Document Delivery Service: 1-800-HAWORTH. E-mail address: <docdelivery@haworthpress.com> Website: <http://www.HaworthPress.com> © 2003 by The Haworth Press, Inc. All rights reserved.]*

KEYWORDS. Gay, lesbian, bisexual, adolescents, sexual minority youth

It is generally accepted that approximately 10% of the population is gay, lesbian, or bisexual (GLB) (Robinson, 1994; Uribe & Harbeck, 1991; Dempsey, 1994). However, among school-aged youths, only one to three percent identify themselves in these categories (DeRane, Krowchuk, & Sinal, 1998; Garofalo, Wolf, Kessel et al., 1998). There are likely various reasons for this disparity between adult and youth populations; however, it has been suggested that adolescents fear being rejected by their peers and hide their sexual orientation until after graduating from high school (Marrow, 1993). Youths may also be unwilling to classify themselves as gay, lesbian, or bisexual because they dislike the label, feel it is a simplistic term for their sexuality, or are unclear concerning their sexual identity (Savin-Williams, 2001).

Not surprisingly, many researchers of GLB adolescents describe them as an "invisible" minority. These youth are also one of the most "at risk" youth populations (Savin-Williams, 2001; Mac an Ghaill, 1994; O'Connor, 1995; Harris, 1997), as they often experience a range of problems related to society's stigmatization of same-sex orientation. Although sexual orientation is not necessarily related to increased difficulties, their lack of social support, infrequent positive interactions, and chronic stress may lead to increased problem behaviors for these youth (Safren & Heimberg, 1999).

Research aimed at understanding and preventing youth problems has recently utilized an organizing approach focusing on risk/protective factors. The essence of this approach is that identifying the processes that increase the risk of the problem's occurrence can prevent or eliminate further difficulties (Hawkins, Catalano, & Miller, 1992). Risk and protective factors related to human behavior within the social environment include social bonding with parents, peers, and society in general (Hawkins & Weis, 1985; Hawkins et al., 1992; Kazdin, 1990). Protective factors, such as prosocial bonding with family, peers, and institutions such as schools and churches, safeguard against prevailing risks that may otherwise contribute to problem behaviors. Risk factors often progressively accumulate and often include combinations of school failure, substance use, smoking, and mental health problems, and precocious involvement in adult behaviors such as risky sexual behavior (Whitbeck, 1999). These multiple risk processes increase the odds or probability that greater high-risk and problematic behaviors will occur (Werner, 1990).

Understanding the impact of individual and family risk and protective factors on adolescent development and behavior provides knowledge necessary for development of effective interventions to improve the lives of this particularly high-risk group of youths. Young gay, lesbian, and bisexual individuals not only struggle internally with their sexual identity, but also face numerous stressors or risk factors related to the stigma attached to homosexuality (Savin-Williams, 1994). As there is no evidence that homosexuality impacts adolescents' progress through biological and cognitive changes, it is psychological and social development that frequently puts GLB adolescents at risk for problem behaviors. To further understand the risk and protective factors experienced by sexual minority adolescents, this article explores a number of these factors and reviews the current empirical research that focuses on the specific topic areas, including: family, peer and school, substance use, suicide, and HIV/AIDS issues. Finally, practice implications will be discussed to guide clinicians in working more effectively with this youth population.

FAMILY ISSUES

One of the most significant issues for GLB youth populations is disclosure of their sexual orientation to their family. Family interactions can be considered both a risk and protective factor, depending on the family's response. The adolescents typically experience considerable tension and anxiety when deciding whether they should 'come out' to their parents, and if so, how they should do it. In some cases, there is fear of disavowal and disownment (Borhek, 1988). Adolescents who receive negative reactions when disclosing to their parents may respond by running away, isolating themselves from others, becoming depressed or suicidal, and engaging in high-risk sexual behaviors (Gibson, 1989; Hammelman, 1993; Remafedi, French, Story et al., 1998; Dube & Savin-Williams, 1999). Some research (D'Augelli, Hershberger, & Pilkington, 1998) has shown that one of every three gay youths experience verbal abuse from family members. The picture is much different for adolescents whose parents are accepting and supportive of their sexual orientation. These youth are much less likely to exhibit many of the problems listed above. They also tend to have higher levels of self-esteem than adolescents whose parents react negatively to their 'coming out' (D'Augelli et al., 1998).

Research Studies of Family Issues

Waldner and Magruder (1999) proposed a model to predict the various responses of parents to the news that their adolescent is gay or lesbian. This model, based on exchange theory and the concepts of costs and rewards, posited that the higher the costs to the adolescent, the less likely they are to "come out" to their family. Conversely, the greater the perceived reward, the more likely the adolescent will disclose their sexual orientation to their family as "rewards are skewed towards heterosexual relations and costs towards lesbian/gay relations" (Waldner & Magruder, 1999, p. 85). Results of this study of 172 gay and lesbian adolescents indicated that "coming out" to parents was influenced by adolescents' perceptions of the availability of pro-gay resources, identity expression, and the positive or negative nature of their family relations. However, adolescents who perceived close relationships with parents were less likely to seek gay/lesbian social support networks because they noted greater fear in violating their family's heterosexual norms and values by revealing their gay identity.

Another study, conducted by Armesto and Weisman (2001), employed Weiner's (1980) attribution theory which states that believing one can control the causes of an event decreases the affective and emotional responses. Three hundred fifty-six college students were asked to imagine they were parents of an adolescent son who had recently disclosed he was gay. Findings showed that those who believe homosexuals are not to blame for their sexual orientation and who are more guilt-prone were most likely to exhibit emotional responses to the information. Males were more likely to ascribe the cause of being gay as something one has control over, and to experience unfavorable emotions toward gay individuals than did females.

D'Augelli et al. (1998) examined the experiences of 105 gay and lesbian youths between the ages of 14 and 21 who were still living at home when they disclosed their sexual orientation to their family. Only 9% reported disclosing their sexual orientation to a parent, and that parent was always the mother. The overwhelming majority of respondents (77%) disclosed first to a close friend. Almost all mothers already knew or suspected their child was gay, but fathers were more likely to be unaware of their child's sexual orientation. When respondents did self-disclose to their parents, 65% told their mothers, 9% their fathers, and 25% informed both. Verbal abuse most often came from mothers. Family members threatened lesbians most often; they were also the most frequent recipients of assault–typically by their mothers. However, brothers of gay males made the most threats and committed the most assaults of any group.

PEER AND SCHOOL ISSUES

Adolescents who are 'out,' 'coming out,' or are privately developing and/or recognizing GLB preferences are often effected by peer homophobia, which may especially impact the youth's self-esteem (Thurlow, 2001). Negative peer communication often becomes internalized and may cause feelings of self-contempt and self-criticism, leading to social and psychological alienation. In addition, the incidence of harassment of young men and women who do not fit into pervasive norms for behavior and appearance is well documented (i.e., Pilkington & D'Augelli, 1995; Rosario, Rotheram-Borus, & Reid, 1996; Rothblum, 1994; Merina, 1995). Disturbing stories of physical and psychological harassment have been widely publicized and touch all levels of education (Henning-Stout, James, & Macintosh, 2000). For GLB youth, these destructive attacks occur on multiple levels and take a significant social and psychological toll (Henning-Stout et al., 2000). According to a recent study (Center for Disease Control and the Massachusetts Department of Education, 1997), 97% of students in public schools report hearing homophobic remarks from peers and 80% of gay and lesbian youth report feelings of severe social isolation. State and national task forces and coalitions estimated that 33-49% of lesbian and gay youth experienced school-based victimization (Aurand, Adessa, & Bush, 1985; Gross, Aurand, & Adessa, 1988). The lack of acceptance by their peers puts GLB youth at greater risk for a variety of social, emotional, physical, and educational hardships (Roffman, 2000).

Research Studies on Peer and School Issues

One study (Thurlow, 2001) asked 377 ninth graders to identify pejorative comments heard at school and to list those they considered most offensive. The convenience sample from five high schools in Wales and England reported nearly 6000 individual derogatory words. Homophobic items accounted for 10% of all items reported, smaller than sexist pejoratives (28%), but larger than racially negative comments (7%). The vast majority of the homophobic derogatory words were aimed at gay men, while 14% were specifically directed at females. In analyzing these data, Thurlow stated that "the relentless, careless use of homophobic pejoratives will most certainly continue to compromise the psychological health of young homosexual and bisexual people by insidiously constructing their sexuality as something wrong, dangerous, or shameworthy" (p. 36).

Another author (Rivers, 2000) conducted a retrospective study of 119 GBL adults to assess their experiences during adolescence. Information was sought concerning absenteeism from school, experiences of harassment from peers, and ideations of self-harm and suicide. Seventy-two percent of the subjects indicated that the anti-lesbian/gay abuse they experienced at school lead them to skip school or pretend to be sick in order to avoid such harassment. However, when compared to gay and lesbian youth who did not use such tactics to avoid anti-GLB abuse, it was found that both groups experienced almost similar levels of harassment. Those who experienced greater absences were more likely than 'non-absentee' youth to report being frightened by looks or stares from others, being ridiculed in public, and having items stolen. Both groups reported having two or three close friends at school; however, those with greater absences were much more likely to spend lunch time and other breaks alone rather than interacting with others. Thirty-six percent of those experiencing greater absences indicated they had attempted to harm themselves on several occasions as compared to 15% of the non-absentee group.

Russell, Seif, and Truoung (2001) analyzed the first nationally representative study of U.S. adolescents to understand same-sex romantic attraction. These researchers assessed school issues within the contexts of family, peers, teachers, and social networks. More than 11,000 students in grades 7 to 12 participated in this national study, along with one parent of each student. Analyses revealed that 7.4% of boys and 5.3% of girls indicated they had attractions to people of the same sex. When examining school outcomes, sexual minority girls identified more problems with school than their heterosexual colleagues. Boys that identified themselves as bisexual reported greater school difficulties. Perhaps the most unexpected outcome was that boys who identified same sex attractions exclusively did not differ from their heterosexual counterparts on school outcomes. Bisexual youth reported spending more time with their friends than did heterosexual or gay males, but these youth also reported being disliked and rejected more often than the other two groups.

Pilkington and D'Augelli (1995) conducted a study of 194 lesbian, gay, and bisexual youth between 15 and 21 years of age. Findings demonstrated that 30% of gay and bisexual young men and 35% of lesbian and bisexual young women had experienced some form of harassment or verbal abuse from peers in school due to their sexual orientation. A peer had physically injured 29% of males and 29% of females, and approximately one-fourth of the respondents indicated that their openness about their sexual orientation was influenced by their fear of physical violence. Many attempted to hide their sexual orientation from their peer group, and the fear of being socially isolated from a peer group was one of the strongest reasons why these GLB youth did not disclose their sexual orientation.

SUBSTANCE USE

Research has shown that substance abuse is a major problem during adolescence and GLB youth may be at increased risk due to negative social attitudes concerning homosexuality (Shifrin & Solis, 1992). However, little is known concerning the prevalence of cigarette, alcohol, and drug use among these youth. Some have speculated that GLB youth might be more likely to use substances to escape the stress of negative societal attitudes and feelings of unhappiness created by the stigma of homosexuality (Rosario, Hunter, & Gwadz, 1997). They may also feel marginalized by society, and seek relief for feelings of depression and isolation through substance use (Jordan, 2000).

On the other hand, some believe that GLB youth may use substances to feel a part of the gay and lesbian subculture, which may be localized around bars (Faltz, 1992). Adolescents, however, who cannot legally access drinking environments may be pushed into inadequately supervised and marginalized subcultures which also increases the likelihood of exposure to substance use and other high-risk situations (Jordan, Vaughn, & Woodworth, 1997).

Research Studies of Substance Use

Rotheram-Borus and Rosario (1994) recruited 136 gay-identified males between 14 and 19 years of age from a community-based social service agency in New York City. Utilizing a semi-structured interview approach, 89% of the respondents reported being sexually active, 87% with other males and 49% with females. Participants reported high rates of alcohol use (76%), marijuana use (42%), and cocaine use (25%). Approximately one-third of these youth used alcohol or drugs on a weekly basis. Correlations suggested that engaging in unprotected oral or anal sex with numerous male partners was associated with greater use of alcohol, marijuana, or cocaine/crack.

Another group of researchers (Rosario et al., 1997) conducted a study of 154 youth between the ages of 14-21 years who were using three community-based agencies that provided social and recreational services to GLB youth. Standardized measures revealed that substance use was significantly related to coping with psychological issues, such as using substances to relax, to be happier or less sad, and to escape problems. Ninety-eight percent of female and 89% of male respondents reported using illicit substances; alcohol was the most frequently used. Sixty-seven percent of females and 59% of males indicated they used illicit drugs, typically marijuana. When this usage was compared to national data, lesbian, and bisexual females were 6.4 times more likely than their heterosexual counterparts to use drugs. The prevalence rate for gay and bisexual males was 4.4 times higher than for heterosexual males.

Other studies have included both heterosexual and homosexual adolescents. Noell and Ochs (2001) employed semi-structured interviews of 532 adolescents. Forty-five percent of females self-identified as lesbian or bisexual, but only 14% of the males reported being gay or bisexual. Lesbian and bisexual females were more likely to have used injection drugs, amphetamines, marijuana, and LSD than their heterosexual counterparts. Overall, GLB youth were at risk for having recently used amphetamines and injected drugs; however, heterosexual youth were more likely to have recently used marijuana.

SUICIDAL BEHAVIOR

The issue of depression and suicide among GLB youth has received increased focus in the empirical literature (Kulkin, Chauvin, & Percle, 2000). Estimates suggest that more than 5,000 adolescents in the U.S. between 15-24 years of age take their lives each year (Ramfedi, Farrow, & Deisher, 1991) and suicide appears to be the leading cause of death for the GLB youth population. It has been reported that GLB youth are 2-3 times more prone to attempt suicide than their heterosexual counterparts and as many as 20% to 35% of gay youth have contemplated suicide. Thirty percent of completed suicides are gay or lesbian youth (Gibson, 1989; Rich, Fowler, Young, & Blenkush, 1986).

Research Studies of Suicidal Behavior

Rotheram-Borus and Hunter (1994) examined suicidality, stress and gay-related stress among consecutive entrants of a youth social service agency focusing on GLB adolescents. Through a semi-structured interview of 131 participants, findings indicated that over one-third (39%) of the adolescents had attempted suicide and more than one half (52.1%) of this group had made multiple attempts. Additionally, 37% indicated they had thought about suicide on a daily basis for at least one week. Adolescents who had attempted suicide were two and one-half times more likely to be school dropouts, to live separately from their parents, and to have friends or family members who had also attempted suicide. Attempters also reported greater gay-related stressors, such as coming out to parents and/or siblings, being discovered they were GLB, or being ridiculed for their sexual orientation.

Remafedi et al. (1991) recruited 137 self-identified gay or bisexual males between 14 and 21 years of age to complete a structured interview regarding demographics, education, home environment, sexuality, psychosocial history, suicidal ideation, and depression. Thirty percent of the participants reported at least one suicide attempt, and almost fifty percent of this group reported multiple attempts. The most common methods reported were taking prescription/non-prescription medications and self-laceration. Other methods included hanging, carbon monoxide poisoning, jumping, using firearms, and automobile crashes. An examination of the causes of the suicide attempts revealed that 44% were motivated by "family problems," including conflict with family members, parents' marital problems, divorce, or alcoholism. One third of the attempts occurred during the first year following the adolescent identifying as gay or bisexual. Other triggers for suicide attempts included depression, problems in a romantic relationship, and dysphoria associated with personal substance abuse.

Hershberger, Pilkington, and D'Augelli (1997) identified predictors of past suicide attempts among 194 GLB youth 15 to 21 years of age involved in social and recreational groups across 14 urban community settings. The researchers compared youth who reported at least one suicide attempt, no attempts, and several attempts through a self-report questionnaire. Forty-two percent of the sample reported at least one suicide attempt, and 23% reported multiple attempts. A comparison of those who had at least one suicide attempt with those who had never attempted suicide revealed commonality among attempters: They had their first same-sex experience at an earlier age, had a greater number of same-sex partners, were more open about their sexual orientation, had more close gay and lesbian friends, had lost more friends due to their sexual orientation, and reported better current overall family relationships. Attempters also reported lower levels of self-esteem, more current suicidal ideation, more substance use, less satisfaction with their sex lives, more problems with close relationships, and greater depression. In addition, subjects that self-identified as bisexual were five times more likely to have made multiple suicide attempts.

Van Heeringen and Vincke (2000) aimed to determine the risk of attempted suicide and the effect of potential risk factors on the occurrence of suicidal ideation and behavior among GLB youth. Four hundred and four youth were recruited from a holiday camp for GLB youth and secondary and high school classes. GLB subjects comprised the majority (54%) of the sample. Findings from questionnaires indicated that a larger percentage (37.7%) of the GLB individuals reported suicidal ideations than their heterosexual counterparts (21.5%) and more GLB adolescents (17.2%) reported a history of suicidal behavior than did heterosexual youths (5.6%). The risk of attempted suicide grew to a fivefold increase when gender was examined–one fourth of all lesbian and female bisexual youth reported occurrence of suicidal behavior as compared to approximately five percent of heterosexual females.

Proctor and Groze (1994) explored risk factors for suicide among GLB youths through a survey instrument completed during youth group meetings across the U.S. Of the 221 participants, findings showed that GLB youth were at highest risk for suicide. Adolescents who had never attempted or contemplated suicide had the highest scores on measures of health, social environment and self-perception, demonstrating that some GLB youth possessed qualities that enabled them to cope with the negative experiences and discrimination associated with being a sexual minority.

HIV/AIDS RISK

Adolescents in general have a higher incidence of sexually transmitted diseases than any other population, as they typically have short-term perspectives of the future and are often impulsive (Dempsey, 1994). Since the early 1990s, intensive targeted HIV prevention strategies have been initiated and a great deal of research has been conducted concerning this issue among GLB populations (Travers & Paoletti, 1999). However, understanding the issues concerning sexual activity of gay young people is hindered by their lack of visibility, the social stigma of homosexuality, and their fears of disclosure (Remafedi, 1987). Despite intervention efforts, young gay and bisexual males continue to present with new infections (Lemp, Hirozawa, Givertz et al., 1994) and HIV prevalence rates among young gay men range from 2.4% to 18.7% (Povinelli, Remafedi, & Tao, 1996; Seage, Mayer, Lenderking et al., 1997). The incidence of new infections among 20-24 year old gay males is twice (4.4% annually) that of older groups of gay men (CDC HIV/AIDS Prevention, 1995). Similar data of incidence and prevalence of HIV among lesbian female youth are not readily available, and these adolescents are not considered 'high-risk' for these problems. However, among highly vulnerable females, such as those who are homeless, runaways, or use substances, the risk may be greater as they may engage in survival prostitution and injection drug use (Gibson, 1989).

Research Studies of Adolescent HIV/AIDS Risk

Seal, Kelly, Bloom et al. (2000) conducted a study to solicit information and recommendations from young gay men regarding what types of HIV prevention programs would best meet their needs and would address risk issues critical to this group. Employing purposive sampling, 72 gay males completed semi-structured interviews that centered on HIV prevention programs. Results indicated that the young men preferred HIV prevention topics to be integrated into other concerns, such as dating and emotional intimacy, the development of relationships, self-esteem, substance abuse, and gaining acceptance by others. Participants reported that unsafe sexual practices often occurred when they were using alcohol or drugs, but were most likely to occur within the context of a regular dating relationship.

Rotheram-Borus, Gillis, Reid, Fernandez, and Gwadz (1997) examined HIV testing behaviors and predictors among adolescents considered at high-risk for HIV. Two hundred seventy-two homeless and GLB youth between 14 and 22 years of age participated from three community-based agencies in New York City, San Francisco, and Los Angeles. Results indicated that 61% of the participants were sexually active during the previous three months and had an average of four sexual partners and 8.4 sexual acts where a condom was not used. Almost two-thirds of the participants had been tested at least once for HIV, with an average of 3.6 tests. Youth who had not ever been tested for HIV gave the following reasons: (1) lack of importance of the test (14%); (2) fear, such as fear of losing their current housing (10%); (3) being under increased stress (47%); and (4) becoming suicidal (21%).

Allen, Glicken, Beach, and Naylor (1998) studied 102 self-identified gay, lesbian and bisexual youth to understand their health care experiences when they were 14 to 18 years of age. Participants completed a questionnaire regarding their sexual orientation and experiences regarding health care. Results indicated that 85% of the male subjects self-identified as gay, 63% of females labeled themselves as lesbian and the remaining subjects considered themselves bisexual. Of those adolescents who received health care, 78% reported they never discussed their sexual orientation with their health care provider, even though they desired to do so. Only half of the males were given information about safe sex and HIV prevention; none were referred to GLB support groups.

Travers and Paoletti (1999) interviewed 32 HIV positive GLB youth 17 to 25 years of age regarding the challenges of living with HIV/AIDS and barriers to youth services. The in-depth, semi-structured interviews were audio-taped and transcribed to reveal concerns faced by these youth, including societal stigma, emotional concerns, fear of disclosure to others, social isolation and loneliness, possible rejection by potential partners, and service barriers in AIDS service organizations. Results demonstrated the difficulty HIV positive youth have in (1) coping with stigma, misinformation, and negative stereotyping, (2) emotional issues resulting from self-blame and shame regarding the infection, (3) social isolation and loneliness as they see themselves as the "only one" their age with HIV and having little peer interaction concerning their problem, and (4) anxiety concerning future sexual and dating relationships. In addition participants identified barriers to youth services focusing on HIV/AIDS. They reported services were useful for practical supports and general information, but were perceived as "adult oriented," and youth felt uncomfortable seeking these services. Many were not connected to a primary care physician.

Blake, Ledsky, Lehman, Goodenow, Sawyer, and Hack (2001) compared GLB youth and heterosexual youth on high-risk behaviors and gay-sensitive

HIV instruction. A multistage cluster sample of 4159 adolescents enrolled in 59 public high schools in Massachusetts completed The Youth Risk Behavior Survey. One hundred seventy-nine HIV education teachers also completed surveys. Analyses revealed that GLB youth were significantly more likely to report lifetime and recent (previous three months) sexual experiences. When only sexually active adolescents were considered, GLB youth reported an earlier age for their first sexual experience, greater lifetime and recent sexual partners, and, interestingly, higher pregnancy rates. GLB youths were more likely to have used alcohol or drugs during their last sexual encounter, but there was little difference between the two groups regarding the general use or nonuse of condoms. GLB youth were significantly less likely to have received HIV prevention instruction in school; however, GLB students in schools with gay-sensitive HIV instruction were less likely to have had sex during the previous three months, had fewer sexual partners, and to have used alcohol or drugs prior to their last sexual experience.

IMPLICATIONS FOR PRACTICE WITHIN THE SOCIAL ENVIRONMENT

The empirical literature concerning high-risk behaviors among GLB youth is still in its early stages. As demonstrated from the previous sections, relatively few studies address the various risk factors associated with being a gay, lesbian, or bisexual adolescent. However, the growing awareness of sexual-minority youths will undoubtedly lead researchers to conduct increasingly rigorous and scientifically valid studies in the future (Savin-Williams, 2001). Despite concerns over the limited scope and methodological rigor of many of these studies, practitioners providing services to youth need appropriate intervention methods and policy makers require further information to address the needs of these youth.

Practitioners must become aware of their own feelings toward sexuality and how it affects their work with clients of any sexual orientation. As Appelby and Anastas (1998) indicate, the coming out process "usually involves overcoming some degree of internalized homophobia for both the worker and the individual client" (p. 291). Further, examination of one's value system is especially important for heterosexual clinicians who have been socialized in ways that often insulate "them against sensitivity to the situations gay people confront in society" (Wirth, 1978, p. 7). As GLB adolescent clients are likely becoming aware of their non-mainstream sexual orientation, it is important that practitioners engage in discussions with them about their possible confusion, uncertainty, and dissonance concerning this awareness. Practitioners who understand that dissonance is an expected phase of the coming-out process will be in a position to support clients as they clarify feelings about their sexual orientation (Morrow, 1993). Assisting youth to develop positive self-acceptance and self-esteem is essential to the successful development of these young people.

Parents are an important part of an adolescent's life, and acceptance by parents is a strong desire for most. However, parents typically react quite negatively upon learning that their child is questioning their heterosexuality (Goldfried & Goldfried, 2001), and family dynamics are likely to be affected. Stommen (1989) describes stages that parents typically experience as they face the true sexual orientation of their GLB son or daughter: (1) subliminal awareness–a vague suspicion based on failure to fit typical gender role characteristics, (2) impact–the actual discovery of child's sexual identity that frequently includes shock, denial, confusion, and/or blame, (3) adjustment–attempts to deal with the crisis, often by trying to get their child to change or hide the information from others, (4) resolution–acceptance of the child for who they are. Clinicians assisting parents to understand their child's sexual orientation may find working through these steps is necessary for parents to reach full acceptance of their child's sexual identity (Goldfried & Goldfried, 2001).

It is crucial that practitioners pay attention to the stories of GLB youth and avoid the temptation to construe the stories from a heterosexual or other biased perspective (Johnston & Jenkins, in press). GLB adolescents' stories may include references to a variety of experiences, such as rape, substance use, unsafe sexual acts, rejection by family and friends, alienation from organized religion, suicidal ideation, and depression. The role of advocacy must not be overlooked as many have experienced such actions from their social environment. There are times when the practitioner must actively work "to adjust the (social) environment to the needs of the individual" (Middleman & Goldberg, 1974, p. 9). Environmental change is needed in order to address such issues as violence in schools, sodomy laws, job discrimination, hate crimes, condom distribution, and recognition of same sex relationships. Advocacy can take the form of the counselor organizing GLB adolescents to assert their own entitlements or arguing for their own personal rights; however, GLB adolescents need practitioners they can trust and depend on who will provide the necessary encouragement and affirmation. Being non-judgmental, proffering acceptance, and offering affirmation to these adolescents are the most significant intervention skills practitioners can employ. The importance of honestly accepting GLB adolescents for who they are and affirming these youth as they grow and develop into young adults cannot be overlooked.

Other structures in the social environment, such as schools, religious organizations, and community groups are important in the lives of GLB youth. Within schools, written and formal policies are being developed to prevent discrimination, harassment, and verbal abuse of these young people (Mallon, 1997). Professionals, such as school administrators and teachers, require clearly stated policies that overcome preconceptions based on personal experiences, culture, religion, or societal biases. School-initiated programming has lead to including such activities as collecting literature on sexual orientation for use by school staff members, addressing sexual orientation as a part of sex education, and creating support and discussion groups (James, 1998). In addition, community-based efforts have become a growing movement among GLB-conscious groups as community action groups offer training to professionals and nonprofessionals concerning sexual orientation issues. Continuing these efforts is needed to enable GLB youths' successful development.

REFERENCES

Allen, L.B., Glicken, A.D., Beach, R.K., & Naylor, K.E. (1998). Adolescent health care experience of gay, lesbian, and bisexual young adults. *Journal of Adolescent Health, 23,* 212-220.

Appelby, G.A., & Anastas, J.W. (1998). *Not just a passing phase: Social work with gay, lesbian, and bisexual people.* New York: Columbia University Press.

Armesto, J.C., & Weisman, A.G. (2001). Attributions and emotional reactions to the identity disclosure ("Coming out") of a homosexual child. *Family Process, 40*(2), 145-161.

Aurand, S.K., Adessa, R., & Bush, C. (1985). *Violence and Discrimination against Philadelphia Lesbian and Gay People.* Unpublished report: Philadelphia Lesbian and Gay Task Force.

Blake, S.M., Ledsky, R., Lehman, T., Goodenow, C., Sawyer, R., & Hack, T. (2001). Preventing sexual risk behaviors among gay, lesbian, and bisexual adolescents: The benefits of gay-sensitive HIV instruction in schools. *American Journal of Public Health, 91*(6), 940-947.

Borhek, M.V. (1988). Helping gay and lesbian adolescents and their families. *Journal of Adolescent Health Care, 9,* 123-128.

Center for Disease Control HIV/AIDS Prevention (1995). *HIV/AIDS among young gay and bisexual men.* Atlanta: Centers for Disease Control, US Department of Health and Human services.

Center for Disease Control and Prevention & Massachusetts Department of Education (1997). *The Massachusetts Youth Risk Behavior Survey.* Department of Education, Just the Facts Coalition, 1999. Boston, MA: Massachusetts.

D'Augelli, A.R., Hershberger, S.L., & Pilkington, B.A. (1998). Lesbian, gay, and bisexual youth and their families: Disclosure of sexual orientation and its consequences. *American Journal of Orthopsychiatry, 68*(3), 361-371.

Dube, E., & Savin-Williams, R.C. (1999). Sexual identity development among ethnic sexual-minority male youths. *Developmental Psychology, 35,* 1389-1399.

DuRane, R.H., Knowchuk, D.P., & Sinal, S.H. (1998). Victimization, use of violence, and drug use at school among male adolescents who engage in same-sex sexual behavior. *Journal of Pediatrics, 132*, 113-118.

Dempsey, C.L. (1994). Health and social issues of gay, lesbian, and bisexual adolescents. *Families in Society: The Journal of Contemporary Human Services, 75*, 160-167.

Faltz, B.G. (1992). Counseling chemically dependent lesbians and gay men. In S.H. Dworkin & F.I. Gutierrez (Eds.), *Counseling gay men and lesbian: Journey to the end of the rainbow* (pp. 245-258). Alexandria, VA: American Association for Counseling and Development.

Garofalo, R., Wolf, R.C., Kessel, S., Palfrey, J., & Durant, R.H. (1998). The association between health risk behaviors and sexual orientation among a school-based sample of adolescents. *Pediatrics, 101*, 895-902.

Gibson, P. (1989). Gay male and lesbian youth suicide. *Report on the Secretary's Task Force on Youth Suicides, 3, 110-142*. Washington, D.C.: U.S. Department of Health and Human Services.

Goldfried, M.R., & Goldfried, A.P. (2001). The importance of parental support in the lives of gay, lesbian, and bisexual individuals. *JCLP/In Session: Psychotherapy in Practice, 57*(5), 681-693.

Gross, L., Aurand, S., & Adessa, R. (1988). *Violence and Discrimination against Lesbian and Gay People in Philadelphia and Commonwealth of Pennsylvania*. Unpublished report: Philadelphia Lesbian and Gay Task Force.

Hammelman, T.L. (1993). Gay and lesbian youth: Contributing factors to serious attempts or considerations of suicide. *Journal of Gay & Lesbian Psychotherapy, 2*(1), 77-89.

Harris, M.B. (1997). *School Experiences of Gay and Lesbian Youth*. New York: The Harrington Press.

Hawkins, J.D., Catalano, R.F., & Miller, J.Y. (1992). Risk and protective factors for alcohol and other drug problems in adolescent and early adulthood: Implications for substance abuse prevention. *Psychological Bulletin, 112*, 64-105.

Hawkins, J.D., & Weis, J.G. (1985). The social development model: An integrated approach to delinquency prevention. *Journal of Primary Prevention, 6*, 73-97.

Henning-Stout, M., James, S., & Macintosh, S. (2000). Reducing harassment of lesbian, gay, bisexual, transgender, and questioning youth in schools. *School Psychology Review, 29*(2), 180-192.

Hershberger, S.L., Pilkington, N.W., & D'Augelli, A.R. (1997). Predictors of suicide attempts among gay, lesbian, and bisexual youth. *Journal of Adolescent Research, 12*(4), 477-497.

James, S.E. (1998). Fulfilling the promise: Community response to the needs of sexual minority youth and families. *American Journal of Orthopsychiatry, 68*(3), 447-454.

Johnston, L.B., & Jenkins, D. (in press). Coming out in mid-adulthood: Building a new identity. *Journal of Gay and Lesbian Social Services*.

Jordan, K.M. (2000). Substance abuse among gay, lesbian, bisexual, transgender, and questioning adolescents. *School Psychology Review, 29*(2), 201-206.

Jordan, K.M., Vaughn, J.S., & Woodworth, K.J. (1997). I will survive: Lesbian, gay, and bisexual youths' experience of high school. *Journal of Gay and Lesbian Social Services, 7*(4), 17-33.

Kazdin, A.E. (1990). *Prevention of conduct disorder.* Rockville, MD: National Institute of Mental Health.

Kulkin, H.S., Chauvin, E.A., & Percle, G.A. (2000). Suicide among gay and lesbian adolescents and young adults: A review of the literature. *Journal of Homosexuality, 40*(1), 1-29.

Lemp, G.E., Hirozawa, A.M., Givertz, D., Nieri, G.N., Anderson, L., Linegren, M.L., Janssen, R.S., & Katz, M. (1994). Seroprevalence of HIV and risk behaviors among young homosexual and bisexual men: The San Francisco/Berkeley Young Men's Survey. *Journal of the American Medical Association, 272,* 449-454.

Mac an Ghaill, M. (1994). Invisibility: Sexuality, race, and masculinity in the school context. In *Challenging Lesbian and Gay inequalities in Education,* D. Epstein (Ed.). Buckingham: Open University Press.

Mallon, G.P. (1997). Toward a competent child welfare service delivery system for gay and lesbian adolescents and their families. *Journal of Multicultural Social Work, 5*(3/4), 177-194.

Merina, A. (1995). A case study in gay bashing. *The NEA Today, 13*(9), 6.

Middleman, R.R., & Goldberg, G. (1974). *Social service delivery: A structural approach to social work practice.* New York: Columbia University Press.

Morrow, D.R. (1993). Social work with gay and lesbian adolescents. *Social Work, 38*(6), 655-660.

Noell, J.W., & Ochs, L.M. (2001). Relationship of sexual orientation to substance, suicidal ideation, suicide attempts, and other factors in a population of homeless adolescents. *Journal of Adolescent Health, 29,* 30-36.

O'Connor, A. (1995). Breaking the silence: Writing about gay, lesbian, and bisexual teenagers. In *The Gay Teen: Educational Practice and Theory for Lesbian, Gay, and Bisexual Adolescents,* G. Unks (Ed.). New York: Routledge.

Pilkington, N.W., & D'Augelli, A.R. (1995). Victimization of lesbian, gay, and bisexual youth in a community setting. *Journal of Community Psychology, 23,* 34-42.

Povinelli, M., Remafedi, G., & Tao, G. (1996). Trends and predictors of Human Immunodeficiency Virus antibody testing by homosexual and bisexual adolescent males, 1989-1994. *Archives of Pediatrics and Adolescent Medicine, 150,* 33-38.

Proctor, C.D., & Groze, V.K. (1994). Risk factors for suicide among gay, lesbian, and bisexual youths. *Social Work, 39*(5), 504-513.

Remafedi, G. (1987). Male homosexuality: The adolescents' perspective. *Pediatrics, 79,* 326-330.

Remafedi, G., Farrow, J.A., & Deisher, R.W. (1991). Risk factors for attempted suicide in gay and bisexual youth. *Pediatrics, 87*(6), 869-875.

Remafedi, G., French, S., Story, M., Resnick, M.D., & Blum, R. (1998). The relationship between suicide risk and sexual orientation: Results of a population-based study. *American Journal of Public Health, 88,* 57-60.

Rich, C.L., Fowler, R.C., Young, D., & Blenkush, M. (1986). San Diego suicide study: Comparison of gay to straight males. *Suicide and Life-Threatening Behaviors, 16,* 448-457.

Rivers, I. (2000). Social exclusion, absenteeism, and sexual minority youth. *Support for Learning, 15*(1), 13-18.

Robinson, K.E. (1994). Addressing the needs of gay and lesbian students: The school counselor's role. *The School Counselor, 41,* 326-332.

Roffman, D.M. (2000). A model for helping schools address policy options regarding gay and lesbian youth. *Journal of Sex Education & Therapy, 25*(2/3), 130-137.

Rosario, M., Hunter, J., & Gwadz, M. (1997). Exploration of substance use among lesbian, gay, and bisexual youth: Prevalence and correlates. *Journal of Adolescent Research, 12*(4), 454-476.

Rosario, M., Rotheram-Borus, M.J., & Reid, H. (1996). Gay-related stress and its correlates among gay and bisexual male adolescents of predominately Black and Hispanic background. *Journal of Community Psychology, 24*, 136-143.

Rothblum, E.D. (1994). I only read about myself on bathroom walls: The need for research on the mental health of lesbians and gay men. *Journal of Consulting and Clinical Psychology, 62*, 213-220.

Rotheram-Borus, M.J., Gillis, J.R., Reid, H.M., Fernandez, M.I., & Gwadz, M. (1997). HIV testing, behaviors, and knowledge among adolescents at high risk. *Journal of Adolescent Health, 20*, 206-225.

Rotheram-Borus, M.J., & Hunter, J. (1994). Suicidal behavior and gay-related stress among gay and bisexual male adolescents. *Journal of Adolescent Research, 9*(4), 498-508.

Rotheram-Borus, M.J., & Rosario, M. (1994). Sexual and substance use acts of gay and bisexual male adolescents in New York City. *Journal of Sex Research, 31*(1), 47-58.

Russel, S.T., Seif, H., & Truong, N.L. (2001). School outcomes of sexual minority youth in the United States: Evidence from a national study. *Journal of Adolescence, 24*, 110-127.

Safren, S.A., & Heimberg, R.G. (1999). Depression, homelessness, suicidality and related factors in sexual minority and heterosexual adolescents. *Journal of Consulting and Clinical Psychology, 67*, 859-866.

Savin-Williams, R.C. (1994). Verbal and physical abuse as stressors in the lives of lesbian, gay males, and bisexual youths: Associations with school problems, running away, substance abuse, prostitution, and suicide. *Journal of Consulting and Clinical Psychology, 62*, 261-269.

Savin-Williams, R.C. (2001). A critique of research on sexual-minority youths. *Journal of Adolescence, 24*, 5-13.

Seage, G.R., Mayer, K.H., Lenderking, W.R., Wold, C., Gross, M., Goldstein, R., Cai, B., Heeren, T., Hingson, R., & Holmberg, S. (1997). HIV and Hepatitis B infection and risk behavior in young gay and bisexual men. *Public Health Reports, 112*, 158-167.

Seal, D.W., Kelly, J.A., Bloom, F.R., Stevenson, L.Y., Coley, B.L., & Broyles, L.A. (2000). *AIDS Care, 12*(1), 5-27.

Shifrin, F., & Solis, M. (1992). Chemical dependency in gay and lesbian youth. *Journal of Chemical Dependency Treatment, 5*, 67-76.

Stommen, E.F. (1989). "You're a what?" Family member reactions to the disclosure of homosexuality. *Journal of Homosexuality, 18*, 37-58.

Thurlow, C. (2001). Naming the "outsider within": Homophobic pejoratives and verbal abuse of lesbian, gay, and bisexual high-school pupils. *Journal of Adolescence, 24*, 25-38.

Travers, R., & Paoletti, D. (1999). Responding to the support needs of HIV positive lesbian, gay and bisexual youth. *Canadian Journal of Human Sexuality, 8*(4), 271-285.

Uribe, V., & Harbeck, K.M. (1991). Addressing the needs of lesbian, gay, and bisexual youth: The origins of PROJECT 10 and school based intervention. *Journal of Homosexuality, 22,* 9-28.

Van Heeringen, C., & Vincke, J. (2000). Suicidal acts and ideation in homosexual and bisexual young people: A study of prevalence and risk factors. *Social Psychiatry and Psychiatric Epidemiology, 35,* 494-499.

Waldner, L.K., & Magruder, B. (1999). Coming out to parents: Perceptions of family relations, perceived resources, and identity expression as predictors of identity expression as predictors of identity disclosure for gay and lesbian adolescents. *Journal of Homosexuality, 37*(2), 83-128.

Weiner, B. (1980). A cognitive (attribution)-emotion action model of motivated behavior: An analysis of help giving. *Journal of Personality and Social Psychology, 39,* 186-200.

Werner, E.E. (1990). Protective factors and individual resilience. In *Handbook of early childhood intervention,* S.J. Meisels & J.P. Shankoff (Eds.) (pp. 97-116). Cambridge: Cambridge University Press.

Whitbeck, L.B. (1999). Primary socialization theory: It all begins with the family. *Substance use and misuse, 34*(7), 1025-1032.

Wirth, S. (1978). Coming out close to home: Principles for psychotherapy with families of lesbians and gay men. *Catalyst, 3,* 6-22.

Gay Adolescents in Rural Areas: Experiences and Coping Strategies

Darrell G. Yarbrough

SUMMARY. The purpose of this qualitative study was to explore issues faced by gay adolescents in rural areas, to gain knowledge regarding support systems of these young persons and to begin to understand the need for "gay-friendly" social services in rural areas. Eight young adults (18-25) from rural areas were interviewed. Common themes that emerged include isolation, supportive teachers, abuse, and resiliency. Implications for social work practice include utilizing generic phrases and interventions that were supportive of these students' diversity without placing the professional at risk and advocating for policy changes through the state legislative process aimed at reducing institutionalized homophobia. *[Article copies available for a fee from The Haworth Document Delivery Service: 1-800-HAWORTH. E-mail address: <docdelivery@haworthpress.com> Website: <http://www.Haworth Press.com>* © *2003 by The Haworth Press, Inc. All rights reserved.]*

KEYWORDS. Gay, adolescents, rural, coping, coming out

Darrell G. Yarbrough, LMSW, is affiliated with Health Horizons of East Texas, Inc., Rural HIV/AIDs Prevention & Treatment, P.O. Box 631346, Nacogdoches, TX 75693.

[Haworth co-indexing entry note]: "Gay Adolescents in Rural Areas: Experiences and Coping Strategies." Yarbrough, Darrell G. Co-published simultaneously in *Journal of Human Behavior in the Social Environment* (The Haworth Social Work Practice Press, an imprint of The Haworth Press, Inc.) Vol. 8, No. 2/3, 2003, pp. 129-144; and: *Sexual Minorities: Discrimination, Challenges, and Development in America* (ed: Michael K. Sullivan) The Haworth Social Work Practice Press, an imprint of The Haworth Press, Inc., 2003, pp. 129-144. Single or multiple copies of this article are available for a fee from The Haworth Document Delivery Service [1-800-HAWORTH, 9:00 a.m. - 5:00 p.m. (EST). E-mail address: docdelivery@haworthpress.com].

Journal of Human Behavior in the Social Environment, Vol. 8(2/3) 2003
http://www.haworthpress.com/web/JHBSE
© 2003 by The Haworth Press, Inc. All rights reserved.
Digital Object Identifier: 10.1300/J137v8n02_08

All young people undergo the developmental process of growing up and becoming adults. However, gay and lesbian youth experience the additional developmental struggles of disclosing their sexual orientation to others and developing a gay identity (Anderson, 1995; Hunter & Schaecher, 1995). This process, often called "coming out," is extremely difficult for gay adolescents due to a lack of environmental support. These adolescents often are subjected to hate words, slurs, and discrimination without anyone to turn to. Furthermore, they have few adult role models and no special programs to assist them in "coming out" (Hunter & Schaecher, 1995; O'Conor, 1995). It is not surprising that many of these adolescents drop out of school, abuse drugs and alcohol, and attempt suicide (Hunter & Schaecher, 1995; Travers & Schneider, 1996; Unks, 1995).

Rural adolescents may experience even greater obstacles to the processes of coming out than their counterparts in larger cities. Rural areas tend to be bastions for conventional virtues and prejudices (Southern Regional Education Board, 1998). Many persons in rural areas, especially in the South, still consider homosexuality as a deviant lifestyle. Rounds (1998) stated that gay persons often only have the choices of staying in rural areas and assuming low visibility or leaving. Furthermore, limited access to support systems contributes to a deep sense of isolation among rural gays (Rounds, 1998).

Research into the experiences of gay adolescents in rural areas may increase awareness of the issues facing this minority population and act as a catalyst for new, creative social services for these young people. Therefore, the purpose of this study is to explore the nature of issues faced by gay adolescents in rural areas and to explore the need for services. Qualitative interviews were conducted with a sample of young gay adults to gain insight as to their experiences growing up gay in rural communities.

HOMOPHOBIA AND HETEROSEXISM

In most rural areas the gay community is invisible due to the effects of homophobia and heterosexism (D'Augelli & Hart, 1987). Homophobia is the term used to describe oppression against gay, lesbian, and bisexual persons. This term is defined as the dread of being in close quarters with gay persons or the revulsion toward these individuals, often including a desire to inflict punishment (Sears, 1997). Homophobia exists at every level of society, but especially in the institutions of organized religion and education. Furthermore, "internalized homophobia" is defined as the self-hatred felt by gay persons in response to negative feelings and attitudes toward them by society (Dupras, 1994; Sears, 1997). Fear of discovery, low self-esteem, aggression against other lesbians and gay men, and rejection of all heterosexuals are manifestations of internalized homophobia (Sears, 1991). Moreover, internalized homophobia interferes with the coming out process in adolescents and adults (Dupras, 1994).

Heterosexism, on the other hand, is the belief that heterosexuality is the only acceptable form of sexual orientation and that non-heterosexual persons should be excluded from all society's structures and institutions (Appleby & Anastas, 1995; Fassinger, 1991; Sears, 1997). Millions of lesbian, gay, and bisexual individuals are at risk of discrimination and violence due to the effects of heterosexism (NASW, 1997). Furthermore, adolescents are at a much greater risk of experiencing the effects of heterosexism and homophobia due to their lack of maturity and dependence on school and family (Travers & Schneider, 1996). These effects include oppression, discrimination, increased levels of substance abuse, familial difficulties, and suicide ideation (Proctor & Groze, 1998).

GAY, LESBIAN, AND BISEXUAL ADOLESCENTS

Drug and alcohol use among lesbian, gay, and bisexual adolescents has been shown to be significantly higher than among their heterosexual counterparts (Travers & Schneider, 1996). In one study, 60 percent of gay and bisexual male youth surveyed used illegal substances on an ongoing basis (Savin-Williams, 1994). Some alcohol use can be contributed to the environment in which many gay people meet. Bars continue to be an important social gathering place for gay males, including adolescents (Hunter & Schaecher, 1995; Savin-Williams, 1994). Also, gay young people who are thrown out of their homes or run away to escape abuse often use drugs and/or turn to prostitution on the street (Hunter & Schaecher, 1995; Travers & Schneider, 1996).

Gay adolescents abuse substances for different reasons than do their heterosexual counterparts. Heterosexual adolescents most often use drugs or alcohol for the purpose of thrill-seeking or due to peer pressure. However, gay adolescents engage in substance abuse in attempts to "fog an increasing awareness that they are not heterosexual, to defend against the painful realization that being lesbian or gay means a difficult life lies ahead, and to take revenge against parents and society for rejecting them" (Savin-Williams, 1996, p. 265).

Because heterosexuality and patriarchy are the norm in most public and private schools (Smith, 1998), openly gay youth and those suspected of being gay experience name-calling and social ostracism (Anderson, 1995). "Faggot" and "queer" are examples of terms used by students to negatively label and verbally abuse gay adolescents (Hunter & Schaecher, 1995; Smith, 1997). Qualitative interviews with gay, lesbian, and bisexual adolescents have revealed the extreme emotional pain and psychological scarring that verbal abuse in high school inflicts upon this population (O'Conor, 1995; Sears, 1991).

School administrators and teachers often refuse to address the harassment of gay adolescents by other students. Instead, these youth are told that they brought these problems upon themselves. This lack of action on the part of school officials often contributes to the escalation from verbal abuse to physical abuse of these students by their peers (Hunter & Schaecher, 1995). A U.S. Justice Department Report from the 1980s reported that school is one of the primary setting for hate crimes against gay, lesbian, and bisexual adolescents (O'Conor, 1995). One survey conducted in the Los Angeles County school system found that the incidence of antigay abuse inflicted by other adolescents was rising dramatically (Savin-Williams, 1994). Furthermore, abuse of gay youth in high school, both verbal and physical, often results in serious academic problems such as missing classes, poor grades, and dropping out of school (Hunter & Schaecher, 1995; Travers & Schneider, 1996).

GAY, LESBIAN, AND BISEXUAL PERSONS IN RURAL COMMUNITIES

Large numbers of lesbians and gay men moved from rural communities to urban areas in the years following World War II seeking the greater anonymity of larger communities. Most gay people who grew up in rural areas believed they had to exile themselves to urban centers if they wanted to live openly, or even discreetly, as gay people (Miller, 1989). By the time of the 1969 Stonewall riots in New York City (often considered the beginning of the gay rights movement), there were significant gay communities in most large cities (Lindhorst, 1997).

However, many gay, lesbian, and bisexual individuals have chosen to remain or return to rural communities where the gay rights movement has had little, if any, effect. Lindhorst (1997) examined the characteristics of life in rural communities and the basic mental health issues faced by lesbians and gay men in these areas. Social workers provide many of the mental health services that exist in rural areas. Unfortunately, large-scale studies have shown that social workers, in general, are more homophobic than psychiatrists or psychologists, at least during the time when the studies were performed (DeCrescenzo, 1984).

Gay persons in rural areas must adhere to a posture of low visibility, avoiding public declarations of their sexual orientation, in order to appear to fit into rural life (Smith, 1997). Rural communities often place a much higher emphasis on traditional moral values based in fundamentalist religious beliefs than do urban centers (Lindhorst, 1997; Smith, 1997), and conformity to traditional values is demanded (Foster, 1997). These communities are also characterized by a lack of tolerance for diversity (Rounds, 1998).

Although several articles have been published in recent years regarding issues facing the gay population in rural areas, few of these have been empirical in nature. Cody and Welch (1997) published findings from a qualitative study that described the life experiences of 20 gay men in rural New England. Common themes present in the narratives of these rural, gay men included early awareness of difference, internalized homophobia, positive aspects of rural living, negative aspects of rural living, positive family of choice, compulsory heterosexuality, isolation, current life partner, and family censorship.

Early awareness of difference is perhaps the most relevant factor to studying rural gay adolescents. Nineteen out of the 20 respondents in the New England study (Cody & Welch, 1997) reported an early sense of feeling different from other males. Several of these respondents felt this "differentness" as early as three years of age, and this feeling gained momentum throughout childhood and adolescence. They reported having few close male friends, having little interest in athletics, and being emotionally attracted to males. Furthermore, these respondents described how they knew early on that same-sex attraction was considered "bad" by society. Also, internalized homophobia is extremely relevant to studying this population because the majority of these rural respondents claim to be deeply affected by hate rhetoric they had heard from parents, teachers, members of the clergy, and peers.

In a qualitative study of gay and lesbian youth in South Carolina, Sears (1991) utilized both face-to-face interview techniques and survey instruments during three-hour sessions with participants. These gay men and lesbians ranged in age from 18 to 28, and were from both rural and urban areas. The findings of the study provided a plethora of rich data regarding the experiences, both negative and positive, of 36 gay, lesbian, and bisexual individuals from the South.

Although there was an increase during the 1990s of empirical studies that address the needs and issues of gay adolescents, few of these had a predominately rural focus. Savin-Williams (1994) reported that the majority of research concerning gay, lesbian, and bisexual adolescents has been based upon non-representative samples consisting of urban/help-seeking individuals or college activists. Additional knowledge must be gained in order to determine if the problems experienced by gay, lesbian, and bisexual adolescents in rural areas are similar to the documented issues of this population in urban centers so that social workers and others can advocate effectively for this population. Through the use of qualitative interviews, this study explored common problems or issues experienced by gay adolescents in rural areas by interviewing young adults about their experiences growing up gay in these areas. The research questions addressed in this study are:

- What issues and problems do rural gay adolescents encounter that inhibit the coming out process?
- What do rural gay youth self-describe as traumatic experiences of adolescence?
- Are there examples of rural adults who provide support to this population and in what roles do they provide this support?
- What services or helping networks already exist that might provide needed support to this population?

METHODOLOGY

Qualitative research was the logical choice of methods to investigate the research questions in this study. Both O'Conor (1995) and Sears (1991) utilized ethnographic techniques to carry out their studies of gay, lesbian, and bisexual adolescents. In ethnographic studies, the researcher uses "conversations" with participants to gather data. Interviewees are treated as experts and are allowed to describe experiences in great detail (Franklin & Jordan, 1997).

Several reasons existed for the choice of an ethnographic design to study the issues faced by gay adolescents in rural areas. First, as mentioned earlier, little empirical evidence existed regarding the experiences of gay adolescents in rural areas. Qualitative approaches most often work best when little is known about a particular subject (Allen-Meares & Lane, 1990; Padgett, 1998). Because little is known, as much data must be collected as possible on different issues in order to discover recurring themes among the responses of participants. The next reason for choosing this type of method is that qualitative approaches are useful for exploring sensitive or emotionally charged issues due to the requirement that researchers first gain some level of acceptance from respondents (Padgett, 1998). Minorities have been exploited by researchers in the past; therefore, these individuals are often suspicious of more traditional research projects. Furthermore, a qualitative approach was used because one of the intents of this study was to provide data that might be used to advocate for gay youth at both the organizational and societal level. The richness of the data collected through qualitative approaches can often be used to make powerful statements about the plight of oppressed populations. Padgett (1998) states that action, or participatory, research is a primary tool to be used by social workers to fight oppression and social injustice.

Sampling Method

The research sample was identified in several ways: through a gay, lesbian, and bisexual student organization on a college campus in rural East Texas, personal contacts, fliers posted describing the study with contact numbers for those interested, and recruitment in an Internet chat room frequented by young gay males from East Texas. First, the researcher gained access to the student organization by joining as a fellow member. After a trusting relationship was built between the researcher and potential participants over the course of several months, the study and its importance were explained to the group and volunteers were requested. Next, contacts were made and participants screened from responses to the fliers placed on campus. Finally, the researcher logged on the chat room and set up a screen name requesting participants for the study and listing a contact e-mail address. After the study was explained to potential participants by e-mail, interested parties provided their telephone numbers and were screened for the sample by telephone. Additionally, snowball sampling was used to identify gay friends and acquaintances of these young adults who might also be willing to participate.

One of the problems with studying gay adolescents is the fact that due to homophobic attitudes in the environment they often cannot be interviewed safely. In addition, obtaining the consent of parents of adolescents under the age of 18 would be difficult, at best. Therefore, the only feasible way to conduct this type of research is in retrospect. However, data collected through retrospective studies is subject to distortion due to the passage of time and the evolving attitudes of respondents (Hunter & Schaecher, 1995; Sears, 1991). Research such as this always runs the risk of having historical biases. In a quantitative study regarding parental influences on the self-esteem of gay and lesbian youth, Savin-Williams (1998) controlled for this variable by limiting the age of respondents to 23 years old. Similarly, the present study attempted to reduce this bias by limiting the age of respondents to between 18 and 25.

Eight male participants were recruited and actually completed the interviews for this study. Five of the participants were African American and three were European American. All but one of the participants were from rural communities, communities of less than 50,000 inhabitants not adjacent to metropolitan areas, except for one participant who was from a small city in East Texas of over 50,000 inhabitants, but which is surrounded by rural areas and in which rural attitudes are prevalent. All of the participants were between 18 and 25 years old. A consent form was presented both orally and in writing to all participants outlining the purpose of the study, the requirements that must be met to be included in the sample, possible benefits to participation, risks of participation, what steps were taken to minimize these risks, and notification that the participant could withdraw from the study at any time.

The primary risk for many gay participants in rural areas is disclosure of their sexual orientation. Therefore, confidentiality might even be considered more important than in other studies regarding topics that are perhaps less controversial. O'Conor (1995) reduced this risk by only publishing his qualitative data in the form of two narratives, one female and one male. The verbal responses of all the females he interviewed were combined under the fictitious name "Christi" and all of the males were listed under the name "Tommy." This approach provided the richness of data associated with qualitative studies and reduced the risk to these young gay persons of being identified by others. The present study protected confidentiality by only interviewing participants in neutral, private places such as offices in the School of Social Work in the evenings or on weekends when few people are on campus. Participants were assured, both in the consent form and verbally, that their names or other identifying information would not be included on the audio tapes or other documentation related to the study, including final reports of the findings. Additionally, a list was provided to each participant with resources such as "gay-friendly" practitioners and web-site addresses of gay support networks. This was to empower participants to deal with any emotional or psychological issues that could arise due to reliving past experiences.

One benefit of participation for the respondents was the opportunity to utilize personal past experiences in order to help possibly create an environment for future generations which is less homophobic and heterosexist. In addition, often just the act of talking about painful experiences and identifying strengths that were survival tools can be beneficial to individuals.

Finally, participants were assured in the consent form that participation is voluntary and that they have the right to withdraw at any time without fear of repercussion. Audiotapes and consent forms will be kept in a secure location for three years and then destroyed.

Data Collection and Instruments

Several open-ended questions were used to begin the interviewing process and were used to keep the "conversation" on track. In addition, spontaneous probes were utilized to follow a lead. The primary questions that were asked of each participant are listed below:

- Can you describe what growing up gay in a rural community was like?
- Who were you "out" to in high school if anyone?
- Did you have any significant experiences during high school related to your sexual orientation? If so, would you describe? How were you able to cope with them?
- Do you remember any adult(s) who seemed supportive? How were they supportive?
- Were there any organizations or clubs at school or away from school that were supportive of you developing a gay identity? If so, describe.

- Were there any organizations or clubs at school or away from school that seemed oppressive to gay adolescents? If so, in what way?
- What advice would you give to a gay adolescent based on your experiences?

Data Analysis

Unlike quantitative studies where data are in the form of numbers, the data from qualitative studies are in the form of words (Unrau & Coleman, 1997). After each interview, the audiotape recording was transcribed. Also, the audiotaped interviews in this study were transcribed verbatim in order to capture all possible meanings of the conversation (Unrau & Coleman, 1997).

The researcher read and reread the transcriptions, searching for common themes. However, these manuscripts were not read all at once. Due to the lengthiness of these manuscripts, only a few pages from each interview were read at a time so that the researcher could remain focused. Also, reading sessions began at different portions of the manuscripts because individuals usually read most effectively when they first begin (Unrau & Coleman, 1997).

After several readings common patterns and themes began to emerge. Common themes were assigned codes to assist with the data analysis process. Codes are labels for "assigning units of meaning to the descriptive or inferential information compiled during a study" (Miles & Huberman, 1994, p. 56). These themes will be outlined in the following sections, along with secondary themes that might warrant further exploration in future studies.

RESULTS

Several common themes that emerged from the interviews included isolation, coming out issues, interactions with parents, abuse from others, supportive adults, and suggestions for other adolescents dealing with these issues. These common themes will be discussed in depth in the following sections. Participants are only identified by ethnicity, age at which they came out and to whom, and by the region of Texas in which they grew up in order to allow the reader to conceptualize how these factors might have played a part in the coming out process.

Isolation

Two of the participants, one African American and one European American, specifically described isolation as a major factor in growing up gay in rural areas. One of these young men described adolescence as " . . . like on a raft on the ocean, but there's no one to throw you a line . . . no one to talk to . . . really alone . . . big time isolation." The other participant described it as "total isolation." Although the other participants did not specifically mention isolation, five of the other participants mentioned a lack of individuals to share feelings and thoughts related to their sexual orientation.

Coming Out

Three of the participants came out to everyone in high school. The two that came out the earliest, both European American and approximately 15 years of age when they came out, reported the greatest number of negative experiences. One of these participants stated, "I thought that by coming out I would have been a role model for others and that it would be a more positive experience and it wasn't . . . it wasn't positive at first at all." This participant is currently involved in activism on the local college campus. The other participant who came out to everyone in high school, an African American, came out at the age of 16 and states that "everyone" began to accept him. However, this participant attended a high school near an army base and stated that there were many "out" people in the town. He was, however, rejected by his father when he finally came out to his family, and he ran away from home for a few months. Even this participant stated that he did not come to terms with his sexual orientation until after he was in college.

Three of the other participants came out to at least one or a few close friends in high school. Two of these, African American males, were from small towns in rural East Texas; the other, European American, was from a rural Central Texas town, also near an army base. All of these participants expressed relief when they finally came out to close friends, although fear of discovery was expressed as a major psychological factor in the development of one of the East Texas participants. He described adolescence in a small town in the Piney Woods of East Texas as "rather tough . . . everybody knows everybody . . . you've basically got to watch your back at all times . . . you're afraid of what people are going to say about you, you know, it's just a never ending thing." The European American adolescent male from Central Texas reported a healthier coming out process; he stated that he was involved in color guard and theatre–both organizations that were accepting of gay men.

The final two participants, both African American, never came out to anyone in high school. However, both of these came out to friends shortly after entering college, right out of high school. Both reported playing sports and "acting straight" in high school in order to fit in. They described the process of coming out to friends in college as a fairly uneventful transition. However, neither of these participants was out to his parents at the time of the interviews.

Interactions with Parents

Interestingly, the two participants who came out at the earliest age were from single parent homes (mothers as head of the household), and both stated that their mothers came to terms with the fact that they were gay. In fact, one of these mothers actually confronted her son at fifteen years old and demanded that he tell her what was going on when he started skipping school and dropping out of classes. She had adult gay friends and told her son, "I know what's going on . . . you're gay." However, this participant was initially rebuked by his older brother and was told that he would never be able to come over to see his brother's children. The other participant's mother did not believe him when he came out to her. He states, "she didn't believe it: she thought that I was emotionally upset; she even wondered if someone had done something to make me have these feelings . . . but, she was supportive, I could always talk to her."

One of the African American participants from a small town in rural East Texas stated that he came out to his parents during his senior year of high school and that they were supportive. He stated, "being able to express your feelings to your parents . . . it's just a big relief. And if they accept you–it's like this total burden is lifted off you and you could care less what other people say about you."

Abuse from Others

As mentioned earlier, the two students who came out at an earlier age than the others experienced the most abuse and harassment from their peers. One of these stated, "I got in a few fights over it; called faggot . . . and you know I defended myself . . . so I had built myself up so that stuff really didn't hurt me that bad." This participant dropped out of high school shortly after coming out. The other participant who came out early in high school experienced abuse in the form of other students attaching post-it notes on his backpack that stated "Die Fag," or "Queer." He was humiliated when students called campus police and reported that he had a gun in his backpack; he was removed from class on more than one occasion (in front of other classmates) and searched for a gun. He was even asked to leave a Baptist church that he was attending because he was openly gay.

Other participants experienced less covert forms of harassment and humiliation. One of the African American participants from East Texas stated that he saw how an openly gay student was treated by other students and that this dissuaded him from coming out to others. This participant reported, "everybody knew that he was gay, and he was always picked on and people made his life a living hell. I mean . . . everyday . . . name-calling or picking on him, or somebody wanted to fight with him. . . . I felt it was wrong the whole time, but if I was to butt in somebody else would say why are you taking up for him unless you are that way yourself."

Conversely, two of the other participants, who reported being very popular in small East Texas schools, stated that they attempted to try to be supportive of others who were out and who experienced name calling and other forms of abuse, although they were not out themselves. One participant expressed it in the following way, "a lot of people who were picked on in high school, I took to them, I don't know why . . . I was very popular in high school and a lot of them folks were not popular, and were picked on all the time, came to me; yeah, I took to them."

Supportive Adults

Four of the eight participants reported at least one teacher or counselor in high school that was supportive of the coming out process, at least in some way. One participant stated that a teacher who was a lesbian was openly gay to him and even stayed after school and provided him with support. He described it in the following way:

> There was a teacher who was a lesbian on campus and she knew my circumstances and she knew that I was going through a rough time. . . . I would stay after school and talk to her . . . [we] got along fine, got along great. But, the faculty in the school began wondering what she was doing talking to me after school and stuff . . . she was given strict orders by the principal of the school to no longer communicate with me and that she was being unprofessional in her teaching position to provide support to a gay student on campus.

The other participants reported teachers and counselors who discreetly provided support through the use of phrases such as, "to thine own self be true."

Suggestions to Other Adolescents

All of the participants had suggestions to give to other gay and bisexual adolescents who are dealing with sexual orientation issues. Only one of the eight participants advised other adolescents to come out to others at an early age. He described it in this manner, "I respect people that are in the closet, but it's just not healthy, it's not healthy for the soul, its like being in jail . . . sure your parents are going to freak out and sure your parents are going to disown; but it's nature and nature is going to take its course." This participant was one of the two that came out at an early age, experienced the most violence, dropped out of high school, and reported more substance abuse than the other participants. The other seven participants advocated a much slower coming out process that included "take it slow," "don't make it your whole life."

Formal Supports

Only one type of existing service or helping network was identified by a participant as a support during the coming out process. This was a nationwide outreach organization for gay youth with a website and mailing address. Adolescents are able to obtain information regarding their rights as sexual minority youth and can meet other gay adolescents through a pen-pal program. However, no local social services that were gay-friendly were identified by the participants.

A few clubs and organizations on high school campuses were identified as being more accepting of gay adolescents than other organizations. These included choir, theatre, and color guard. One gay adolescent described theatre as a way to escape the reality of being a member of an oppressed population by pretending to be someone else.

DISCUSSION

The negative effects associated with the primary themes of isolation, coming out, and interactions with parents appeared to be endured, in party, by resiliency on the part of the participants. This seemed to be a secondary theme throughout the interviews. Barker (1999) defines resiliency as the ability to recover after encountering problems and stresses. Even the two participants who came out at a very early age and reported suffering the greatest amount of name-calling, violence, and other forms of abuse have achieved goals since high school such as obtaining a Graduate Equivalency Diploma (in the case of the participant who dropped out of high school), or entering college and becoming active in the campus gay, lesbian, and bisexual student organization.

The participants who were not out in high school reported fewer negative experiences. Smith (1997) reports that staying unknown and not visible in rural areas becomes a means of coping with discrimination, oppression, and physical abuse. Participants who were either not out to anyone or only a few people reported achievements in high school such as senior class president or membership in honor societies, even though some of these mentioned experiencing some level of internalized homophobia and fear. Almost all of the participants reported active engagement in the pursuit of personal goals. Intrapersonal and environmental factors that support resiliency and coping strategies in this rural population warrant further research.

School social workers, counselors, or teachers cannot specifically address sexual orientation issues in most rural schools without fear of reprisal, including termination of their positions. However, these professionals can carefully word their interventions with adolescents to include generic quotes and phrases that provide support in identity development without specifically mentioning sexual orientation. Social workers and other mental health practitioners in private or group practice might experience fewer restrictions providing services to gay adolescents than professionals working for schools or other agencies.

Social workers are encouraged to become politically active to effect change at the state and national level in the form of legislation protecting the rights of gay students and the rights of professionals who provide services to these young persons to speak openly about these issues without fear of reprisal. The National Association of Social Workers and lobby groups such as the Lesbian/Gay Rights Lobby of Texas are examples of organizations that social workers could work with to advocate for the rights of these individuals. At the time of this study a bill that would prohibit discrimination against students or teachers in Texas public schools based on gender identity and sexual orientation (along with other factors) had been passed by the House Public Education committee of the Texas Legislature and was awaiting a vote on the floor of the Texas State House of Representatives.

Limitations of this study include the fact that individuals who agreed to participate in this study were already "out" to some friends or family. This study does not reflect the high school experiences of sexual minority youth who are still "in the closet" during their early twenties and unwilling to participate in this study. Several gay and bisexual young adults refused to participate in the current study due to fear of disclosure to others, even though the steps that were taken to protect confidentiality were discussed with these persons. Another limitation of this study was the lack of lesbian participants; one lesbian did agree to participate but then failed to show up for the interviews on at least two occasions with no reason given. Future studies should utilize female, as well as male, interviewers in order to possibly gain more female participation.

Most of the participants in this study advise gay adolescents in rural areas to be cautious of coming out too young and only coming out to trusting, supportive individuals. The results of this study would indicate that finding individuals who are willing to support these adolescents is difficult. In addition, social services in rural Texas that are supportive of gay adolescents appear to be non-existent. Social workers are encouraged to work with all system levels to help create a society where gay youth, even in rural areas, can undergo developmental processes such as coming out without experiencing oppression and discrimination.

REFERENCES

Allen-Meares, P., & Allan-Meares, B. A. (1990). Social work practice: Integrating qualitative and quantitative data collection techniques. *Social Work, 35*(5), 385-480.

Anderson, D. A. (1995). Lesbian and gay adolescents. In G. Unks (Ed.), *The gay teen: Educational practice and theory for lesbian, gay, and bisexual adolescents* (pp. 17-30). New York, NY: Routledge.

Appleby, G. A., & Anastas, J. W. (1995). Social work practice with lesbians and gays. In A. T. Morales & B. W. Sheafor (Eds.), *Social work: A profession of many faces* (7th ed., pp. 333-366). Boston, MA: Allyn & Bacon.

Bawer, B. (1995). Notes on Stonewall. In R. M. Baird & M. K. Baird (Eds.), *Homosexuality* (pp. 23-30). Amherst, NY: Prometheus Books.

Cody, P. J., & Welch, P. L. (1997). Rural gay men in northern New England: Life experiences and coping styles. *Journal of Homosexuality, 33*(1), 51-68.

D'Augelli, A. R., & Hart, M. M. (1987). Gay women, men, and families in rural settings: Toward the development of helping communities. *American Journal of Community Psychology, 15*(1), 79-93.

DeCrescenzo, T. A. (1984). Homophobia: A study of the attitudes of mental health professionals toward homosexuality. In R. Schoenberg, R. S. Golber, & D. A. Shore (Eds.), *With compassion towards some: Homosexuality and social work in America* (pp. 115-136). New York: Harrington Park Press.

Dupras, A. (1994). Internalized homophobia and psychosexual adjustment among gay men. *Psychological Reports, 75*, 23-29.

Fassinger, R. E. (1991). The hidden minority: Issues and challenges in working with lesbian women and gay men. *The Counseling Psychologist, 19*(2), 157-176.

Fontaine, J. H., & Hammond, N. L. (1996). Counseling issues with gay and lesbian adolescents. *Adolescence, 31*(124), 817-830.

Foster, S. J. (1997). Rural lesbians and gays: Public perceptions, worker perceptions, and service delivery. In J. D. Smith & R. J. Mancoske (Eds.), *Rural gays and lesbians* (pp. 23-35). New York: The Haworth Press, Inc.

Franklin, C., & Jordan, C. (1997). Qualitative approaches to the generation of knowledge. In R. M. Grinnell, Jr. (Ed.), *Social work research & evaluation: Quantitative and qualitative approaches* (5th ed., pp. 106-140). Itasca, IL: Peacock.

Ginsberg, L. H. (1998). *Social work in rural communities* (3rd ed.). Alexandria, VA: CSWE.

Hunter, J., & Schaecher, R. (1995). Gay and lesbian adolescents. In *The encyclopedia of social work* (19th ed., pp. 1055-1063). Washington, DC: NASW.

Lindhorst, T. (1997). Foundation knowledge for work with rural gays and lesbians. In J. D. Smith & R. J. Mancoske (Eds.), *Rural gays and lesbians* (pp. 1-12). New York: The Haworth Press, Inc.

Logan, C. R. (1996). Homophobia? No, homoprejudice. *Journal of Homosexuality, 31*(3), 31-53.

Miller, N. (1989). *In search of gay America: Women and men in a time of change*. New York, NY: The Atlantic Monthly Press.

NASW. (1997). *Social work speaks: NASW policy statements.* Washington, DC: NASW.

Newton, D. E. (1994). *Gay and lesbian rights.* Santa Barbara, CA: Instructional Horizons.

O'Conor, A. (1995). Who gets called queer in school? Lesbian, gay, and bisexual teenagers, homophobia, and high school. In G. Unks (Ed.), *The gay teen: Educational practice and theory for lesbian, gay, and bisexual adolescents* (pp. 95-104). New York, NY: Routledge.

Olson, E. D., & King, C. A. (1995). Gay and lesbian self-identification: A response to Rotheram-Borus and Fernandez. *Suicide & life-threatening behavior, 25,* 35-38.

Padgett, D. K. (1998). *Qualitative methods in social work research: Challenges and rewards.* Thousand Oaks, CA: Sage.

Proctor, C. D., & Groze, V. K. (1994). Risk factors for suicide among gay, lesbian, and bisexual youths. *Social Work, 39*(5), 481-624.

Rofes, E. (1995). Making our schools safe for sissies. In G. Unks (Ed.), *The gay teen: Educational practice and theory for lesbian, gay, and bisexual adolescents* (pp. 79-84). New York, NY: Routledge.

Rounds, K. A. (1998). AIDS in rural areas: Challenges to providing care. *Social Work, 33*(3), 257-261.

Royce, D. (1991). *Research methods in social work.* Chicago, IL: Nelson-Hall.

Savin-Williams, R. C. (1989). Parental influences on the self-esteem of gay and lesbian youths: A reflected appraisals model. In G. Herdt (Ed.), *Gay and lesbian youth* (pp. 93-109). New York: The Haworth Press, Inc.

Sears, J. T. (1991). *Growing up gay in the South: Race, gender, and journeys of the spirit.* New York: The Haworth Press, Inc.

Sears, J. T. (1997). *Overcoming heterosexism and homophobia.* New York, NY: Columbia.

Shriver, J. M. (1998). *Human behavior and the social environment: Shifting paradigms in essential knowledge for social work practice.* Boston, MA: Allyn & Bacon.

Smith, G. W. (1988). The ideology of "fag": The school experience of gay students. *The Sociological Quarterly, 39*(2), 309-335.

Smith, J. D. (1997). Working with larger systems: Rural lesbians and gays. In F. D. Smith & R. J. Mancoske (Eds.), *Rural gays and lesbians* (pp. 13-22). New York: The Haworth Press, Inc.

Travers, R., & Schneider, M. (1996). Barriers to accessibility for lesbian and gay youth needing addictions services. *Youth & Society, 27*(3), 356-378.

Unks, G. (1995). Thinking about the gay teen. In G. Unks (Ed.), *The gay teenager: Educational practice and theory for lesbian, gay, and bisexual adolescents* (pp. 3-12). New York, NY: Routledge.

Unrau, Y. A., & Coleman, H. (1997). Qualitative data analysis. In R. M. Grinnell, Jr., (Ed.), *Social work research & evaluation: Quantitative and qualitative approaches* (5th ed., pp. 501-525). Itasca, IL: Peacock.

Williams, M., Grinnell, R. M., Jr., & Tutty, L. M. (1997). Research contexts. In R. M. Grinnell, Jr. (Ed.), *Social work research & evaluation: Quantitative and qualitative approaches* (5th ed., pp. 25-45). Itasca, IL: Peacock.

Providing HIV Education and Outreach via Internet Chat Rooms to Men Who Have Sex with Men

Samuel A. MacMaster
Redford Aquino
Kenneth A. Vail

SUMMARY. This article describes a pilot project that provided Internet-based outreach and HIV educational information to Men Who Have Sex with Men (MSM). The project provided services via chat rooms designated for MSM who meet there anonymously for sexual encounters. Services were designed to support behavior changes as well as serving a gateway function for additional services at the host agency. The experiences of the project suggest that the target population may engage in high-risk sexual activity more than

Samuel A. MacMaster, PhD, is Assistant Professor, University of Tennessee College of Social Work. Redford Aquino is Project Coordinator, and Kenneth A. Vail, MPH, MA, is Director of HIV Outreach, Prevention, and Education, both at AIDS Resources, Information, and Services of Santa Clara County, 106 East Gish Road, San Jose, CA 95112.

Address correspondence to: Samuel A. MacMaster, PhD, Assistant Professor, College of Social Work, University of Tennessee, 193 East Polk Avenue, Nashville, TN 37210.

[Haworth co-indexing entry note]: "Providing HIV Education and Outreach via Internet Chat Rooms to Men Who Have Sex with Men." MacMaster, Samuel A., Redford Aquino, and Kenneth A. Vail. Co-published simultaneously in *Journal of Human Behavior in the Social Environment* (The Haworth Social Work Practice Press, an imprint of The Haworth Press, Inc.) Vol. 8, No. 2/3, 2003, pp. 145-151; and: *Sexual Minorities: Discrimination, Challenges, and Development in America* (ed: Michael K. Sullivan) The Haworth Social Work Practice Press, an imprint of The Haworth Press, Inc., 2003, pp. 145-151. Single or multiple copies of this article are available for a fee from The Haworth Document Delivery Service [1-800-HAWORTH. 9:00 a.m. - 5:00 p.m. (EST). E-mail address: docdelivery@haworthpress.com].

Journal of Human Behavior in the Social Environment, Vol. 8(2/3) 2003
http://www.haworthpress.com/web/JHBSE
© 2003 by The Haworth Press, Inc. All rights reserved.
Digital Object Identifier: 10.1300/J137v8n02_09

what was initially assumed; and that Internet outreach provides a relevant means of conducting outreach to this group. *[Article copies available for a fee from The Haworth Document Delivery Service: 1-800-HAWORTH. E-mail address: <docdelivery@haworthpress.com> Website: <http://www.HaworthPress.com> © 2003 by The Haworth Press, Inc. All rights reserved.]*

KEYWORDS. HIV/AIDS, outreach, Internet, men who have sex with men

INTRODUCTION

The Internet has forever altered our society and culture, and has changed the manner in which individuals interact with each other, and is specifically changing the manner in which they interact sexually (Cooper, Scherer, Boies, & Gordon, 1999). Easy, anonymous access to sexual content on the Internet can facilitate sexual encounters through the exploration of sexual preferences and feelings in an anonymous setting (Leiblum, 1997; Newman, 1997). Since its inception, individuals have used the Internet to interact with each other and develop social networks, either through e-mail, bulletin board postings, personal ads, instant messaging, and/or chat rooms. The Internet also offers a venue for expressing relational needs without prerequisites of physical attractiveness or traditional dating skills (Cooper, Scherer, Boies, & Gordon, 1999). These interactions are increasingly being used to initiate sexual contact (McFarlane, Bull, & Reitmeijer, 2000; Bull & McFarlane, 2000), and are used specifically by men who have sex with men (MSM) to locate potential partners for anonymous sexual encounters (Hospers, Harterink, Van Den Hoek, & Veenstra, 2002; Bull, McFarlane, & Reitmeijer, 2001).

Individuals who seek sex on the Internet constitute a group with specific risk for contracting HIV. Studies have found that individuals who seek sex on the Internet tend to be more sexually active and have more partners than individuals who do not seek sex via the Internet; however, they are also less likely to have been tested for HIV or other STDs (McFarlane, Bull, & Rietmeijer, 2002). This is in spite of the fact that these individuals are also more likely to engage in high-risk sexual behaviors, specifically unprotected anal sex (Hospers, Harterink, Van Den Hoek, & Veenstra, 2002; Benotsch, Kalichman, & Cage, 2002).

Locating potential sexual partners via the Internet has become especially attractive to men seeking sex with other men. The Internet allows disenfranchised groups an avenue to connect with other members of their group, and to even develop a community of acceptance. This is particularly important for members of sexual minorities, who may not have the means to identify or connect with likeminded individuals (Cooper, Boies, Maheu, & Greenfield, 1999). MSM individuals, in general, have relatively few places to meet without fear of negative social consequences (Benotsch, Kalichman, & Cage, 2002). For gay, bisexual and questioning men these connections can be made over the Internet with limited fear of repercussions. This can be an important gateway for bisexual or questioning men who may not immediately feel comfortable in an overtly gay environment, but are seeking social support from individuals with similar sexual preferences.

MSM who primarily utilize the Internet as means for identifying other MSM individuals constitute a subgroup that differs from the general MSM population. Primarily, MSM who utilize the Internet are more likely to be socially isolated, relative to their sexual preferences, than other MSM who do not utilize the Internet in this fashion. MSM responding to Internet surveys were more likely to reside in rural areas, less likely to experience sexual experiences solely with other men, more likely to visit chat rooms and bath houses and erotic book stores, and were more likely to report unmet HIV education needs than MSM respondents to mailed surveys (Ross, Tikkanen, & Mansson, 2000).

Traditional HIV/AIDS outreach to MSM has relied primarily on social networks and venues where MSM individuals congregate (gay bars and other targeted businesses, festivals, parades, etc.) to deliver face-to-face outreach and educational materials. These interventions have helped to facilitate a change in community norms around sexual practices within the gay community; however, these service delivery modes may not reach all potential MSM. It appears that MSM who meet sexual contacts on the Internet through chat rooms may not have access to traditional HIV outreach services, as they may not engage with, or even identify with, the traditional gay community. However, these individuals appear to engage in high-risk behaviors at higher rates than other MSM. While the Internet has been used to distribute HIV/AIDS education and prevention materials (Perry, 1998), there are few interventions specific to Internet chatters (Redmann, 2001). This article will provide a description of one such pilot program in San Jose, California.

PROGRAM DESCRIPTION

In January of 2002, the Asian and Pacific Islander Men Who Have Sex with Men Peer Education Group at AIDS Resources, Information, and Services (ARIS) in San Jose, California began a six month pilot program to test the impact of an Internet based outreach to "high risk" MSM living in Santa Clara County. ARIS's outreach programs utilize a peer driven service delivery model to ensure the authenticity of both the service needs and the delivery of services. The need for Internet-based services was determined following informal discussions among members of the target population. These individuals believed that Internet chat rooms were in need of specific outreach efforts, as it was a venue that was often utilized by members of the target population to access potential sexual partners. Importantly, there was concern that many of these individuals may be initiating MSM sexual contact for the first time and lacked information and social support to adequately reduce their risk of contracting HIV.

A staff person and two volunteers from the Peer Education Group conducted Internet outreach interventions on a weekly to bi-weekly basis. Before the Internet outreach interventions were conducted, the topics to be covered during each event were drafted, a website was chosen, and outreach guidelines were developed to ensure that only factual and relevant information was being disseminated. Websites were selected for outreach on the basis of the availability of a "profile system" that allowed for a check of demographic data of the biological sex and ethnic background of the population targeted and a choice of chat rooms by geographic area. Due to the peer-driven service delivery model, the project primarily targeted chat rooms that were designed for, or frequented by, Asian and Pacific Islander MSM in cities in the Santa Clara County, California area.

During the chat sessions, two outreach team members would engage in a conversation about the topic chosen for that event in the main chat room and entice other chatters to join in. Team members posed as "normal" chatters and were either accepted within the chat room as presenting a topic worthy of conversation or were simply ignored by the other individuals in the chat room. The issues discussed were limited to (1) dispelling myths about the transmission of the human immunodeficiency virus and other sexually transmitted infections, (2) how to make safer sex (sex that included the use of a latex barrier) more pleasurable, and (3) HIV testing information. A one page script was developed before each outreach event that was used to guide the outreach workers with cues to covering as much factual information as possible regardless of the stray conversations that other "chatters" may engage them in. The script allowed outreach workers to work from home and to guide them back to the topic whenever conversations on the main chat room or through individual chat sessions became inappropriate, irrelevant, and/or out of the context of HIV prevention. It must be noted that the staff found that lunch hours or the hours between 12:00 pm and 5:00 pm on weekends were the most productive outreach times. This may be due to the fact that prevention messages are more readily ignored at night when the mood of chatters appeared to be centered more on a physical "hook-ups" or "real time (r/t)" sex. These times were the most beneficial in contacting the target population. As the outreach was primarily focused on individuals who may be experiencing their first man to man sexual encounters, it is also important to note that anecdotally most of the newer chatters to 'Men Only chat rooms' reported that they were often overwhelmed by the explicit sexual nature of evening chatters and preferred the slower advances of the lunch and weekend chatters.

Internet outreach guidelines were developed by the agency to ensure that services were provided in a professional manner. While these were similar to guidelines used by face-to-face outreach workers, due to the faceless, and somewhat more anonymous, nature of Internet outreach work, these guidelines were extensively emphasized by the host agency. The new guidelines stressed zero contact with the individuals out of the Internet chat rooms, i.e., instant messaging and/or non-computer-based interactions. The lack of instant messaging made all information public within the chat room, thus allowing individuals who were only passively engaged in the chat room to receive all of the information. There were exceptions to this directive, as contact could be deemed appropriate by the program coordinator, but only for reasons that related directly to the accessibility to mental health, substance abuse, and/or HIV healthcare services. Contact information that could be provided to individuals requesting additional services was limited to the program coordinator's work email and phone number. Once the person receiving outreach made contact with the program coordinator, follow up services were initiated. In order to ensure the provision of professional services and to provide some level of quality control, all chat sessions were documented via a printed hard copy from the chat room. In order to protect confidentiality and due to the explicit nature of the chats, these documents were only made available to program staff and outreach team members.

DISCUSSION AND CONCLUSIONS

The pilot program ended in June 2002 after meeting its objectives. Most importantly, the program was successful in demonstrating the feasibility and impact of an Internet-based program as a means of accessing a difficult to reach and often overlooked at-risk population. The program was able to provide consistent and factual information to individuals who did not have ready access to such information. The information was also provided in a supportive manner that was meaningful and relevant to the population. While the provision of information and social support was the expressed goal of the program, as with any outreach service, the long-term goal is to ensure that the information continues to be disseminated within the target population once

the outreach event has occurred. The program also sought to provide
face-to-face services, i.e., HIV testing, involvement in agency sponsored
events, etc., with individuals initially contacted through Internet outreach;
and eventually to provide volunteer opportunities for these individuals as
outreach workers. The measurable impact of the program included forty-six
referrals to HIV testing sites for blood-based HIV testing, and the completion
of one Orasure test (the oral antibody test for HIV that test the tissues of the
cheek and gum rather than blood), that was completed at the agency. Additionally, eight individuals became involved in at least one agency sponsored
group event, and two individuals were retained as volunteers to the
API/MSM Peer Education Program. These numbers are remarkable considering (1) that the program was in operation for only six months, and (2) the
anonymous nature of the population.

Although not an intended consequence of the pilot program, the agency
was able to rethink the definition of "high-risk" populations that they serve
with HIV/AIDS services. Following the completion of the demonstration
project, staff and volunteers met to review the program's goals, the formal
and informal data gathered on API/MSM and their sexual behaviors, and to
discuss whether the Internet proved to be a viable venue in disseminating
HIV prevention information to "high risk" API/MSM. During this session,
the conclusion was that the attributes that have come to normally constitute a
"high risk" individual should be revised in outreach specifically to
API/MSM as well as all other MSM groups. Anecdotal information suggested that the individuals reached that were most likely to practice risky behaviors, in particular anal sex without a condom, were those individuals who
were about to or are experiencing their first penetrative sexual contact with
another man. These individuals appeared to be somewhat isolated relative to
their sexual preferences and only had limited bits of information about prac-
ticing safer sex available to them. These individuals also perceived that they
were at low risk for contracting any sexually transmitted infection, much less
HIV/AIDS, due to their practice of only seeking sexual contact with other
men "new" to the MSM scene. They were aware of the existence of
"high-risk" populations, but made no connections with the more publicized
"high-risk" populations of self-identified gay men and active injection drug
users and their own personal risk. A small portion of individuals displayed a
strong knowledge of safer sex practices but disclosed that they were willing
to have unprotected anal sex with men claiming to be new to male-to-male
sexual contact. This presented the staff with the question of whether men are
knowingly having sex with men who have unprotected sex with their female
partners in the assumption that unprotected heterosexual sex does not present
a risk for infection. It is important therefore to not only provide useful and

relevant information regarding the safer sex practices, but it is equally important to raise awareness regarding perceived vulnerability to contracting HIV. It is hoped that the description of this pilot project provides one means for providing these services.

REFERENCES

Benotsch, E., Kalichman, S., & Cage, M. (2002). Men who have met sex partners via the Internet: Prevalence, predictors, and implications for HIV prevention. *Archives of sexual behavior*, 177-183.

Bull, S., & McFarlane, M. (2000). Soliciting sex on the Internet. What are the risks for sexually transmitted diseases and HIV? *Sexually Transmitted Diseases, 27*, 545-550.

Bull, S., McFarlane, M., & Rietmeijer, C. (2001). HIV/STD risk behaviors among men seeking sex with men online. *American Journal of Public Health, 91*, 988-989.

Cooper, A., Boies, S., Maheu, M., & Greenfield, D. (1999). Sexuality and the Internet: The next sexual revolution. In F. Muscarella & L. Szuchman (Eds.), *The Psychological Science of Sexuality: A Research Based Approach*. New York: Wiley.

Cooper, A., Scherer, C., Boies, S., & Gordon B. (1999). Sexuality on the Internet: From sexual exploration to pathological expression. *Professional Psychology: Research and Practice, 30*(2), 154-164.

Hospers, H., Harterink, P., Van Den Hoek, K., & Veenstra, J. (2002). *Chatters on the Internet: A special target group for HIV prevention*, 539-544.

Leiblum, S.R. (1997). Sex and the net: Clinical implications. *Journal of Sex Education and Therapy, 22*(1), 21-28.

McFarlane, M., Bull, S., & Rietmeijer, C. (2000). The Internet as a newly emerging risk environment for sexually transmitted diseases. *Journal of the American Medical Association*, 443-446.

McFarlane, M., Bull, S., & Rietmeijer, C. (2002). Young adults on the Internet: Risk behaviors for sexually transmitted diseases and HIV. *Journal of Adolescent Health*, 11-16.

Newman, B. (1997). The use of online services to encourage exploration of ego-dystonic sexual interests. *Journal of Sex Education and Therapy, 22*(1), 45-48.

Perry, G. (1998). Websites as weapons in the war on HIV: Education and prevention geared to the new at-risk populations. *Health care on the Internet*, 39-51.

Redman, J. (2001). New Orleans AIDS Task Force CAN Internet intervention. *HIV Impact*, 5&12.

Rhodes, S., DiClemente, R., Cecil, H., Hergenrather, K., & Yee, L. (2002). Risk among men who have sex with men in the United States: A comparison of an Internet sample and a conventional outreach sample. *AIDS Education and Prevention*, 41-50.

Ross, M., Tikkanen, R., & Mansson, S. (2000). Differences between Internet samples and conventional samples of men who have sex with men: Implications for research and HIV interventions. *Social science and medicine*, 749-758.

Sex Role Identity and Jealousy
as Correlates of Abusive Behavior
in Lesbian Relationships

Grace A. Telesco

SUMMARY. This article presents the findings of a study from a cross-sectional sample of 105 lesbians taken from a non-clinical setting to investigate to what extent they exhibited abusive behavior toward an intimate female partner and whether the abuse was physical, psychological, or both. This study examined whether an association exists between a lesbian's sex role identity, particularly the dimension of femininity, and her abusive behavior. The hypothesis that jealousy in the relationship would be positively associated with reported incidences of abusive behavior was also examined. The results show that when abuse is broadly defined a sizable minority report high incidences of overall abuse and psychological abuse at some time during their current relationship. The most salient finding of this study was the strong evidence of a relationship between jealousy and abusive behavior. The implications of these findings underscore the need for continued and enhanced delivery of services. Other implications of this study point toward consciousness-raising to the larger community about institutionalized and individual homophobia and heterosexism.

Grace A. Telesco, PhD, Assistant Professor, is affiliated with East Stroudsburg University of Pennsylvania, Department of Sociology, 200 Prospect Street, East Stroudsburg, PA 18301.

[Haworth co-indexing entry note]: "Sex Role Identity and Jealousy as Correlates of Abusive Behavior in Lesbian Relationships." Telesco, Grace A. Co-published simultaneously in *Journal of Human Behavior in the Social Environment* (The Haworth Social Work Practice Press, an imprint of The Haworth Press, Inc.) Vol. 8, No. 2/3, 2003, pp. 153-169; and: *Sexual Minorities: Discrimination, Challenges, and Development in America* (ed: Michael K. Sullivan) The Haworth Social Work Practice Press, an imprint of The Haworth Press, Inc., 2003, pp. 153-169. Single or multiple copies of this article are available for a fee from The Haworth Document Delivery Service [1-800-HAWORTH, 9:00 a.m. - 5:00 p.m. (EST). E-mail address: docdelivery@haworthpress.com].

Journal of Human Behavior in the Social Environment, Vol. 8(2/3) 2003
http://www.haworthpress.com/web/JHBSE
Digital Object Identifier: 10.1300/J137v8n02_10

153

KEYWORDS. Lesbian, sex role identity, masculinity, femininity, jealousy, abusive behavior

INTRODUCTION

Over the past few decades, there has been a great amount of research and literature written on the subject of heterosexual partner abuse. There is much known about the incidence, prevalence, and severity of heterosexual partner abuse. Theorists have looked at various correlates and explanations for abusive behavior between heterosexual intimates, focusing their attention on gender difference and looking at battering using a male batterer paradigm.

This study addresses existing gaps in the research on lesbian partner abuse by looking through a multi-theory lens and shifts the focus from gender differences to explain abusive behavior to examining sex role identity and relationship factors. This research investigates specifically whether a lesbian's sex role identity is associated with her abusive behavior toward an intimate female partner, focusing on whether the dimensions of masculinity and femininity help explain abusive behavior. Additionally, building on existing research in the field of lesbian partner abuse, this study examines to what extent the relationship factor of jealousy in lesbian relationships is related to abusive behavior. Variables of dependency and power in the relationship were also examined.

REVIEW OF THE LITERATURE

Although the research on heterosexual abuse serves to inform theoretical explanations for lesbian partner abuse, the issues surrounding gender difference are not applicable for lesbian intimates. While there is a wealth of research and theoretical models to choose from when investigating heterosexual partner abuse, the lack of research and scarcity of the literature as it relates to lesbian partner abuse is glaring. It is clear that the research on the heterosexual population has been met with fewer challenges than it has for the hidden and under-recognized lesbian population, and as a result of the deficit in the research, practitioners have relied largely on a heterosexual paradigm to understand lesbian partner abuse.

There are currently no national probability studies to research the incidence, prevalence, and severity of lesbian partner abuse. Homophobia and heterosexism continue to keep lesbians a hidden sub-population within society and make generalizations of the findings of non-probability studies conducted with lesbians limiting.

Lesbian, gay, transgender, and bisexual people face verbal and physical assault on the street, face termination from their employment, losing custody of their children, abandonment by their families, and suicide all resulting from reactions to their sexual orientation (Greene, 1994). Moreover, the institutions that serve to protect people at large have often been the very source of oppression and discrimination for lesbian, gay, transgender, and bisexual people (Holmes & Hodge, 1997).

Mainstream religious institutions are often at odds with lesbian, gay, bisexual, and transgender people in the spirit of morality and religiosity, promoting heterosexuality as normative (Holmes & Hodge, 1997). Policies and practices of the courts and the criminal justice system suggest a failure to protect the rights of the lesbian, gay, transgender, and bisexual communities. Allen and Leventhal (1999) examined domestic violence laws in fifty states and concluded that in some states lesbian and gay victims of partner abuse were afforded no protection under the law and in most states were more likely to receive less protection when compared to heterosexual victims. Legislation has also been negligent in failing to protect the civil rights of lesbian, gay, bisexual, and transgender people, particularly in the absence of laws that prohibit discrimination on the basis of sexual orientation (Greene, 1994).

Despite the progressive mentality of the American Psychiatric Association removing "homosexuality" from the *Diagnostic and Statistical Manual of Mental Disorders* in 1973 and "ego dystonic homosexuality" in 1988, efforts to change lesbian and gay clients through conversion therapy continue to persist for some (Greene, 1994). Medical, mental health, domestic violence advocates, and social work professionals often make assumptions that all people are heterosexual (Berkman & Zinberg, 1997; Greene, 1994; Hammond, 1986; Holmes & Hodge, 1997). Because of homophobia and heterosexism, lesbian, gay, transgender, and bisexual people struggle to attain a positive self-identity and often endure lifelong negative self-images, fear, shame, embarrassment, and isolation because of their sexual identity. Some research indicates that lesbian, gay, transgender, and bisexual youth are three times more likely than their heterosexual counterparts to attempt suicide (Hunter & Schaecher, 1995).

Homophobia magnifies the effects of partner abuse. A lesbian, who is a victim of this abuse, may be reluctant to seek help from the police or service providers fearing a homophobic reaction. Anecdotal evidence from service providers suggests that many lesbians deliberately change pronouns when re-

porting partner abuse, in order to safeguard themselves from homophobic reactions from law enforcement officials. Others may also hide the reality of
abuse from their family because they may not be open about their sexuality.
Even the openly lesbian victim may not want family or friends to know about
the abuse for fear that her sexuality will be perceived as the justification for the
abuse. This internalized homophobia may be one of the many reasons why victims of lesbian partner abuse remain hidden (Elliott, 1996; Lie & Gentlewarrier,
1991; Pharr, 1988; Renzetti, 1992).

In the late eighties, some theorists offered explanations for the lack of data
on lesbian partner abuse. Morrow and Hawxhurst (1989) posited that the lesbian community's reluctance to acknowledge that partner abuse is a real problem for them might lie in the notion that lesbian relationships are egalitarian, loving, and not violent. Additionally, the reluctance to acknowledge lesbian partner
abuse may stem from the fear that lesbianism will be seen as pathological.

Lesbian survivors may be reluctant to admit abuse in their relationship, mir-
roring the same dynamics of self-blame, fear, economic and emotional dependency, and low self esteem that are experienced by heterosexual women
who are survivors of partner abuse (Hammond, 1986). Further, the data on lesbian partner abuse from official sources are limited. Police, hospital, and crisis
hotline reporting may not accurately reflect the incidence and severity of lesbian partner abuse and may be minimized by crisis workers, perhaps due to
their own homophobia. Therefore, same sex partner abuse is often left out of
police statistics and is consequently not counted in criminal justice reports
(Hart, 1986; Island & Letellier, 1991).

There has been a considerable increase in the research of lesbian partner
abuse within the last few decades. Findings for these studies suggest that rates
and severity of violence among lesbian partners is comparable to that of heterosexual partners (Brand & Kidd, 1986; Coleman, 1990; Elliot, 1996; Lie &
Gentlewarrier, 1991; Lockhart, White, Causby, & Isaac, 1994; Renzetti, 1992).

With the increase in the research, there has been a substantial growth in the
amount of literature pointing to several explanations for lesbian partner abuse.
Some of these explanations include power imbalance, dependency and autonomy, jealousy, substance abuse, and intergenerational violence (Caldwell & Peplau,
1984; Coleman, 1990; Lynch & Reilly, 1986; Peplau, Rook, & Padesky, 1978;
Peplau, Padesky, & Hamilton, 1982; Reilly & Lynch, 1990; Renzetti, 1992).

The existing research has limitations. The studies investigating lesbian partner abuse have almost exclusively used convenience samples that are comprised of lesbians who are mostly white, middle class, and feminist (Lie &
Gentlewarrier, 1991; Lockhart et al., 1994; Schilit, Lie, Bush, Montagne, &
Reyes, 1991). While some of this research has focused on client populations of
survivors, examining abusive behavior through the eyes of the victim (Lobel,

1986; Renzetti, 1988), other studies have been conducted with client populations of batterers participating in intervention programs (Farley, 1996). The findings from these studies make generalizations to the general lesbian population difficult and limit inferences. Another issue threatening the generalizability of these studies to the larger lesbian population lies within the methodologies used. Some of these studies rely on retrospective accounts of the abuse from the victim. The limited number of studies on lesbian partner abuse that utilize self-report methods in a non-clinical setting make it difficult to obtain an accurate estimate of lesbian partner abuse among the general lesbian population.

In intimate heterosexual relationships where violence is occurring, the primary aggressors are typically men, and the victims are women. Feminist theorists posit that it is patriarchal domination and the control of women that contributes to partner abuse, specifically among heterosexual intimates (Bograd, 1988; Dobash & Dobash, 1979, 1998).

Dobash and Dobash (1979, 1998) dominate the literature in this feminist argument and socio-cultural framework, suggesting that societal belief systems sustain partner abuse at the individual level. They suggest the factors that contribute to partner abuse are embedded in patriarchal privilege and male entitlement and further posit that the sense of entitlement that a husband believes he possesses to punish "his" wife, lies in the very position of husbandry, allowing men to be abusive simply because of their rank in the relationship.

Some feminist theorists suggest that men are inclined to be more abusive than women because this abuse is embedded in an accumulated web of physical strength and male tradition describing masculinity in terms of aggression, power, and a predatory spirit. These theorists suggest that when "masculinity" is threatened, acts of aggression may follow (Thompson, 1998). In the Violent Men Study of 1996, the data reported by Dobash and Dobash (1998) suggest that when men recounted their physical abuse against a female intimate partner, it was usually accompanied by anger and rationalization. The evidence of masculine identity associated with the abusive behavior was indicated through statements made by the batterer which suggested a strong belief system that the batterer was forced to "put the victim in her place," "show her who the boss was," and "could not let a 'woman' get away with anything" (Dobash & Dobash, 1998, p. 144).

Thompson (1998) argues that femininity in this society is viewed as weak and subordinate. Thompson adds:

> The boy who is called a fag is the target of other boys' homophobia as well as the victim of his own homophobia. While the overt message is the absolute need to avoid being femininized, the implication is that females–and all that they traditionally represent–are contemptible. The

United States Marines have a philosophy, which conveniently combines homophobia and misogyny in the belief that "when you want to create a group of male killers, you kill the 'woman' in them." (p. 561)

The paradigm of patriarchy, which is male created and driven, is one of domination and control where the feminine is viewed as subordinate (Dobash & Dobash, 1998). Regardless of one's biological gender or sexual orientation, these messages can become internalized and inform behavior, particularly in a patriarchal setting where the feminine is not valued and is seen as inferior. Coleman (1996) posits that we exist within a heterosexist system where the relationship model is comprised of two roles: one being dominant and the other submissive. Therefore, lesbians are not immune to the potential for one partner to dominate the other.

Traditional stereotypes of masculinity and femininity can be limiting, gender based, and viewed in terms of dress, roles, and personality attributes (Bem, 1993). Further, as these traditional stereotypes of masculinity and femininity are limiting, so is the construct of gender. Lesbian partner abuse should not be framed exclusively in terms of gender because of the unique differences in the dynamics of lesbian relationships and the fact that the partners are the same sex. Coleman (1996) also argues that regardless of gender or sex role identity, patriarchal values are internalized and may play a role in abusive behavior. Since biological gender difference between lesbian partners does not serve as an explanation for abusive behavior, a closer examination of a lesbian's level of masculinity and femininity may help to explain the incidence and severity of abuse in their relationships. Further, building on existing research, this study examines to what extent the relationship factor of jealousy is related to abusive behavior among lesbian intimates. Relationship factors of dependency and power were also examined.

METHODS

This descriptive study makes use of a cross-sectional survey of a convenience sample of 105 lesbians. In order to participate, respondents had to self identify as lesbians and be in a relationship with another woman for at least six months at the time of the study.

Four questions guide the research: (1) To what extent does partner abuse exist among lesbian intimates? (2) What is the nature of this abusive behavior (physical or psychological abuse)? (3) Is there an association between sex role identity and abusive behavior? (4) To what extent is the relationship factor of jealousy related to abusive behavior in lesbian relationships? It was expected that low levels of femininity would be positively associated with high rates of abusive behavior. The relationship of dependency, jealousy, and power imbalance with abusive behavior was also of interest, and it was expected that high levels of dependency, jealousy, and power imbalance in the relationship would be positively associated with higher rates of abusive behavior.

Measures

The self-administered multi-item questionnaire contained 125 questions and asked participants to rate themselves on their perceived level of masculinity and femininity, as well as the level of dependency, jealousy, and power imbalance present in their current relationship. Respondents were also asked to report on whether they have been physically or psychologically abusive toward an intimate partner at any time during their current relationship. Sex role identity was measured utilizing the Bem Sex Role Inventory Scale (BSRI). The BSRI measures 60 different personality attributes related to constructs of masculinity and femininity (Bem, 1974). The masculine items describe traits and characteristics that are considered socially agreed upon, although stereotypical, "masculine" attributes that are related to problem solving, assertiveness, and leadership. Respondents are asked to rate themselves on twenty masculine attributes from "never or almost never true" to "always or almost always true" on statements like "I act as leader," "I am assertive," and "I am ambitious." The feminine items describe traits and characteristics that are considered socially agreed upon, although stereotypical, "feminine" attributes that are related to concern for the well being of others and nurturing. Respondents are asked to rate themselves on twenty feminine attributes from "never or almost never true" to "always or almost always true" on statements like: " I soothe hurt feelings," "I am sensitive to the needs of others," and "I am sympathetic." Twenty questions are fillers and are not counted. Raw scores were totaled for masculinity and femininity separately so that each respondent receives a separate masculine and feminine score. The BSRI for this sample showed an alpha coefficient of .73 for masculinity and .77 for femininity.

Participants were also asked to report whether they have been physically or psychologically abusive at any time toward their current partner at any time during their current relationship. The 30 item Abusive Behavior Inventory was used to measure the construct of abusive behavior (Shepard & Campbell, 1992). Respondents were asked how often they exhibited each of the 30 physical or psychological abusive behaviors from "never" to "very frequently." Some items included "called her names or criticized her," "slapped, hit, or punched her," "put her down," "choked or strangled her," and "drove recklessly when she was in the car." Raw scores were totaled for physical abuse, psychological abuse and overall abuse. Respondents with raw scores in the top twenty-five percentile were categorized as "high abuse" for cross tabulation and categorical purposes. The sample was then categorized into high and low abuse for descriptive purposes. Continuous raw scores were used for correlation and hierarchical regression analysis. Reliability analysis for the ABI indicated an alpha coefficient of .74.

A series of questions about the participants' relationship as it relates to issues of dependency, jealousy, and power imbalance were asked utilizing a combination of items from Renzetti's (1992) research and original items designed for this study. Respondents were asked to rate their behavior from "never" to "very frequently" on characteristics of jealousy, dependency, and power in their relationship. Some jealousy items included "I don't like it when my partner spends time with her friends," and " I don't like it when my partner pays attention to other things and not me." Reliability analysis indicated alpha coefficients of .75 for the dependency items, .71 for the jealousy items, and .73 for the power imbalance items.

SAMPLE

Study participants were volunteers who frequent the New York City Lesbian, Gay, Bisexual, and Transgender Community Center for social events. Although a non-probability sampling strategy, this type of "location" sampling, sometimes referred to as "target" sampling, is often used when studying hidden populations who lack a sampling frame (Watters & Biernacki, 1989). This sample consisted of individual responses from participants in regards to their own behavior and was not a sample of paired couples.

African American lesbians accounted for 22% of the sample, and 11% of the sample identified themselves as Latino. Similar studies investigating abusive behavior among lesbian intimates has primarily been focused on white, middle class, feminist, lesbians, and has largely ignored the experience of lesbians of color.

The mean age of the respondents was 40 years old with ages ranging from 21 to 66 years. Twenty percent of the sample's income fell within the $10,000 to $35,000 income category and 26% of the respondents fell within the $35,000 to $50,000 income category. Eighty-five percent of the respondents said that they were employed and categorized their work in terms of a wide range of white-collar occupations. Twenty-eight percent of the respondents held at least a bachelor's degree.

The mean number of years respondents reported being in their current relationship was an average of 5 years with 84% categorizing the relationship as a committed one. Ninety-seven percent described their relationship as monogamous and 55% reported that they reside with their partner.

Respondents were also asked to report on their partner's demographic characteristics. The same information requested from them was asked about their partners. Results indicated no differences between respondents and partners on demographic variables, as provided by the respondent.

RESULTS

Physical and Psychological Abuse

The results show 34% of the sample categorized as "high" levels of overall abuse. These raw scores of overall abuse were placed in the top twenty-five percentile and represent both physical and psychological abuse. On psychological abuse, 34% were categorized as exhibiting "high" levels of abuse, with 66% reporting "low" levels of abuse. Thirty-seven percent of the sample is categorized as "high" on physical abuse with 63% as low. It is important to note that although 34% of the sample reported high rates of abuse, these specific abuse items fell within a lower range of severity and would not have incurred serious physical or psychological injury. The classifications of high and low abuse percentages are presented in Table 1.

Seventy-five percent of the sample admits to demonstrating more than one incident of overall abusive behavior toward their current partner. As Table 2 indicates, eight percent of the sample report never abusing a current partner in any way, and 17% admit to exhibiting one abusive act toward their current partner at some time during the relationship.

The physical abuse items and the percent of the sample who reported never, occasionally, frequently, or very frequently exhibiting these abusive behaviors toward their current partner within the last year are presented in Table 3. The top items are ranked in the order of those that were most reported by the respondents. Twenty percent of the respondents admitted to occasionally throwing or smashing something or hitting their partner. Twenty percent also admitted to occasionally pushing her.

The six most reported psychologically abusive acts that respondents admitted to either occasionally or frequently/very frequently exhibiting toward their partner were: gave partner angry looks or stares (71%), called partner names or criticized her (55%), ended a discussion with partner and made the decision

TABLE 1. Sample Percentages Based on Top 25% for Levels of Overall Abuse, Psychological Abuse, and Physical Abuse (N = 105)

Variable	Low	High
Overall Abuse	66%	34%
Psychological Abuse	66%	34%
Physical Abuse	63%	37%

TABLE 2. Sample Percentages of Overall Abuse (N = 88*)

Category	n	Percent
Never Abusive	7	8%
1 Incident of Abuse	15	17%
More Than 1 Incident of Abuse	<u>66</u>	<u>75%</u>
	88	100%

*Missing data

TABLE 3. Rank Order of Sample Percentages for Individual Physical Abuse Items (N = 105)

Abuse Item	Never	Occasionally	Frequently/ Very Frequently
Threw/hit/smashed something	78%	20%	2%
Pushed her	79%	20%	1%
Drove recklessly with her in car	85%	15%	-
Slapped, hit, or punched her	92%	8%	-
Pressured her to have sex	95%	3%	2%
Threw her around	96%	4%	-
Attacked sexual parts of her body	98%	2%	-

yourself (50%), accused partner of paying too much attention to others (41%), put partner down (36%), and kept partner from doing what she wanted (21%).

Femininity and Abusive Behavior

To test whether a respondent's low level of femininity would be positively associated with abusive behavior, correlation analysis was conducted. It was expected that the characteristic of femininity contains dimensions that are concerned with the well being of others and thought to contribute to non-abusive behavior. In contrast, individuals who possess low levels of these characteristics may be more likely to demonstrate abusive behavior.

Correlation analysis results are presented in Tables 4 and 5. The findings indicate that femininity is neither positively nor negatively correlated with overall abuse. It was expected that low femininity would be positively associated with abusive behavior. This was not supported by the data. It is difficult to determine why low levels of femininity were not related with high rates of abuse as predicted. Perhaps respondents perceived themselves as having high levels of both masculine and feminine attributes, when in fact they may really possess lower levels of both masculinity and femininity. There may be a difference between the perception one has of the attributes they possess and the reality of their behavior.

Jealousy and Abusive Behavior

To test the hypothesis that jealousy is associated with abusive behavior, correlation analysis was conducted, utilizing a list-wise deletion of data with a two-tailed test of significance and are also presented in Tables 4 and 5.

Correlation analysis shows that jealousy and overall abuse were positively correlated and significant ($r = .37$, $p < .01$). As jealousy increased so did reported abusive behavior. Jealousy and psychological abuse were also positively correlated and significant ($r = .36$, $p < .01$). Neither masculinity nor femininity was correlated with abuse.

Jealousy as a Predictor of Abuse

To examine predictors of abuse, three hierarchical regression models were conducted using continuous scores for all variables. Utilizing two-tailed significance, with a list-wise deletion of missing data, the independent variables of dependency, jealousy, power imbalance, masculinity, and femininity were entered into the first regression model to determine how much of the variance in abuse is explained by these variables.

Tables 6 and 7 summarize the results of the regression models and are presented in this section. As a group, the variables of dependency, jealousy, power imbalance, masculinity, and femininity significantly explain 18% of the variance in overall abuse ($R^2 = .18$, $p < .05$), and jealousy was the strongest predictor when all the other variables were held constant ($t = 3.26$, $p < .01$).

The results of the second regression model, entering psychological abuse as the dependent variable indicate that as a group, the variables of dependency,

TABLE 4. Bi-Variate Correlations Between Masculinity, Femininity, Dependency, Jealousy, Power Imbalance, and Overall Abuse

	1	2	3	4	5	6
1 Masculinity	-					
2 Femininity	−.07	-				
3 Dependency	−.02	.23*	-			
4 Jealousy	−.12	.20*	.07	-		
5 Power Imbalance	.13	.26*	.32**	.12	-	
6 Overall Abuse	.15	−.01	.17	.37**	.12	-

Note: *p < .05 **p < .01

TABLE 5. Bi-Variate Correlations Between Masculinity, Femininity, Dependency, Jealousy, Power Imbalance, and Psychological Abuse (n = 88*)

	1	2	3	4	5	6
1 Masculinity	-					
2 Femininity	−.07	-				
3 Dependency	−.02*	.23*	-			
4 Jealousy	−.12	.20*	.07	-		
5 Power Imbalance	.13	.26*	.32**	.12	-	
6 Psychological Abuse	.12	−.07	.17	.36**	.06	-

Note: *p < .05 **p < .01

jealousy, power imbalance, masculinity, and femininity significantly explain 17% of the variance in psychological abuse ($R^2 = .17$, p < .05). Jealousy was the strongest predictor of psychological abuse when all the other variables were held constant (t = 3.189, p < .01).

DISCUSSION

It was expected that a respondent's femininity would be negatively associated with high rates of abusive behavior that she reported exhibiting toward her partner. The results indicated that femininity was neither positively nor negatively correlated with overall physical and psychological abuse. Although not part of the hypotheses testing, femininity was weakly associated with dependency, jealousy, and power imbalance.

TABLE 6. Multiple Regression Analysis for Variables Predicting Overall Abuse

Variable	SE B	B
Dependency	.10	.12
Jealousy	.37	1.20**
Power Imbalance	.23	.18
Masculinity	.42	.71
Femininity	.64	−.64

Note: For jealousy, $F_{(5, 73)} = .013^*$, $R^2 = .18$, **$p < .01$

TABLE 7. Multiple Regression Analysis for Variables Predicting Psychological Abuse

Variable	SE B	B
Dependency	.08	.12
Jealousy	.31	.98**
Power Imbalance	.19	.06
Masculinity	.35	.52
Femininity	.52	−.82

Note: For jealousy, $F_{(5, 73)} = .016^*$, $R^2 = .17$, **$p < .01$

As a group, the variables of dependency, jealousy, power imbalance, masculinity, and femininity significantly explain 18% of the variance in overall abuse and 17% of the variance in psychological abuse. The correlate of jealousy, in this sample, was the strongest predictor, when all the other variables were held constant. While 18% of the variance in physical and psychological abuse are explained by the variables, there is a substantial percentage that is not explained and requires further examination. Other variables for further examination include lesbians exposed to violence in their family origin, substance use and abuse, and prior abusive relationships.

Consistent with existing research, thirty-four percent of the sample was categorized as exhibiting high rates of physical and psychological abuse toward a current intimate female partner. Thirty-seven percent was classified as demonstrating high rates of physical abuse toward their partner at some time during the relationship.

Despite the finding that a sizable minority reported high rates of physical and psychological abuse, it is important to note that the psychological abuse items that were most reported may not be considered "serious" psychological terror and the physical abuse items most reported would not have required hospitalization.

LIMITATIONS

It is unclear whether respondents were forthcoming about their abuse and whether the instrument used accurately measured the true level of physical and psychological abuse demonstrated by the respondent. Straus (1990) acknowledges that batterers tend to underreport their own abusive behavior. Additionally, the findings indicate that 15% of the respondents failed to accurately complete the Abusive Behavior Inventory portion of the questionnaire suggesting that higher rates of abuse may have been indicated but were not reported. Further, the self-report nature of the research suggests that the actual abuse occurring, both physically and psychologically, may be even higher.

The ability to generalize the findings of this present study is limited by the location and nature of the sample; however, the findings confirm prior research suggesting that the incidence of abuse among lesbian intimates is similar to their heterosexual counterparts. The examination of the extent to which violence in the family of origin, substance use/abuse, and prior abusive relationships is related to a lesbian's abusive behavior in a current relationship was not explored in this research. These may account for the variance that is not explained by the variables investigated in this study and require further examination.

IMPLICATIONS FOR SOCIAL WORK

The present study indicates that not only was jealousy significantly associated with abusive behavior, but it was the strongest predictor of overall (both physical and psychological) and psychological abuse by itself. This finding is consistent with the literature.

For lesbians, issues of attachment, autonomy, and monogamy may serve to complicate jealous tendencies by either of the partners. Further, jealousy among lesbian couples may also be explained by a lack of institutional validation and legitimacy, resulting from institutionalized heterosexism and homophobia.

The results of this study underscore the need to recognize that abuse occurs among lesbian couples and takes the form of psychological abuse as well as physical abuse. The findings also suggest that jealousy may be a strong predictor of abuse. The results of this study highlight the commitment needed for the continued and enhanced delivery of services to battered lesbians, expanded intervention programs for lesbian batterers, and innovative prevention initiatives designed to adequately address the issue of partner abuse in lesbian relationships.

Since assessment is critical in the intervention of partner abuse (Morrow & Hawxhurst, 1989), service providers can benefit from continuing education on how to effectively assess abusive behavior in lesbian relationships. The implications for practice suggest that social workers who serve lesbians and lesbian couples examine how issues of jealousy and its manifestations may serve to create an environment of abuse.

Other implications point toward consciousness-raising to the larger community about institutionalized and individual homophobia and heterosexism and how they can serve to magnify the problem of partner abuse. Additionally, homophobia and heterosexism present unique challenges in researching this hidden population, making inferences from study results complex and generalizations to the larger population of lesbians limiting.

REFERENCES

Allen, C., & Leventhal, B. (1999). History, culture, and identity: What makes GLBT battering different. In B. Leventhal & S. Lundy (Eds.), *Same-sex domestic violence: Strategies for change* (pp. 73-81). CA: NASW Press.

Bem, S. (1974). The measurement of psychological androgyny. *Journal of Consulting & Clinical Psychology*, 42, 155-162.

Bem, S. (1993). *The lenses of gender.* New Haven: Yale University Press.

Berkman, C., & Zinberg, G. (1997). Homophobia and Heterosexism in Social Workers. *Social Work*, 42 (4), 319-332.

Bograd, M. (1988). Feminist perspectives on wife abuse: An introduction. In K. Yllo, & M. Bograd (Eds.), *Feminist perspectives on wife abuse* (pp. 11-28). Newbury Park, CA: Sage.

Brand, P., & Kidd. (1986). A frequency of physical aggression in heterosexual & female homosexual dyads. *Psychological Reports*, 59, 1307-1313.

Caldwell, M., & Peplau, L. (1984). The balance of power in lesbian relationships. *Sex Roles*, 10, 587-599.

Coleman, V. (1990). *Violence between lesbian couples: A between groups' comparison.* Doctoral dissertation (University Microfilms No. 9109022).

Coleman, V. (1996). Lesbian Battering: The relationship between personality & the perpetration of violence. In L. K. Hamberger, & C. Renzetti (Eds.), *Domestic partner abuse* (pp. 77-102). New York: Springer Publishing.

Dobash, R. E., & Dobash, R. (1979). *Violence against wives.* New York: Free Press.

Dobash, R.E., & Dobash, R. (1998). *Rethinking violence against women.* CA: SAGE.

Elliott, P. (1996). Shattering illusions: Same-sex domestic violence. In C. Renzetti, & C. Miley (Eds.), *Gay & lesbian domestic partnerships* (pp. 1-8). New York: The Haworth Press, Inc.

Farley, N. (1996). A survey of factors contributing to gay and lesbian domestic violence. In C. Renzetti, & C.H. Miley (Eds.), *Violence in gay and lesbian domestic partnerships* (pp. 35-42). New York: The Haworth Press, Inc.

Greene, B. (1994). Lesbian and gay sexual orientations: Implications for clinical training, practice, and research. In B. Greene & G. Herek (Eds.), *Lesbian & gay psychology: Theory, research, and clinical applications* (pp. 1-24). CA: SAGE.

Hammond, N. (1986). Lesbian victims and the reluctance to identify abuse. In K. Lobel (Ed.), *Naming the violence: Speaking out about lesbian battering* (pp. 190-197). Seattle: Seal Press.

Hart, B. (1986). Lesbian battering: An examination. In K. Lobel (Ed.), *Naming the violence* (pp. 173-189). Seattle: Seal.

Holmes, K., & Hodge, R. (1997). Gay and lesbian people. In J. Philleo, & F. Brisbane (Eds.), *Cultural competence in substance abuse prevention* (pp. 153-176). Washington D.C.: NASW Press.

Hunter, J., & Schaecher, R. (1995). Gay & lesbian adolescents. In R. Edwards, & J. Hopps (Eds.), *Encyclopedia of Social Work* (19th ed., pp. 1055-1063). NASW Press.

Island, D., & Lettellier, P. (1991). *Men who beat the men who love them: Battered gay men and domestic violence.* New York: Harrington Park Press.

Lie, G., & Gentlewarrier, S. (1991). Intimate violence in lesbian relationships: Discussion of survey findings and practice implications. *Journal of Social Service Research, 15* (2), 41-59.

Lobel, K. (1986). *Naming the violence: Speaking out about lesbian battering.* Seattle, WA: Seal.

Lockhart, L., White, B., Causby, V., & Isaac, A. (1994). Letting out the secret: Violence in lesbian relationships. *Journal of Interpersonal Violence, 9*(4), 469-492.

Lynch, J., & Reilly, M. (1986). Role relationships: Lesbian perspectives. *Journal of Homosexuality, 12,* 53-70.

Morrow, S., & Hawxhurst, D. (1989). Lesbian partner abuse: Implications for therapists. *Journal of Counseling & Development, 68,* 58-62.

Peplau, L., Cochran, S., Rook, K., & Padesky, C. (1978). Loving women: Attachment and autonomy in lesbian relationships. *Journal of Social Issues, 34,* 7-27.

Peplau, L., Padesky, C., & Hamilton, M. (1982). Satisfaction in lesbian relationships. *Journal of Homosexuality, 8,* 23-35.

Pharr, S. (1988). *Homophobia: A weapon of sexism.* CA: Chardon Press.

Reilly, M., & Lynch, J. (1990). Power sharing in lesbian relationships. *Journal of Homosexuality, 19*(3), 1-30.

Renzetti, C. (1988). Violence in lesbian relationships: A preliminary analysis of causal factors. *Journal of Interpersonal Violence, 3,* 381-399.

Renzetti, C. (1992). *Violent betrayal: Partner abuse in lesbian relationships.* CA: Sage.

Schilit, R., Lie, G., Bush, J., Montagne, M., & Reyes, L. (1991). Intergenerational transmission of violence in lesbian relationships. *Affilia, 6* (1), 72-87.

Shepard, M., & Campbell, J. (1992). The Abusive Behavior Inventory: A measure of psychological and physical Abuse. *Journal of Interpersonal Violence, 7,* 291-305.

Straus, M., & Gelles, R. (1990). *Physical violence in American families: Risk factors and adaptations to violence in 8,145 families.* New Brunswick, N.J.: Transaction.

Thompson, C. (1998). A new vision of masculinity. In P. Rothenberg (Ed.), *Race, class, & gender in the United States: An integrated study* (pp. 559-564). NY: St. Martins Press.

Watters, J., & Biernacki, P. (1989). Targeted sampling: Options for the study of hidden population. *Social Problems*, 36 (4), 416-430.

Lesbian-Headed Stepfamilies

Karen I. Fredriksen-Goldsen
Pauline I. Erera

SUMMARY. This paper examines the lesbian stepfamily. It considers the family structure, parenting roles, gender composition of the couple, the distribution of family labor, and the impact of familial and community support. It discusses some of the challenges facing lesbian-headed stepfamilies, their strengths, capacities and competencies, and the strategies these families use for coping with stigma and intolerance. The paper concludes with implications for policy and practice with lesbian stepfamilies. *[Article copies available for a fee from The Haworth Document Delivery Service: 1-800-HAWORTH. E-mail address: <docdelivery@haworthpress.com> Website: <http://www.Haworth Press.com> © 2003 by The Haworth Press, Inc. All rights reserved.]*

KEYWORDS. Lesbian families, gay families, stepfamilies, blended families, family diversity

Karen I. Fredriksen-Goldsen, PhD, and Pauline I. Erera, PhD, are affiliated with the University of Washington.

Address correspondence to: Karen I. Fredriksen-Goldsen, University of Washington School of Social Work, 4101 15th Avenue NE, Seattle, WA 98105-6299 (E-mail: fredrikk@u.washington.edu).

[Haworth co-indexing entry note]: "Lesbian-Headed Stepfamilies." Fredriksen-Goldsen, Karen I., and Pauline I. Erera. Co-published simultaneously in *Journal of Human Behavior in the Social Environment* (The Haworth Social Work Practice Press, an imprint of The Haworth Press, Inc.) Vol. 8, No. 2/3, 2003, pp. 171-187; and: *Sexual Minorities: Discrimination, Challenges, and Development in America* (ed: Michael K. Sullivan) The Haworth Social Work Practice Press, an imprint of The Haworth Press, Inc., 2003, pp. 171-187. Single or multiple copies of this article are available for a fee from The Haworth Document Delivery Service [1-800-HAWORTH, 9:00 a.m. - 5:00 p.m. (EST). E-mail address: docdelivery@haworthpress.com].

INTRODUCTION

In recent years a significant number of lesbian couples have claimed the right to raise children and live as a family. Recent research has demonstrated extensive family relationships and responsibilities among lesbians (Fredriksen, 1999). Studies have found lesbians and their families to be deeply committed to creating strong family environments and emphasizing emotional closeness, love, and security (Hare, 1994). Despite living with prejudice, many lesbians have been successful in fostering and sustaining positive family environments (Patterson, 2000).

Yet to date, lesbians raising children have been considered primarily from the standpoint of deviance, sexuality, and gender while being compared, explicitly and implicitly, to families with heterosexual parents. The majority of studies of lesbian-headed families have examined the influence of lesbian mothers on their children's sexual, psychological, and social development (Belcastro, Gramlich, Nicholson, Price, & Wilson, 1993; Fitzgerald, 1999; Golombok & Tasker, 1996), focusing on issues of oppression, coming out, and living in a homophobic society (Allen, 1997; DiPlacido, 1998). Adverse social stereotypes and attitudes have led some scholars to address such issues as lesbian mothers having legal custody, visitation, and adoption rights (Brienza, 1996; Duran-Aydintug & Causey, 2001; Rubenfeld, 1994).

Recognition of the unique characteristics and strengths of lesbian families–as family structures in their own right–is long overdue. Lesbians become parents through having, fostering, or adopting a child while in a heterosexual relationship or as a single parent, or through donor insemination or adoption as a lesbian couple. To fully understand lesbians and their families, it is essential to differentiate and examine a number of distinct family styles. These include lesbian couples giving birth to children within the context of their family unit, stepfamilies, single parent families, adoptive families, and foster families. While sharing some similarities, lesbian-headed stepfamilies are unique in several respects from both stepfamilies with heterosexual parents as well as lesbian couples who choose to have children within the context of their relationship (Erera & Fredriksen, 1999; Lynch, 2000).

This article will specifically address lesbian-headed stepfamilies[1] and explore various structural issues within the family unit, the distribution of family labor, and the impact of familial and community support. We will explore some of the challenges facing lesbian-headed stepfamilies and the strategies these families use for coping with difference and intolerance. In addition, we will discuss ways in which helping professionals can support lesbian-headed stepfamilies. We conclude with implications for policy and practice based on the strengths, capacities, and competencies of lesbian-headed stepfamilies.

LESBIAN-HEADED STEPFAMILIES

There are two distinct types of lesbian-headed stepfamilies. In the majority of lesbian-headed stepfamilies to date, children are born into a heterosexual relationship and the birth mother later establishes a relationship with another woman (Ariel & McPherson, 2000; Lewin, 1993). In such families, the mother's partner likely functions as a stepparent.

The number of lesbian couples giving birth to children within the context of their relationship is steadily increasing (Flaks, Ficher, Masterpasqua, & Joseph, 1995; Pies, 1989). In the event there is a separation between the lesbian parents and the mothers eventually establish relationships with other partners, these partners will also likely function as stepparents. To date this type of lesbian-headed stepfamily has been virtually overlooked in the literature (Erera & Fredriksen, 1999).[2]

One of the primary differences between lesbian-headed stepfamilies with children conceived in a heterosexual relationship compared to those with children conceived within the context of a lesbian relationship is the issue of the sexual identity of the birth mother. When a child is conceived within the lesbian relationship, the mothers are more likely to be openly identified as lesbian and to have already completed the process of accepting and integrating sexual identities prior to having children and prior to becoming a stepfamily (Nelson, 1996). Most research to date suggests that lesbians who openly identify and successfully integrate their lesbian identity are more comfortable and satisfied with their lives than those who do not (Rand, Graham, & Rawlings, 1982).

For lesbian mothers who conceived the child within an earlier heterosexual relationship, the mother is likely acquiring and adjusting to a new sexual identity while in the process of parenting and becoming a stepfamily (Lynch, 2000; Lynch & Murray, 2000). Acquiring and integrating a new sexual identity while simultaneously transitioning through the developmental tasks of stepfamily formation can create unique challenges for these lesbian-headed stepfamilies. Within an emerging stepfamily context, the issue of coming out can be complicated by issues of if, when, how, and to whom to come out (Lynch & Murray, 2000). Family members in this situation must weigh the potential risks and consequences of these decisions in relation to the security of their family. For example, given societal prejudice and discrimination, the lesbian birth mother could run the risk of losing child custody if her sexual identity became known to her previous husband.

As a protective and adaptive response to societal homophobia and social stigmatization, a child-centered approach is predominant concerning the sexual identity of the mothers and the coming out process, particularly among lesbian mothers who had children within the context of an earlier heterosexual relationship. Decisions regarding identifying as a lesbian or as a lesbian stepfamily, for example, are generally made by these lesbian parents dependent upon the child's comfort level, age, developmental stage, and changing needs (Lynch, 2000).

FAMILY STRUCTURE

Lesbian-headed stepfamilies are diverse, representing all ethnic, social, and economic backgrounds and a variety of structural and custodial arrangements. Lesbian-headed stepfamilies, like all stepfamilies, are created on the basis of the disruption of previous families–through separation, divorce, or widowhood. In most stepfamilies, there are generally two residential parents: a biological parent and a stepparent. Having one residential parent that is not a biological parent is generally considered a unique feature of stepfamilies. This feature is also shared with lesbian-headed families in which the child is conceived within the context of a lesbian relationship. In both cases, there is a biological and a non-biological parent. Lesbian-headed families, like other types of lesbian-headed families, also lack legal legitimization and institutionalized rituals such as marriage that sanction the process of becoming a family.

Lesbian-headed stepfamilies are systems created by the joining of a stepparent. Sometimes the stepparent brings her children to the new family system. Both the joining stepparent and the pre-existing family have their own family connections, rituals, and habits. The resulting stepfamily may comprise two distinct subsystems: the joining and the veteran family members. At least in the early stages, unrealistic expectations tend to characterize the formation of lesbian-headed stepfamilies, and initially the birth mother often reports feeling caught in the middle between the needs of her partner and her children (Lynch, 2000).

Most stepfamilies also include nonresidential family members. In lesbian-headed stepfamilies the nonresidential family member is usually a previous spouse of the birth parent or a previous partner. At times, lesbian-headed stepfamilies also include an additional nonresidential stepparent (i.e., the current partner of either the noncustodial birth parent or of the noncustodial lesbian parent). In lesbian-headed stepfamilies where children were conceived within the context of a lesbian relationship, a nonresidential biological father may sometimes be a known donor or an inaccessible or unknown donor. In the case of an unknown donor, children may develop fantasies and idealize this nonresidential biological father (Erera & Fredriksen, 1999).

Residential parents may share parental responsibilities and authority with the nonresidential parents in stepfamilies. This interdependence may lead to conflict, especially if the residential and nonresidential parents have different goals or priorities (Ahrons & Wallisch, 1987). Although lesbian mothers often tend to have congenial relations with their previous husbands (Hare & Richards, 1993; Kirkpatrick, 1987), visitation and custody can be an arena for mutual antagonism, tension, and competitiveness between the parents. Documentation of custody and visitation trials involving lesbian mothers suggests that in some cases, the birth father tries to prevent the lesbian birth mother from having custody of her children or even from having visitation rights (Brienza, 1996; Duran-Aydintug & Causey, 2001; Rubenfeld, 1994). Such incidents indicate that lesbian mothers are likely to be vulnerable to societal discrimination.

In the event of a separation within a lesbian couple, the nonbiological mother may be particularly vulnerable and may be denied parental rights, custody, and visitation rights (Morton, 1998; Pies, 1989; Rohrbaugh, 1988). Lesbian-headed families are generally disadvantaged in resolving such issues because they lack the legal sanction of marriage, and can confront unsympathetic, heterosexist judicial and administrative bodies. Only a few states currently grant second-parent adoptions to lesbians, and in most cases there is no legally recognized relationship between a child and the nonbiological lesbian mother.

In a ground-breaking decision, however, an Ocean City, New Jersey Superior Court ruled that a lesbian nonbirth mother was to share custody of their child and support costs with the biological mother following the couple's separation. The couple had decided together to have the child, had chosen a sperm donor, had jointly sent out birth announcements, and shared parenting. The court decision, however, was not binding in other jurisdictions, and was in fact at odds with another New Jersey court ruling (Westfeldt, 1998). In most cases the rights, responsibilities, and protections taken for granted by other families are not granted to lesbian-headed families or to lesbian-headed stepfamilies.

ASSUMPTION OF PARENTING ROLES

As parents, lesbian mothers may choose from a wide variety of parenting styles ranging from patriarchal norms that they tend to reject, to egalitarian parenting styles (Dalton & Bielby, 2000; Erera, 2002). The assumption of parenting roles within lesbian-headed stepfamilies tends to be, at least initially, influenced by the differing relationships to the child.

As in all stepfamilies, parenting may be a different experience for the lesbian birth mother and lesbian stepparent. If the responsibilities for the children are unevenly divided, for example, the lesbian birth mother may feel overburdened, perceiving herself as single parent who is living in a two-partner family (Hare & Richards, 1993; Muzio, 1993; Pies, 1989). Furthermore, the birth mother may experience a sense of divided loyalties between her children and her partner (Berger, 1998), which may restrict or prevent stepparent/stepchild intimacy, and eventually interfere with integration of the stepparent into the family.

Lesbian stepparents, like heterosexual stepparents, tend to lack clearly defined behavioral guides about their relationship with their partner's birth children, and have no clear models to turn to for assistance in their performance of the stepparent role (Berger, 1998; Erera & Fredriksen, 1999; Lynch, 2000). In lesbian-headed families, both the birth and the stepparent are mothers, which may add to the stepparents' uncertainty and role confusion (Rohrbaugh, 1988). It is also likely that questions arise in the community as to which of the two is the "real" mother (Morton, 1998). From the stepparent's perspective, the step-role can be highly demanding and problematic. Such step-role complexities can result from lack of clear norms and behavioral standards that stepparents can turn to for guidance, unrealistic notions about step-parenting, unclear expectations between parents, and jealousy and resentment of the stepchildren toward the stepparent (Berger, 1998; Lynch, 2000).

Lesbian relationships, in general, have been found to be relatively adaptive, egalitarian, and flexible. Initial research suggests that the parents in lesbian-headed stepfamilies tend to bring an adaptive orientation to the many challenges facing their families. Despite initial unrealistic expectations and role ambiguity, parents in lesbian-headed stepfamilies demonstrate a strong commitment to their families and tend to incorporate flexibility in terms of allowing mutual roles and relationships to evolve (Erera, 2002; Lynch, 2000). Furthermore, research has found that the parents in lesbian-headed stepfamilies tend to assume a strong child-centered orientation to parenting, often placing the needs of the child over the needs of the couple dyad (Lynch, 2000). While ensuring an inclusiveness and openness within the lesbian stepfamily, such a child-centered approach could inadvertently impact the level of intimacy achieved by the lesbian couple (Lynch & Murray, 2000).

DISTRIBUTION OF FAMILY LABOR

The gender composition of the parental dyad in lesbian-headed stepfamilies may impact these families in several important respects. Studies of lesbian couples found that they tend to have a relatively egalitarian division of labor, regardless of whether they do or do not raise children together (Dalton & Bielby, 2000; Hare & Richards, 1993; Sullivan, 1996). While the tendency of the lesbian couple may be to share household tasks and decision-making (Chan, Brooks, Raboy, & Patterson, 1998; Dunne, 2000), the birth mother has been found to be often more involved in childcare than is the nonbirth mother (Hare & Richards, 1993; Kirkpatrick, 1987; Patterson, 1995; Sullivan, 1996), particularly when the child was conceived within an earlier heterosexual relationship.

This unequal involvement in childcare may be attributed to internalized heterosexual cultural norms where only one parent serves as a primary caregiver (Pies, 1989; Rohrbaugh, 1988); to biological ties between mother and child, resulting in the tendency of birth mothers to assume more parental responsibilities (Hare & Richards, 1993; Kirkpatrick, 1987); and to external as well as internalized homophobia that dictates there can only really be one mother. Parental involvement in childcare is also likely impacted by financial considerations, resulting in the tendency of the higher-earning mothers to spend more time in paid employment and less time with the children (Sullivan, 1996).

The greater involvement of the birth mother in childcare has also been associated with the context of the child's birth. It has been suggested that birth mothers of children born in previous heterosexual marriages tend to assume more parental responsibilities than birth mothers of children born within the lesbian relationship. For children born in the context of the lesbian relationship, parenting tends to be more equally shared, regardless of who is the birth mother or how the child was conceived, for example, such as using a known or unknown male donor (Hare & Richards, 1993).

FAMILY AND COMMUNITY SUPPORT

Contrary to the common stereotype that lesbians are rejected and isolated from their families of origin, research has found that lesbians with children report experiencing fairly high degrees of support from their families of origin (Fredriksen, 1999). Parks (1998) notes that families of origin may be sources of both support and conflict for lesbian parents. While it is well documented that in some cases nonresidential biological family members have sought custody of children being raised in lesbian-headed stepfamilies, research suggests that support from biological family members is often an important resource that is overlooked when addressing the needs of lesbian-headed families.

For many lesbian-headed stepfamilies, another major source of social support is the lesbian community, providing legitimacy as well as tangible, emotional, and social support (Hare, 1994; Lott-Whitehead & Tully, 1993). Because of experiences gained confronting stigmatization and oppression, the lesbian community is often a vital source of support, solidarity, and collegiality. Research has demonstrated that lesbian mothers often tend to consciously "adopt" male friends as male role models for their children, insuring the participation of men in the lives of their children (Hare & Richards, 1993; Kirkpatrick, 1987).

Lesbians often have a close network of both lesbians and supportive men, often regarded as an extended family (Hare, 1994; Lott-Whitehead & Tully, 1993) that is actively involved in the lesbian family's life. Members may assume familial roles toward children of the lesbian couple. The extended family of lesbians generally provides lesbian-headed stepfamilies with support, tending not to engender conflicts over sharing familial responsibilities.

FACING THE CHALLENGE OF STIGMA

Berger (2000) suggests that lesbian-headed stepfamilies run the risk of triple stigmatization due to negative societal attitudes regarding homosexuality, enduring myths about stepfamilies, and a perceived lack of support for parenthood within the gay community. Lesbian-headed families experience homophobic stereotypes, discrimination, and prejudice. Such stigmatization is expressed in persistent beliefs, contrary to empirical evidence, that being raised in a lesbian family may adversely affect the social, psychological, or sexual and gender role development of the child (Belcastro et al., 1993; Golombok & Tasker, 1996; Patterson, 2000).

Lesbian mothers are often stereotyped as unfit parents, emotionally unstable, or unable to assume a maternal role (Fitzgerald, 1999). Negative assumptions are further reflected in persistent beliefs that lesbian relationships are temporary; therefore, a lesbian couple is less stable than a heterosexual one and provides less stability to the child (Gallagher, 1993). Although these stereotypes run counter to the available empirical evidence, they continue, at times, to be used within the legal system to deny lesbian mothers child custody and visitation rights (Brienza, 1996; Duran-Aydintug & Causey, 2001; Rubenfeld, 1994).

Law and public policy have yet to acknowledge the reality of the lesbian family, and they provide lesbian-headed families little protection, as they may be denied parental rights, custody, and visitation rights in the event of separation (Pies, 1989; Rohrbaugh, 1988). To date, lesbian couples are not entitled to formal marriage in the U.S., and without the protection of formal marriage, lesbian partners are denied such basic rights as community property, inheritance, and dependent social security benefits.

In response to social stigma, lesbian-headed families have incorporated various strategies for coping with intolerance. As discussed earlier, lesbian-headed stepfamilies have responded by incorporating an adaptive flexibility with a child-centered approach (Lynch & Murray, 2000). Having faced social stigma, these families tend to understand the personal costs of discrimination and oppression, and the importance of inclusiveness, openness, and fairness. To cope with intolerance, the development of a strong sense of self is paramount. With the incorporation of flexibility, inclusiveness, and a child-centered approach within the family unit, the children raised in these families are likely to internalize these important values. Further, while heterosexual step-families usually need to maintain flexible enough boundaries to include nonresidential members, lesbian-headed stepfamilies may need to maintain more rigid boundaries than heterosexual stepfamilies in order to assure the family's survival in the face of heterosexism, stigma, and discrimination (Erera, 2002). The greater the level of perceived threat and rejection, the more the couple attempts to keep the social hostility at bay and "fortify the bonds of love" (McVinney, 1988, p. 216). Although this kind of closed family system may put considerable pressure on the family members to feel responsible for fulfilling one another's needs, this closeness is usually adaptive (Erera, 2002).

STRENGTHS OF LESBIAN-HEADED STEPFAMLIES

While lesbian-headed stepfamilies do face unique challenges, it is important to recognize their strengths. Most often these families have responded to the challenges they face in a creative manner by integrating flexibility in adaptation, utilizing a child-centered approach to parenting and family life, and incorporating strategies for confronting intolerance and difference. They often draw support from biological as well as extended family members. The strengths and adaptations utilized by these lesbian-headed stepfamilies provide important examples for heterosexual stepfamilies and, more generally, for the field of family studies.

Lesbian-headed families give cause to reexamine our views about parenting roles, caregiving, and couple relations. Once the family has children, members of traditional families, especially women, have been consistently found to experience a decrease in marital satisfaction (see, for example, White & Booth, 1985). In contrast, research on lesbian families suggests that having children increases the couple's satisfaction (Koepke, Hare, & Moran, 1992). These divergent findings may be due to the tendency of traditional heterosexual families to become more patriarchal following the birth of a child (Acock & Demo, 1994), while lesbian families maintain their egalitarian division of labor following the addition of children to the family (Bigner, 1996; Hare & Richards, 1993; Kurdek, 1995; Patterson & Chan, 1997; Sullivan, 1996). Both lesbian parents and their children are more satisfied when childcare responsibilities are evenly distributed between both parents (Chan et al., 1998; Patterson, 1995; Sullivan, 1996). Furthermore, compared with heterosexual couples, lesbian couples tend to relate to each other more as friends who are assumed to be equal in power and status (Demo & Allen, 1996; Kurdek, 1995). This equity is highly valued and regarded as an important source of intimacy and family satisfaction.

IMPLICATIONS FOR PRACTICE

To assist lesbian-headed stepfamilies effectively, providers themselves may need support, direction, and training to address their own sexuality and re-examine their attitudes and beliefs about homosexuality. It is particularly important for family practitioners to examine their assumptions regarding lesbianism, child development, and family diversity. Furthermore, it is important for practitioners to have an understanding of the larger context (such as the consequences of homophobia and heterosexism in this society) within which lesbian-headed step families exist.

To provide appropriate services to lesbian-headed stepfamilies, service providers will need to understand the strengths and challenges that may be unique to lesbian-headed stepfamilies as well as to recognize that these families share many issues common to most families. These include, for example, communications, parenting issues, finances, sex, division of household tasks, and use of leisure time. Lesbian parents may need help with negotiation and conflict resolution skills in addressing these common couple and family issues.

Lesbian-headed stepfamilies, like stepfamilies in general, face multiple challenges as they transition through family formation, such as establishing new family configurations as well as maintaining ties with family members from previous households and families (Ganong, Coleman, & Weaver, 2002). Stepfamily life is not static; relationships within stepfamilies change over time. Thus, family practitioners need to consider several important factors that may influence stepfamily functioning, such as previous individual and family experiences, developmental issues for individual family members, and the developmental progression of the family unit. Several critical practice issues are relevant to helping stepfamilies including the strengthening of the couple, parenting, parent/stepparent-child relations, and nonresidential parent and extended kin relations (Bray, 1999; Chase-Lansdale, Gordon, Coley, Wakschlag, & Brooks-Gunn, 1999; Smith, 1999).

Generally, in stepfamilies, from the beginning of the couple relationship, there are demands of caring for children. As a result the couple generally has less time alone to create a bond prior to meeting parental responsibilities. Thus, the maintenance and enhancement of the couple relationship is paramount (Ganong et al., 2002), and providers may need to help these couples find ways to develop and maintain intimacy. Support groups for couples where the facilitator can use modeling, role playing, and real life situations can be effective (Erera, 2002). Stepfamily couples may also benefit from discussing and understanding the relationships between current and former partners (Gold, Bubenzer, & West, 1993).

Both birth parents and stepparents may benefit from understanding their parenting styles more fully. For example, parents should be encouraged to consider their own personality, the expectations of their partner and children, the stage of stepfamily formation, the age and gender of the children, and the nature of the bond between the stepchildren and the nonresidential parent as they search for the most suitable parenting style (Bray & Kelley, 1998; Erera, 2002; Ganong et al., 2002). The family practitioner can discuss alternative parenting styles, helping these parents to understand and identify an effective parenting style.

Relationships in stepfamilies provide ample opportunities for conflict as well as the potential for forming of coalitions and triangles between family members. For example, if a biological parent spends more time with a new partner, children may feel a sense of abandonment or competition with the stepparent. As a result, the biological parent may then ignore the new couple relationship in order to meet the increasing needs of their children. The stepparent may be perceived as well as experience oneself as an outsider and as a result become more distant. Family practitioners can help stepparents, their partners, and the stepchildren to clarify their expectations of each other, as well as acknowledge openly their respective feelings toward one another and the nonresidential parent (Erera & Fredriken, 1999). These may include unresolved feelings of loss, anger, disappointment, abandonment, rejection, and divided loyalties.

Stepfamilies need reassurance that it takes time to develop a sense of cohesion, integration, and emotional closeness between family members (Bray & Kelly, 1998). As new relationships are being formed, family counselors should consider individual developmental issues, with special attention to the developmental stage of the children (Bray, 2001; Schwartz & Kaslow, 1997). Children need to be able to mourn the absence of the nonresidential parent at their own pace (Kompara, 1980). Stepparents and stepchildren should be encouraged to gradually establish a parent-child dyad. A repertoire of shared activities may facilitate bonding between stepparents and stepchildren.

The dissolution of an earlier relationship may bring forth conflict and issues of custody, visitation, and child support. The dissolution of a lesbian couple may be especially difficult to resolve in view of the failure of the legal system to adequately address the issues posed by the increasing prevalence of lesbians raising children. Thus, it is essential that both service providers and lesbian parents understand the related legal issues, rights, and constraints involved and be aware of the need for professional legal planning to ensure, as much as possible, the protection of all family members and their relationships (Fredriksen, 1999).

In order to join together as a family, the extended kin, both past and present, must have their place in the stepfamily (Ganong & Coleman, 1994). Practitioners should, if necessary, help lesbian couples to strengthen the intergenerational emotional boundaries that protect their relationship from parents' and in-laws' disapproval and hostility, and take advantage of biological family members' support. To assist lesbians and nonsupportive family members, it is important for helping professionals to understand the process and adaptation involved when a family member discloses her sexual orientation (Strommen, 1989).

Initially, parents and other family members often experience concerns regarding social stigma, self-blame, and fears of loss and isolation in relation to having a lesbian family member (Bernstein, 1990). Support groups, educational materials, and talking to other family members of lesbians have been used successfully to help family members explore their fears and prejudices and become more accepting of lesbian lifestyles. For service providers, it is important to respect a family's privacy and to provide ample opportunities for disclosure and the honest sharing of information. To promote such an environment, it is essential to ask questions in a nonthreatening and inclusive manner, without making assumptions concerning the sexual orientation, gender, or marital status of family members (Fredriksen, 1999).

The practitioner also needs to recognize the significance of extended family networks in the lesbian community, and the importance of defining family broadly to encompass the critical role and functions that others can play in the life of a family. The concept of family of choice, which includes partners, significant friends, as well as biological family members, is relevant (Bonuck, 1993). Some lesbian parents may be in need of information and social support from other lesbian-headed families and knowledgeable service providers in terms of how to negotiate their unique family life (Erera & Fredriksen, 1999; Pies, 1989). Such providers can provide useful information directly, and can also facilitate mutual exchange through group interventions. Likely topics for such groups are issues pertinent to adult lesbians, including lesbian identity development, homophobia, relationships, parenting, and other family concerns (Morrow, 1996).

IMPLICATIONS FOR POLICY

Lesbians lack legal protection against discrimination in employment, housing, and education. Extending basic civil rights guarantees against discrimination on the basis of sexual orientation is an essential first step toward normalizing the status of lesbian families. Beyond this, lesbians should be granted the legal right to marry, or to have legal recognition of their relationships as is now available in Vermont. This will serve to legitimize their status, their relationships, and their families. It will also facilitate application of appropriate laws regarding divorce, custody, and child support, as well as inheritance and eligibility for public benefits. It should be noted, however, that the issue of marriage as a heterosexist institution is controversial among some lesbians.

Court decisions regarding child custody and visitation should be based solely on parental abilities rather than the parents' sexual orientation. Courts have sent mixed messages with respect to the legal protection of lesbian parental rights. The prejudice and discrimination encountered by lesbian parents in the legal system needs to be eliminated by law and through the promulgation of objective legal standards (Rubenfeld, 1994). Lawyers and judges need to be educated about the realities of homosexuality and the implications of lesbian parenting. Legal professionals need additional education regarding the diversity of American families, the current empirical knowledge base regarding lesbian-headed families, and the strengths as well as the challenges concerning lesbian-headed stepfamilies.

As with heterosexual families, mediation should be available as an alternative or adjunct to court adjudication for settling family disputes (Smith, 1999). Laws and explicit policies about adoption and foster parenting by lesbians are also needed. Basically, these should not differ from those applied to both single and coupled heterosexual applicants.

CONCLUSION

Given the increasing heterogeneity among American families, helping professionals will increasingly be called to assist family members living in a variety of family types, including lesbian-headed families. Although most research has focused on the needs of family members within traditional families, we need to further understand the similarities as well as unique needs and experiences of lesbian-headed stepfamilies. In order to support these families, family practitioners need to find ways to effectively sustain the strength of these families while supporting them in the various challenges they face. Practice methods and public policies are needed to promote the legitimization and acceptance of the lesbian family.

NOTES

1. In this paper we will use the term lesbian-headed stepfamilies rather than lesbian stepfamilies since families are not lesbian, gay or heterosexual, but rather are families that may include a mix of lesbian, gay, and heterosexual members (Fredriksen, 1999).

2. It is important to note that stepfamilies are also created within other types of lesbian-headed families such as adoptive and foster families, and the unique experiences of these families also warrant attention in future research.

REFERENCES

Acock, A. C., & Demo, D. H. (1994). *Family diversity and well-being*. Thousand Oaks, CA: Sage.

Ahrons, C. A., & Wallish, L. (1987). Parenting in the binuclear family: Relationships between biological and step-parents. In K. Pasley & M. Ihinger-Tallman (Eds.), *Remarriage and step-parenting: Current research and theory* (pp. 225-256). New York: Guilford Press.

Allen, K. R. (1997). Lesbian and gay families. In T. Arendell (Ed.), *Contemporary parenting: Challenges and issues* (pp. 196-218). Thousand Oaks, CA: Sage.

Ariel, J., & McPherson, D. W. (2000). Therapy with lesbian and gay parents and their children. *Journal of Marital and Family Therapy, 26*(4), 421-432.

Belcastro, P. A., Gramlich, T., Nicholson, T., Price, J., & Wilson, R. (1993). A review of data based studies addressing the affects of homosexual parenting on children's sexual and social functioning. *Journal of Divorce & Remarriage, 20*(1-2), 105-133.

Berger, R. (2000). Gay stepfamilies: A triple-stigmatized group. *Families in Society, 81*(5), 504-516.

Berger, R. (1998). The experience and issues of gay stepfamilies. *Journal of Divorce & Remarriage, 29*(3/4), 93-102.

Bernstein, B. E. (1990). Attitudes and issues of parents of gay men and lesbians and implications for therapy. *Journal of Gay and Lesbian Psychotherapy, 1*(3), 37-53.

Bigner, J. J. (1996). Working with gay fathers: Developmental, postdivorce parenting, and therapeutic issues. In J. Laird & R. J. Green (Eds.), *Lesbians and gays in couples and families: A handbook for therapists* (pp. 370-403). San Francisco, CA: Jossey-Bass.

Bonuck, K. (1993). AIDS and families: Cultural, psychological, and functional impacts. *Social Work in Health Care, 18*(2), 75-89.

Bray, J. H. (2001). Therapy with stepfamilies: A developmental systems approach. In S. McDaniel, D. Lusterman et al. (Eds.) *Casebook for integrating family therapy: An ecosystemic approach* (pp. 127-140). Washington, DC: American Psychological Association.

Bray, J. H. (1999). From marriage to remarriage and beyond: Findings from the Developmental Issues in StepFamilies Research Project. In E. M. Hetherington (Ed.), *Coping with divorce, single parenting, and remarriage: A risk and resiliency perspective* (pp. 253-271). Mahwah, NJ: Lawrence Erlbaum Associates.

Bray, J. H., & Kelly, J. (1998). *Stepfamilies: Love, marriage, and parenting in the first decade*. New York: Broadway Books.

Brienza, J. (1996). 'Best interests' test met in guardianship case. *Trial, 32*(1), 16-18.

Chan, R. W., Brooks, R. C., Raboy, B., & Patterson, C. J. (1998). Division of labor among lesbian and heterosexual parents: Associations with children's adjustment. *Journal of Family Psychology, 12*(3), 402-419.

Chase-Lansdale, P. L., Gordon, R. A., Coley, R. L., Wakschlag, L. S., & Brooks-Gunn, J. (1999). Young African American multigenerational families in poverty: The contexts, exchanges, and processes of their lives. In E. M. Hetherington (Ed.), *Coping with divorce, single parenting, and remarriage: A risk and resiliency perspective* (pp. 253-271). Mahwah, NJ: Lawrence Erlbaum Associates.

Dalton, S. E., & Bielby, D. D. (2000). "That's our kind of constellation:" Lesbian mothers negotiate institutionalized understandings of gender within the family. *Gender and Society, 14*(1), 36-61.

Demo, D. H., & Allen, K. R. (1996). Diversity within lesbian and gay families: Challenges and implications for family theory and research. *Journal of Social & Personal Relationships, 13*(3), 415-434.

DiPlacido, J. (1998). Minority stress among lesbians, gay men, and bisexuals: A consequence of heterosexism, homophobia, and stigmatization. In G. M. Herek (Ed.), *Stigma and sexual orientation: Understanding prejudice against lesbians, gay men, and bisexuals* (pp. 138-159). Thousand Oaks, CA: Sage.

Dunne, G. A. (2000). Opting into motherhood: Lesbians blurring the boundaries and transforming the meaning of parenthood and kinship. *Gender and Society, 14*(1), 11-35.

Duran-Aydintug, C., & Causey, K. A. (2001). Child custody determination: Implications for lesbian mothers. In J. Lehmann (Ed.), *The Gay & Lesbian Marriage and Family Reader: Analyses of Problems and Prospects for the 21st Century* (pp. 47-64). Nebraska: University of Nebraska Press.

Erera, P. I. (2002). *Family diversity: Continuity and change in the contemporary family*. Thousand Oaks, CA: Sage.

Erera, P. I., & Fredriksen, K. I. (1999). Lesbian stepfamilies: A unique family structure. *Families in Society, 80*(3), 263-170.

Fitzgerald, B. (1999). Children of lesbian and gay parents: A review of the literature. *Marriage and Family Review, 29*(1), 57-75.

Flaks, D. K., Ficher, I., Masterpasqua, F., & Joseph, G. (1995). Lesbians choosing motherhood: A comparative study of lesbian and heterosexual parents and their children. *Developmental Psychology, 31*(1), 105-125.

Fredriksen, K. I. (1999). Family caregiving among lesbians and gay men. *Social Work, 44*(2), 142-155.

Gallagher, J. (1993). Raw deal. *Advocate, 641*, 24-26.

Ganong, L. H., Coleman, M., & Weaver, S. (2002). Relationship maintenance and enhancement in stepfamilies: Clinical applications. In J. Harvey, & A. Wenzel (Eds.) *A clinician's guide to maintaining and enhancing close relationships* (pp. 105-129). Mahwah, NJ: Lawrence Erlbaum Associates.

Ganong, L. H., & Coleman, M. (1994). *Remarried family relationships*. Thousand Oaks, CA: Sage.

Gold, J. M., Bubenzer, D. L., & West, J. D. (1993). Differentiation from ex-spouses and stepfamily marital intimacy. *Journal of Divorce & Remarriage, 19*(3-4), 83-96.

Golombok, S., & Tasker, F. (1996). Do parents influence the sexual orientation of their children? Findings from a longitudinal study of lesbian families. *Developmental Psychology, 32*(1), 3-12.

Hare, J. (1994). Concerns and issues faced by families headed by a lesbian couple. *Families in Society: The Journal of Contemporary Human Services, 75*(1), 27-36.

Hare, J., & Richards, L. (1993). Children raised by lesbian couples: Does context of birth affect father and partner involvement. *Family Relations, 42*(3), 249-256.

Kirkpatrick, M. (1987). Clinical implications of lesbian mother studies. *Journal of Homosexuality, 14*(1-2), 201-211.

Koepke, L., Hare, J., & Moran, B. (1992). Relationship quality in a sample of lesbian couples with children and child-free lesbian couples. *Family Relations, 41*(2), 224-230.

Kompara, D. R. (1980). Difficulties in the socialization process of step parenting. *Family Relations, 29*, 69-73.

Kurdek, L. (1993). The allocation of household labor in homosexual and heterosexual cohabiting couples. *Journal of Social Issues, 49*, 127-139.

Kurdek, L. A. (1995). Lesbian and gay couples. In A. R. D'Augelli & C. J. Patterson (Eds.), *Lesbian, gay, and bisexual identities over the lifespan: Psychological perspectives* (pp. 243-261). New York: Oxford University Press.

Lewin, E. (1993). *Lesbian mothers: Accounts of gender in American culture*. Ithaca, N.Y.: Cornell University Press.

Lott-Whitehead, L., & Tully, C. T. (1993). The family lives of lesbian mothers. *Smith College Studies in Social Work, 63*(3), 265-280.

Lynch, J. M. (2000). Considerations of family structure and gender composition: The lesbian and gay stepfamily. *Journal of Homosexuality, 40*(2), 81-95.

Lynch, J. M., & Murray, K. (2000). For the love of the children: The coming out process for lesbian and gay parents and stepparents. *Journal of Homosexuality, 39*(1), 1-24.

McVinney, L. D. (1988). Social work practice with gay male couples. In G. P. Mallon (Ed.), *Foundations of social work practice with lesbian and gay persons* (pp. 229-248). New York: Harrington Park Press/The Haworth Press, Inc.

Morrow, D. F. (1996). Coming-out issues for adult lesbians: A group intervention. *Social Work, 41*(6), 647-656.

Morton, S. B. (1998). Lesbian divorce. *American Journal of Orthopsychiatry, 68*(3), 410-419.

Muzio, C. (1993). Lesbian co-parenting: On being/being with the invisible (m)other. *Smith College Studies in Social Work, 63*(3), 215-229.

Nelson, F. (1996). *Lesbian motherhood: An exploration of Canadian lesbian families*. Toronto: University of Toronto Press.

Parks, C. A. (1998). Lesbian parenthood: A review of the literature. *American Journal of Orthopsychiatry, 68*(3), 376-389.

Patterson, C. J. (2000). Family relationships of lesbians and gay men. *Journal of Marriage and the Family, 62*(4), 1052-1069.

Patterson, C. J. (1995). Families of the lesbian baby boom: Parents' division of labor and children's adjustment. *Developmental Psychology, 31*(1), 115-124.

Patterson, C. J., & Chan, R. W. (1997). Gay fathers. In M. E. Lamb (Ed.), *The role of the father in child development* (3rd ed., pp. 246-260). New York: John Wiley & Sons.

Pies, C. A. (1989). Lesbians and the choice to parent. *Marriage and Family Review, 14*(3-4), 137-154.

Rand, C., Graham, D. L. R., & Rawlings, E. I. (1982). Psychological health and factors the court seeks to control in lesbian mother custody trials. *Journal of Homosexuality, 8*, 27-39.

Rohrbaugh, J. B. (1988). Choosing children: Psychological issues in lesbian parenting. *Women & Therapy, 8*(1-2), 51-64.

Rubenfeld, A. R. (1994). Sexual orientation and custody. *Human Rights, 21*(1), 14-18.

Schwartz, L. L., & Kaslow, F. W. (1997). *Painful partings: Divorce and its aftermath.* New York: John Wiley and Sons.

Smith, H. (1999). *Children, feelings, and divorce: Finding the best outcome.* London, Great Britain: Free Association Books.

Strommen, E. F. (1989/1990). You're a what? Family member reactions to the disclosure of homosexuality. *Journal of Homosexuality, 18*(1/2), 37-58.

Sullivan, M. (1996). Rozzie and Harriet? Gender and family patterns of lesbian coparents. *Gender & Society, 10*(6), 747-767.

Westfeldt, A. (1998, November 4). Lesbian ex-partners to share custody. *The Seattle Times*, A9.

White, L. K., & Booth, A. (1985). The transition to parenthood and marital equality. *Journal of Family Issues, 6*, 435-449.

Life Course Analysis–
The Courage to Search for Something More:
Middle Adulthood Issues in the Transgender
and Intersex Community

Tarynn M. Witten

SUMMARY. In this paper we discuss middle-to-late life issues of the transgender and intersex communities. We demonstrate that these mid-to-late life issues are richly complex, full of courage, coping, risk, and resilience, and are grounded in a socio-ecological landscape of systemic actual and perceived violence and abuse. We examine how this socio-ecological environment affects the "normative" mid-life cycle processes. Practical examples are drawn from the author's field interviews and survey research over the past decade. We close by examining the effects of such a landscape on the middle-age life stage and examine its potential ramifications for old age as well. *[Article copies available for a fee from The Haworth Document Delivery Service: 1-800-HAWORTH. E-mail address: <docdelivery@haworthpress.com> Website: <http://www.HaworthPress.com> © 2003 by The Haworth Press, Inc. All rights reserved.]*

Tarynn M. Witten, PhD, is Executive Director, TranScience Research Institute, P.O. Box 28089, Richmond, VA 23228 (E-mail: transcience@earthlink.net; Web: http://www.transcience.org).

[Haworth co-indexing entry note]: "Life Course Analysis–The Courage to Search for Something More: Middle Adulthood Issues in the Transgender and Intersex Community." Witten, Tarynn M. Co-published simultaneously in *Journal of Human Behavior in the Social Environment* (The Haworth Social Work Practice Press, an imprint of The Haworth Press, Inc.) Vol. 8, No. 2/3, 2003, pp. 189-224; and: *Sexual Minorities: Discrimination, Challenges, and Development in America* (ed: Michael K. Sullivan) The Haworth Social Work Practice Press, an imprint of The Haworth Press, Inc., 2003, pp. 189-224. Single or multiple copies of this article are available for a fee from The Haworth Document Delivery Service [1-800-HAWORTH, 9:00 a.m. - 5:00 p.m. (EST). E-mail address: docdelivery@haworthpress.com].

Journal of Human Behavior in the Social Environment, Vol. 8(2/3) 2003
http://www.haworthpress.com/web/JHBSE
© 2003 by The Haworth Press, Inc. All rights reserved.
Digital Object Identifier: 10.1300/J137v8n02_12

KEYWORDS. Adulthood, ageism, aging, discrimination, gender, gender identity, gender presentation, gender self-perception, hate crimes, health inequality, hermaphrodite, heterosexual, intersex, legal status, LGBT, life course, life cycle, middle adulthood, middle age, old age, power, race, sex, sexuality, sexual orientation, social theory, socio-economic status, transsexual, transgender, violence

INTRODUCTION

Overview

Normative Understandings

Numerous texts and articles have discussed ways of constructing a contextual basis for human behavior (Hutchinson, 1992ab; Robbins, Chatterjee, & Canda, 1998). However, theory does not exist in absentia of context and context carries with it embedded dialectics that impose meaning and values on the context. In fact, one of the primary arguments of feminist science is the fact that modern day science is grounded in a "male" dominated phenomenological approach (context) to the world (Harding, 1987; Smith & Mahfouz, 1994; Keller & Longino, 1996).

The fields of medicine and biomedical research are no less susceptible to contextually based theoretical constructions and to the historical impact of that contextual basis than any other field (Basu, 2000; Cassell, 1998; DeJong, 2000; Doyal, 2001; Fulmer et al., 1999; Gannon et al., 1992; Grant, 2001; Ritzer, 1992; Sands, 2001; Watt, 2001; Weiss & Lonnquist, 2000). The same arguments can be made for the contextual evolution of the fields of psychology and psychoanalysis (Smith & Mahfouz, 1994).

The historical development of modern day psychology and psychoanalysis is bound up in the complexity of a Eurocentric, heterosexual, Judeo-Christian viewpoint. Obviously, restriction of the theoretical construct to males eliminates all research on women (Goodnow, 2000a, b, and previous references) and on the intersex population (Witten, 2001b). It also eliminates all research on transsexuals, transgenders, and other gender-variant individuals (Jacobs & Cromwell, 1992; Kirk & Rothblatt, 1995; Cahill, South, & Spade, 2000; Witten, 2002b; Witten & Eyler, 1999).

Clearly, limiting the discussion to heterosexuality (Fernandez, 1998; Bowles, 1995) buys into the Judeo-Christian paradigm (Witten, 2001a; 2002b) of the family and consequently eliminates all theoretical constructs that would deal with non-normative sexualities (gay adoption, for example), genders, and the potential variety of combinations that emerge from pairing them off as partners (Kurtz, 2000; Littleton v. Prange, 2000; Pesquera, 1999; Hull, 2001) and their embedding into families (both immediate and extended, i.e., Kantaras v. Kantaras–a transsexual fighting for custody of his two children; Ettner, 1999). For example, such a restriction could not realistically attempt to address the behavioral, psychosocial, or developmental pathways of children in same-sex parental households. Nor could it address issues of eldercare for transgendered elders within the family or in any type of retirement, assisted living, or nursing home facility (Witten, Eyler, & Weigel, 2000). Assumption of heterosexuality also eliminates any theoretical constructs dealing with the dynamics of aging for non-normative sex and gender roles in a heterosexual society (Adelman, 1987; Ahmed, 1999; Ayala & Coleman, 2000; Barrett, 1999; Butler & Hope, 1999; Currah, Minter, & Jamison, 2000; Dempsey, 1994; Fulmer, 1995; Grossman, D'Augelli, & Hershberger, 2000; Kaminski, 2000; Slusher, Mayer, & Dunkle, 1996). These issues are further complicated when one considers the impact of intersex (Greenberg, 1998) on gender roles, gender self-perception, and gender identity as it is perceived by individuals external to the intersex individual. Cassell (1997) elucidates this complexity quite nicely when she states:

> Although I believe gender differences are deep and relatively resistant to change, I am convinced that social factors can explain my findings. To supplement explanations that describe gender as an ongoing social construction, I use the notion of embodiment–meaning the way in which people experience and inhabit their bodies, and the way in which these bodies incorporate and express social information. I argue that certain male-identified death-haunted pursuits, such as surgery, test piloting, race car driving, are embodied occupations, and that the body of a woman who aspires to be subject (she who acts) rather that object (she who is acted upon) seems bizarrely out of place to their martial masculine practitioners. (Cassell, 1997, p. 12)

Cassell's comment accurately reflects the complexities of the interaction between the body, as a physical entity in space and time, as it is self-perceived in an abstract internal way, and as it is understood through reflexive interaction in both a symbolic interactionist construct and a socially constructed metaphor of reality. Hence, the subtleties of meaning evoked by members of the transgender and intersex communities in this context can be difficult, if not confusing to understand (Pryzgoda & Chrisler, 2000). Moreover, in a moment, we shall demonstrate that these subtleties are viscerally provocative in terms of precipitated violence and abuse against these communities and it is within this socio-ecological construct that transgender and intersex individuals must navigate both the normative biomedical processes of aging as well as the concomitant issues arising from their perceived position as sociologically deviant, not just sociologically, but also biomedically as well.

Pathologizing Intersex and Transgender: Two Sides of the Same Coin

Briefly summarized, intersex is seen as a chromosomal and/or metabolic pathology. The ancient Greeks (Harvey, 1997, pg. 32) recognized that there was a "third sex." They called it "hermaphrodite," which is now considered a pejorative term for an individual who displays both sexual organs at birth (actually, the anatomical presentation can be quite varied and does not necessarily require both complete organs to be displayed). The preferred current terminology is "intersexed" (ISNA, 2002). The prevalence of intersexuality is estimated at 1/2000 births. Additionally, it is estimated that there are nearly 65,000 intersex births worldwide per year. Intersexed individuals can be generally categorized into two groups: "genetically intersexed" or "hormonally intersexed."

We have all been taught that the male chromosomal structure is XY, while the female chromosomal structure is XX. However, it is possible to have a genetic mosaic in which the individual has a chromosomal structure XX/XY. In this case, the individual is said to be "genetically intersexed." However, it is possible that an individual may be XX (genetically female) and be subjected to elevated in utero levels of testosterone thereby partially masculinizing the individual. Likewise, an individual may be XY and be subjected to reduced levels of testosterone, thereby feminizing the body. These individuals are said to be "hormonally intersexed." However, an individual can be intersexed in other ways. For example, in congenital adrenal hyperplasia the adrenal glands make too much male hormones and the individual, while genetically female, may appear and develop intersexed. Partial androgen insensitivity is a genetic male fault that causes the testosterone receptors not to bind testosterone as efficiently as they should. Consequently, the individual subsequently develops as an intersexed person. In some small villages in the Dominican Republic, there is an elevated prevalence of another genetic fault in that there are individuals who cannot convert testosterone to dihydrotestosterone, and while born genetically XY, they are born looking female. However, at the onset of puberty, they eventually start looking male. These people are given the name "ouevodolce" (eggs at 12) meaning the testicles descend at twelve years of age.

As such, intersex can be medicalized in the context of being a sanctionable pathology (Weberian sense) that, because it is of the body (see Table 1) it can be dealt with, in this case by surgical intervention. However, this "interven-

TABLE 1. Biomedical pathologization of transgender and intersex.

Variable	Condition	
	Intersex	*Transgender*
Body *vs.* Mind	Body[2]	Mind
Origin of condition	Genetic/Physiological	Unknown, probably multi-factorial
Psychological Designation	No DSM IV-TR codes. Condition is considered to be a medical condition.	DSM IV-TR code "Gender Identity Disorder" with exclusive statement that client displaying intersex condition is not to be classified as having gender identity disorder[3.]
Intervention	Operation typically performed at birth. Frequently performed without consent of parents and undesired by child.	Operation desired by individual and typically beyond individual's ability to attain due to numerous psycho-social and financial constraints.
Medical Coverage	Typically covered under most healthcare plans.	Not covered under any healthcare plan.
Social Acceptability	Socially reasonable with marginal stigmatization.	Socially highly stigmatized.

tion" can create profound later-life difficulties for the intersexed individual (Goodnow, 2000a, b; Witten 2001a). However, the dichotomy of mind/body vis à vis individual versus group/society automatically pathologizes trans-phenomena as they are of the mind. Such an association is inherently a stigmatization as rational positivist science cannot "touch"–with any instrument currently known–a discernable "body-bound" explanation for trans-behaviors; thus, unable to ground trans-phenomena within the historic Western biomedical, monotheistic, heterosexual, Eurocentric traditions of medicine. Consequently, the healthcare system, with few exceptions, pathologizes trans-behaviors and intersexed bodies–"right mind/right body vs. wrong mind/right body or right mind/ambiguous body" (Cassell, 1997). Unlike the pathologization of intersex via medicalization, "trans" is invisiblized, as well as pathologized, through a classification of mental pathology (302.85, 302.6-DSM-IV; APA, 2000, p. 849). This is further evident from the denial of healthcare coverage. For example, respondents to the TLARS (TranScience Longitudinal Aging Research Study) stated that

> My insurance specifically excludes TS care, so I'm having trouble with money for medical care. Oregon Health plan excludes mental health, so I can't afford therapy, which I need for surgery. I obtained an inappropriate surgery because I lied to my MD about being a TS. I did this because the last time I told a medical professional (University student mental health counselor) the truth they wanted to institutionalize me. I had seri-

ous complications from the surgery, possibly because I was on birth control pills because I could not get testosterone.

Another respondent reported that

> Notations re: gender are always disclosed in medical records. Whenever insurance applications are filled out, an authorization for release of all medical records is included. Once the info is disseminated to the insurance carrier, all hope of confidentiality is lost . . . providers are not TG friendly.

Additionally, there is the inability to access Medicare/Medicaid coverage (Cahill, South, & Spade, 2000) and the legal system's failure (see *http://www.ngltf.org/library/index.cfm* for current Civil Rights and Hate Crimes maps) to respond to violence and abuse against the trans/intersex communities. For more on transgender hate crimes see *http://www.gender.org/remember/about/core.html*.

Transgender and Intersex Violence and Abuse: What Is Known?

Witten and Eyler (1999) point out that population estimates for the gender community are difficult to obtain and verify, due principally to the currently highly stigmatized nature of transsexualism, transgenderism, and cross-dressing identifications and behavior, as well as the lack of available resources for the gender community in many geographic regions. (The latter phenomenon leads to the choice of private solutions, such as "passing" as the other sex without medical or mental health assistance, and therefore to "*epidemiological invisibility*.") Similar data are available on an international scale (Witten et al., 2003).

By means of example, Witten and Eyler report that in a sample of 174 individuals (sample biased towards middle to upper-class individuals and having age range 22-79 years) there was a high degree of violence and abuse suffered. With regard to the definitions of abuse that most accurately described these situations (respondents n = 135; multiple answers permitted), results were as given in Table 2. Sadly, much abuse and violence is suffered prior to the age of eighteen years old. Of the 86 respondents, 60 of them stated that they had suffered some sort of violence or abuse (multiple choices could be checked) prior to age 18. Furthermore, the top perpetrators were the father, another adult followed by a relative, the mother, and finally a peer. The implications of this multiple violence and abuse for health services personnel is also discussed in Witten and Eyler (1999).

Respondents were also asked to identify whether or not they had ever told another person about the violence, abuse, or mistreatment that they had received, and to whom these events had been reported. Of the n = 121 partici-

TABLE 2. Prevalence of violence types among respondents of the TLARS study.

Violence Type	n =	%
Physical	62	25%
Emotional	91	37%
Sexual	26	11%
Neglect	35	14%
Exploitation	11	5%
Not Applicable	22	9%

pants who answered this question, n = 93 (77%) indicated that they had told others of their abuse experiences, and n = 28 (23%) stated that they had not. With respect to reasons for non-reporting, (n = 132; multiple responses permitted) n = 28 (21%) indicated that they were afraid to report for fear of reprisal by the perpetrator, n = 14 (11%) feared abuse by the medical/legal system, n = 5 (4%) were unable to report, n = 38 (29%) felt that it would not make a difference if they had reported the incident or incidents, n = 10 (8%) wanted to protect the perpetrator, and n = 22 (17%) indicated that there had been reasons other than those listed in Table 3.

In addition, several items were included which pertained to any acts of abuse, mistreatment or violence that had occurred in social settings. Typically, such acts take place in the workplace, on the street, in bars, or in any other public, interpersonal scene. Religious institutions, educational settings, other public environments, organizations, or institutions were also included in this section. When asked whether or not the respondent had had any acts of mistreatment, abuse, or violence perpetrated against them in social settings, survey participants responded as follows: Yes (= 89; 66%), No (= 42; 31%), and Not Applicable (= 4; 3%; n = 135).

Stigma and Reports of Transgender Life Experiences

The Witten and Eyler survey asked the respondents to share, if they were willing, some examples of their real-life experiences with respect to violence and abuse. The survey participants, in response to open-ended questions, reported the following vignettes. Many respondents experienced abuse during childhood or adolescence which they attributed to being a "different" child, as well as violence which was less specifically targeted:

TABLE 3. Prevalence of respondents citing violence as hate crime related (TLARS study).

Violence Type	Percentage of Respondents
Street Harassment	48%
Followed/Stalked	41%
Mugged	29%
Beaten	39%
Sexual Harassment	23%
Sex Abuse/Attempt	15%
Rape	6%

> Step father used to beat me because as a child I didn't play with the boys or get into manly things. I wanted to play with the girls. I didn't play school games–I was a "sissy." I got a broken nose for 1959 Christmas. (52-year-old transsexual woman)

> My early experiences in cross-dressing were discovered . . . and reported to my father. He caus[ed] me great embarrassment in front of the whole family. The second [time] I was caught resulted in a private consultation where I was issued the ultimatum: Stop dressing or be sent to a psychiatric institution . . .

> I watched my father physically beat an older sibling on numerous occasions and did fear physical abuse as well as emotional abuse from dad. Because of this we were never close though I worked hard at conforming to dad's desires for me (Varsity football, college scholarship, the military). (38-year-old biologically male cross-dresser)

Many study participants also reported multiple-victimization as well as victimization/abuse across the lifecycle. Consider the following response by a 43-year-old gender-blended individual (respondent's errors are retained without editing):

> At the BE-ALL weekend [a cross-dressing event] in Detroit I was verbal abused while walking from my room across the courtyard when I was [illegible] by two men. I was verbal harassed often. Beaten by my mother . . . I was raped once by [illegible] in college.

Social victimization included harassment in employment settings, with its attendant confusion for the victim for example, consider the following response by a 45-year-old biologically male cross-dresser:

> ... I got involved with a professional who wanted to 'tutor' me. I had already identified myself as bisexual, and when gender play was offered, I willingly went along ... But it was exploitive and embarrassing and my boss paraded his power in front of the company.

This same individual also reported a history of intra-familial abuse as well as an associated sense of loss persisting into adult life:

> If my brother had been helped in his [sexual orientation] when he was young, he would have been a better person. Maybe I wouldn't have been such a 'victim' at a young age. And if I had different avenues of gender expression, maybe my life would have been different.

Other respondents who had experienced abuse throughout childhood and adult life expressed a defensive and cynical worldview, as did the young adult female-to-male transsexual who simply stated: "*People have tried to kill me since I was a child.*"

Furthermore, reports of social mistreatment, including street harassment and violence, are so prevalent in the gender community that many individuals begin the transition process (from female to male, or male to female living) with a mixture of joy (due to the anticipation of being able to be true to their deepest self-perceptions) and dread (regarding the potential consequences):

> I have been one of the lucky ones. I've only experienced verbal abuse/harassment. I hope to start transition within a few months. We'll see what happens then. (35-year-old male-to-female transsexual)

Transgender Hate Crimes Violence

Individuals who responded as having suffered some sort of violence were asked a series of clarifying items that addressed whether or not the respondents believed that any of these acts of violence constituted "hate crimes" (i.e., that the acts occurred because of hatred of the respondent's race, gender, sexual orientation, or gender presentation, multiple responses were allowed). Of n = 143 responses, n = 101 (70%) stated Yes, n = 23 (16%) indicated No, and n = 19 (13%) chose Not Applicable. At this time, correlations between type of violence and perception as a hate crime are not available.

Results of the WTNAS (Washington Transgender Needs Assessment Survey; Xavier & Simmons, 2002) are equally disturbing. The WTNAS study reports 26% harassment, 18% intimidation, 17% assault with a weapon, 14% sexual assault/rape and minor percentages in other areas such as police entrapment, police sweep, blackmail/extortion, and unjustified arrest. Of the n = 89

TLARS respondents who indicated that they had experienced an act of social mistreatment, abuse or violence, n = 62 (70%) indicated that they had suffered some form of street harassment or verbal abuse at some time in their lives and n = 16 (18%) had suffered an act of rape or attempted rape. Survey items also addressed the reporting of social violence, and satisfaction with the response. Of the n = 89 respondents who had experienced social violence, n = 20 (22%) indicated that they had reported these occurrences, n = 66 (74%) stated that they had not done so, and n = 3 (4%) indicated that they had "sometimes" reported these crimes. Of the (n = 22) survey participants who had made reports to the appropriate authorities, n = 8 (35%) expressed satisfaction with the action taken in that case (or cases) while n = 15 (65%) reported dissatisfaction.

Given that the Witten and Eyler results were based upon a sample biased towards the more advantaged of the transgender population, it is within reason to conclude that–in point of fact–the situation is significantly worse for the bulk of the unreported population. The likely validity of this assumption is born out by the recent results of the Washington Transgender Needs Assessment Survey. In this study, n = 109 victims who fell victim to violence or crime were instructed to check any and all categories of motives they thought applied to their experiences. The WTNAS data is reported in Table 4.

Sadly, violence and abuse against the transgender community continues. The high profile murders of Tyra Hunter, Brandon Teena, Debra Forte, Chanel Pickett, and Carmen Marie Montoya serve to underscore the ongoing problem. Estimates as to how many other transgender-related murders go unreported are currently unknown. Nevertheless, as we have pointed out earlier, high profile homicides (in which hatred of transgenderism is believed to be the motivation for murder) are reported in the media. As is common in hate crime assaults, these episodes involved severe violence (such as multiple stab wounds, strangulation, and genital assault) but in contrast to the norm for investigation other hate crimes (e.g., neo-Nazi attacks), response by the law enforcement and medical providers was allegedly sub-standard in several of these cases. Furthermore, as anti-transsexual violence and related criminal behaviors are not reportable as hate crimes, investigating police often do not consider bias as a pertinent motivation. Additionally, most transgender people conceal the difference between their social and biological genders from the general population (and since this discrepancy is usually discovered only post-homicide by the investigating law enforcement agencies), it must be assumed that these few highly visible cases represent the "*tip of the iceberg*" with regard to severe (and sometimes fatal) acts of violence against this community.

Results from the work of Witten and Eyler (1999) have demonstrated the profound public health hazard associated with the violence and stigma against the transgender community. However, their research supports the argument

TABLE 4. Prevalence percentages of category of violence or crime motive, as perceived by the victim, in respondents of the WTNAS.

Category of Motive for Crime as Applied to WTNAS Respondent Experience	Percentage of WTNAS Respondents
Homophobia	41.3%
Transphobia	33.9%
Don't know motive	27.5%
Economic gain	20.2%
Domestic violence	10.1%
Racism	8.3%
Other motive not listed	4.6%

that the stigma extends into other areas as well. In particular, it has profound impact on the financial and medical well-being of this population. While the sample population from our longitudinal study was both reasonably well off financially, it was only through this success that they were able to pay for the necessary drugs and other medical interventions necessary to both begin and subsequently maintain the transition. The wave 1 TranScience Longitudinal Aging Research Study (TLARS) respondents replied as follows: Of the n = 175 individuals who answered the employment question, responses were as follows: n = 15 unemployed, n = 12 employed part-time, n = 131 employed full-time, n = 10 retired, and n = 7 receiving disability. Individuals were also asked to describe their most recent employment, with the following results: n = 9 corporate executives, n = 85 managerial or professional positions (e.g., accountant, engineer, scientist, lawyer, etc.), n = 19 service occupations (e.g., cook, child care worker, police, firefighter, etc.), n = 0 farming/forestry/fishing related employment, n = 14 precision production, craft, and repair (e.g., mechanics, phone repair, locksmith, etc.), n = 16 operator, fabricator, or laborer (e.g., typesetter, assembly worker, crane operator, taxi driver, etc.), n = 10 independent freelancer or consultant, n = 7 students, n = 3 receiving alternative income, and n = 19 "other." Results from the Washington Transgender Needs Assessment Study (2000) document significantly lower educational levels, 42% unemployment, and significantly lower income-earning levels (48% of the WTNAS respondents state that they could not afford care, 29.6% state that they have either no insurance or insurance that does not cover the transgender healthcare related needs). Additionally, in the WTNAS study, 37% of those employed worked as service industry workers, 14.5% as private sector office workers, 5.5% as sex industry workers, and the rest in other categories, with only 9% working as private sector professionals. Clearly, the type of employment will have significant impact on the mid-to-later life issues, of both the transgender and intersex populations.

Before we move into the details of the mid-to-late life experiences from the field research, let us take a moment to put this violence and abuse into a life-cycle context. First, violence and abuse are prevalent in the transgender community (Witten & Eyler, 1999; Lombardi et al., 2001; Russell et al., 2001). If we assume that undesired surgical intervention to alter ambiguous genitalia is also violence and abuse perpetrated against the intersex person, then while no real estimates can be made as to how many surgical interventions are being performed, it can be reasonably speculated that there exists a high degree of abuse and violation in the intersex population as well. This is consistent with the remarks of Cheryl Chase and with the statistics of the ISNA (2002) website.

Failure to respond to the violence and abuse, along with the denial of coverage, serves as sanctioning hatred and violence through absence of policy and, in doing this, serves to allow/sanction by silence societal policing of this visceral "deviance." This is evident in the lack of prosecution of numerous transgender murders over the past decade.

With this contextual sociology in mind, let me now provide a brief overview of the normative knowledge of the launching phase (Carter & McGoldrick, 1999, p. 287) and follow that discussion with the results of a small field study of a group of mid-to-late life trans- and intersex persons. From this discussion, we will see that while the normative heterosexual life cycle phases provide us with some useful information, and while the results of studies on lesbian and gay populations further our understandings of midlife issues, the transgender and intersex populations carry with them a unique collection of confounding issues that make their mid-to-late life cycle particularly complex and rich with potential learning experiences and history.

MIDLIFE ISSUES

Normative Knowledge

Midlife, as seen by most individuals in research, is a time in which a number of tasks must be completed and a number of issues must be faced. One of the life cycle tasks of this period is the completion of the "launching" phase. Carter and McGoldrick (1999, p. 287) address this issue with respect to launching of children and significant realignment of family roles. Tasks of this phase include becoming a couple again, developing adult relationships with adult children, accepting new family members through marriage and birth, and the resolving of issues with, providing for, and finally the burying of their parents. It will be important, in the upcoming field discussion, to keep these tasks and issues in mind, as we shall see that these supposedly "common/normative" processes are not generative across all population types. Carter and McGoldrick's discussion, while it does give mention to the particular issues of the Gay and Lesbian environment (Carter & McGoldrick, 1999, pp. 302-303, and Chapter 20) still quite clearly predicates its analytical constructions upon normative Judeo-Christian, Western biomedical, Eurocentric constructions of sex and gender roles, and the concomitant definitions of what it means to be a family and to have adult relationships within that context. As such, it is illuminating to note that this text tacitly perpetuates, for its reader, a means with which to buy into this very stereotype and, as such both marginalizes and invisibilizes those with atypical sex/gender/sexuality constructions. Such a phenomenon is not, as we have already documented, uncommon in the healthcare literature.

What Carter and McGoldrick do provide us with is a means by which we can examine the complexities of the launching phase for the intersexed and transgender individual within the framework of how the normative society views the launching phase. In essence, the transgender/intersex community can serve as a countersystem (Lyng, 2001) with which to examine the underlying definitions of the life cycle roles and issues presented by Carter and McGoldrick. It is beyond the scope of this discussion to address, in any extensive fashion, all of the similarities and differences. In order to provide an insight into this stage of life cycle development and to highlight some of the salient features of this stage, we will now present the results of some recent field interviews with members of the mid-to-late life LGBT community.

RESULTS

The Players[1]

Babes, the designated Lesbian hangout, sits on a corner in Carytown, VA. Inside Babes it is stark, most of the walls painted black and beige, a single disco reflector ball hangs from the black dance-room ceiling waiting to be given life. Friday nights, the crowd is dense, the air smoky, and the music loud. On Tuesdays, it is far more quiet, far less smoky, and the only place in town for the LGBT crowd to hang out and mingle with a relative degree of safety. In the back of the main dance area sits a large circular table, seating ten, that has become the designated meeting place of the transgendered of the area.

This evening, sitting around the table are Tracy (51-year-old male-to-female, post-operative, transsexual), Istvan (48-year-old, gay male), Rebecca (45-year-old male-to-female, pre-operative, transsexual), Lance (55-year-old, male cross-dresser), Paula (54-year-old, male-to-female, post-operative transsexual), Noreen (58-year-old, male-to-female, pre-operative transsexual), Janice (48-year-old, male-to-female, post-operative transsexual), Stan (57-year-old, female-to-male, post-operative transsexual), and Marissa (33-year-old, male-to-female, post-operative transsexual). In the booth next to us sit Carl (43-year-old, gay male), Kristin (57-year-old, lesbian female), and Allie (50-year-old, lesbian female). Barry (43-year-old, female-to-male transsexual) provided commentary on the pre-final version of this manuscript. Cigarettes burn, dinner plates rattle, and the air is rife with multiple conversations that weave in and out of each other, some dropping away only to return at a latter point, others intermingling with whatever the main stream of consciousness happens to be at the moment. During a lull in the conversation, I whip out my notepad and inform my table colleagues that I have volunteered to write an article on mid-life LGBT issues for the American Society on Aging and I ask them if they are willing to provide some personal anecdotes to ground the story in reality. Nods of heads indicate yes, as long as I use no names; to which I readily agree. I pose the following question: *"What is it that you worry about now that you are in the middle part of your lives?"*

The Field and Survey Data and Discussion

It is no surprise that the answers differ between the different respondent categories. And yet, they do fall into certain themes: Financial stability (short and long-term), Social isolation (partnership and community), Safety, Healthcare, Independence and Living environment. Intertwined with the gender/sexuality issues is an emergent theme of ageism illustrated by Istvan's comment *"The young ones don't want to talk to you. They feel that you are not knowledgeable. You haven't been Queer long enough."*

Tracy responded with a strong nod of the head and recounted a story in which some teenager at the local grocery store had called her an *"old tranny hag."* Notice the multiple agent-target "isms" embedded in this statement. There is the ageist comment "hag" (not only ageist, but a commentary on the body and lack of usefulness and youth/beauty). Moreover, it is coupled to the pejorative "tranny" (which carries with it numerous "isms" including the inherent social segregation due to both perceived social deviance and age). David Valentine (2000), in his recent doctoral dissertation, points out that the common binding of the transgender community is violence and abuse. This sense of social isolation and of being a target is critical to the understanding of the basis of operation of the transgender community. It is important to understand this common binding as it affects the life cycle of all transgender and intersex individuals.

Data from the Gerontological literature contain a well-documented fact base supporting the argument that social conditions (Kubzamsky, Berkman, &

Seeman, 2000), social network support (Everard et al., 2000; Pinquart & Sorenson, 2000), socio-economic status (Rautio, Heikkinen, & Heikkinen, 2001), and even social role (Krause & Shaw, 2000) can all have significant impact, positively or negatively, on mortality, morbidity, health status, depression prevalence (overall psychological well-being, Zhang and Hayward, 2001), successful aging, and numerous other life course outcomes that are of current importance in the Healthy People 2010 Project. The results of these studies can be summarized as follows, the lower the income, the less social support (friends, spiritual activity, supporting organizations, neighbors upon whom one can depend, for example), the less habitable to social conditions (isolation, poor environment), the less education, the higher the risk for psychological dysfunction, long-term poor quality of life, poor health status, increased morbidity and mortality, and the less likely to be "a successful ager" in the sense of the MacArthur Foundation's Successful Aging Project.

In the upcoming discussion, we will address both intersex and transgender violence. With that in mind, let us examine some recent research in transgender violence and abuse.

The Problem of Transgender Stigma and Violence

In and of itself, violence and abuse need to be stopped, no matter what the situation. However, the impact of the type of trans-intersex related violence and abuse can be measured across the life cycle in that early and mid-life violence and abuse can have direct impact on health, well-being, and quality of life in the mid-to-later life years. Stallings et al. (1997) elaborates a theory of well-being involving life-events and psychological well-being (see also Turner, 1996). For example, Bengtsson and Lindstrom (2000) demonstrate that childhood misery can have significant effects on mortality in old age. Dressler and Bindon (1997) examine the effects of social status, social context, on arterial blood pressure, finding a direct link between blood pressure and the other two variables. Kraaij, Arensman, and Spinhoven (2002) demonstrate a profound relationship between negative life events and depression in elderly persons. Kubzansky, Berkman, and Seeman (2000) illustrate a significant relationship between social conditions and stress in elderly persons. Pinquart and Sorenson (2000) demonstrate that there is a significant relationship between socio-economic status, social network, and competence on subjective well-being in later life, while Rautio, Heikkinen, and Heikkinen (2001) further strengthen the understanding by demonstrating a significant relationship between socio-economic factors and physical and mental capacity in elderly men and women. Turrell et al. (2002) demonstrate the effects of socioeconomic position across the life course and its effect on cognitive function in late middle age. Based upon the data presented in the previous sections, it is not difficult to posit that the trans and intersex populations are at a significant disadvantage when it comes to biomedical and psycho-socio-cultural well-being given the degree of difficulties that they face.

Yet, despite the magnitude of problems, many trans and intersex individuals not only cope, they survive and are successful. No work has been done on the coping strategies, the resilience, and spirituality/religiosity of these communities and how they positively affect the outcome of the trans/intersex lifecycle. For example, as Barusch (1997) posits, could mid-to-late life members of these two communities recast their viewpoint to see themselves as "not old and poor" but "fortunate and blessed?" While there is research performed on life-cycle aspects of poverty among older women (Choudhury & Leonescio, 1997; Clark et al., 1996), and while there is some understanding of the older Lesbian condition (Ayala & Coleman, 2000; Butler & Hope, 1999; Fulmer, Shenk, & Eastland, 1999; Grant, 2001; Kaminski, 2000; Kehoe, 1989), little is understood about how this literature can–if at all–impact our knowledge of the transgender/transsexual/intersex woman in her life cycle. One could, for example, hypothesize that social control and definition of sex and marriage (Littleton vs. Prange, 2000; Hull, 2001) as well as other gender/sex/body type roles (see the previous discussion on embodiment and right mind/right body vs. right mind/wrong body, Cassell, 1997) could easily lead to confusion and conflict for transgender/transsexual and intersex persons in their daily life course. Such confusion could, as Krause and Shaw (2000) postulate, lead to problems with role-specificity and feelings of control that, they demonstrate, can have a significant affect on mortality.

Questions of resilience, coping strategy, spirituality, and religiosity bring to the fore questions of social network support, peer-relationships, support groups, network structures, and friendship circles. Little work has been done in these areas either. While it is clear that these two communities are epidemiologically difficult to sample in a meaningful way (either cross-sectionally or longitudinally), it is critical that we begin to understand the intersex and trans-communities from these perspectives as well. Such information can not only inform us as to how we might strengthen the abilities of those who are unable to cope or are having a hard time coping, but perhaps the results of such a study could be of wider use, as techniques derived from new knowledge could inform the Geriatric and Gerontological communities as a whole.

Finally, it is important to understand how the "normative" life course biomedical changes of the human body, as mediated by cross-hormonal/surgical intervention, plastic surgery, and "atypical" chromosomes/metabolism, can affect long-term quality of life and life cycle passage. In the transgender community, little is known about long-term mortality/morbidity rates (Assherman,

Gooren, & Eklund, 1989). Christmas et al. (2002) point out that growth hormone and sex steroid effects bone metabolism and bone mineral density in healthy aged women and men. There is no research on the cross-hormonal effects on bone in trans-persons, nor is there any research on atypical metabolic effects on bone in intersex individuals. Anecdotal evidence in the transgender community among male-to-female transsexuals indicates that there well may be loss of height and bone mass. However, there is no formal research in this area. Financial aspects of the trans-person's/intersex person's life also can play a part in lifespan development (Vitt & Siegenthaler, 1996). Out-of-pocket healthcare costs also have an effect on medical treatment and hence on numerous mid-to-late stage life course factors. With these basic concepts in mind, I would now like to focus on the issues surrounding growing older in the transgender and intersex population.

Mid-to-Late Life Issues: The Field Study

It is hard to undo the Gordian knot of emergent themes. Nor should we necessarily attempt to do so, as it is this very reductionist approach to understanding human nature (sex, gender, sexuality) that imposes an historic lens of the type we discussed earlier in this paper. Denying complexity and interaction is to deny the very nature of the transgender/intersex lifecycle experience. Moreover, it is this very complexity that differentiates the trans/intersex trajectory from the normative dynamics discussed in Carter and McGoldrick.

Financial stability implied greater access to healthcare. Strong social circles implied less worry about "*who would take care of me if something were to happen?*" They also implied an ongoing degree of independence. As Nancy Nystrom of Michigan State University's Lesbian Aging Project points out,

> Midlife Lesbians begin to worry about getting older. In particular, they worry about three things. First, can they keep their housing? Will they be able to maintain the housing that they have? This implies second, keeping their independence. Will they be able to take care of themselves? And this implies third, a certain quality of health. However, independence is the key and it is maintained through health and housing. Notice that it is not about money, about finances. And, while partnering is important, it is on the side.

Finances make health and independence more possible. Certainly, meeting someone with whom to partner was critical, not just in diminishing worry about healthcare-related issues, but also in diminishing social isolation as well.

Istvan is worried about "*. . . meeting the right person. As you get older, you worry about what will happen to you if something bad were to happen in your life.*"

Carl, Kristin, and Marissa echoed this sentiment as well. Beyond the worry of having a partner to advocate for you if you are ill, hospitalized, or incapacitated, is the well-established Gerontological knowledgebase supporting the fact that social support has a major impact on long-term quality of life. Social isolation can have a strong negative impact on morbidity and mortality. Moreover, even if someone in midlife is fortunate to find a partner, there is still a fear of loss due to lack of rights. Fear of loss due to lack of rights was also frequently mentioned. Istvan did not hesitate to point out his fear of "*family members challenging (his) partnership, if his partner were to become severely ill, disabled, or to die.*" Carl states that, "*I have a great fear of being wiped out by biological family, even though my partner and I have sewed everything up with legal documents. They (the biological family) could just back a truck up to the house and empty it. And that scares me to death.*"

In and of itself, this statement informs us of a complex interweaving of midlife issues. The gravity of Carl's statement is magnified further by the continuing comment that "*. . . to solve this problem, I maintain two houses, in case I will need to go somewhere.*"

Paula, Noreen, Tracy, and Lance all echoed similar sentiments thereby indicating that this is an important midlife theme and not an isolated incident.

Partnership also brings with it interpersonal issues and worries. Judy Bradford, Director of the Survey Research Laboratory at VCU and head of the Lesbian Health Project points out that

> Intimacy issues among Lesbians at midlife are in every midlife lesbian's mind. 'Lesbian bed death' is a great fear. How does one transition from a hot sexual relationship with a companionship component, to a relationship that is based solely upon friendship? How do you handle a lesbian couple who are both menopausal and what is the sexual response about?

Judy Bradford's research has demonstrated that independence and social support are critical issues that have been seen in her study as well.

> Social support in the sense of community in which they don't have to return to the closet (so that they don't have to become sexless and genderless), where there are open, joyous places to maintain their ability to be a Lesbian is paramount in midlife Lesbian worry.

The idea of social isolation, not just in terms of partnership, but also in terms of community, cannot be overemphasized in its importance. Community is seen as a complex interaction of friendship circles, social support networks, and a more generalized "*ecological*" community. For the transgendered, the lack of social interaction is frequently found to be one of the greatest sources of difficulty. Marissa was forbidden to see her brother, when she finally outed herself to her parents. Janice and Lance further emphasized the importance of a sense of community and a need to have peers. Most transgendered people have a personal story about loss of a wife, of children, of parents, or of all of them, or they know a transgendered person who has suffered such a loss. Support groups are few and far between. Lack of trans community in most geographic areas means a dearth of social supports. This is particularly true in most countries outside of the United States. Consequently, a large number of transgendered individuals use the web chat rooms as a place in which to derive a sense of community, kinship, friendship, and social support. Despite some trans-people finding support online, many do not because of race, class, age, and gender barriers. However, social isolation is not limited to the transgender community. Istvan's experience is worthy to note.

> Loss of friends to death or to moving away from the area is gut-wrenching. It represents a loss of safety and companionship as well as diminishing the chances to find a partner. It is like being in a closet with the walls closing in.

For the intersex population, which has an approximate prevalence of 1/2000 births worldwide, many adults have a hard time finding anyone who knows about intersex or who is willing to talk about it.

This is not to say that financial issues were not important. However, financial issues were almost inseparable from health and independence issues. Noreen states, "*I am lucky, I have my healthcare benefits through the VA. It isn't great, but at least I have them.*" However, everyone around the table was worried about what would happen if their healthcare coverage were lost (most transgenders, who have healthcare coverage, have it through their work) for some reason. Moreover, finances were also intimately tied to life decisions. Noreen stated, "*I will have to worry about making a decision. Do I save for surgery or for retirement?*"

Rebecca heartily agreed. Noreen is also worried about "*how to pay for the house when I retire and how will I handle paying for healthcare?*" It is particularly crucial to understand that nearly all transgender related healthcare costs are not covered by healthcare insurance of any kind. Hence, transgender related medical expenses are out of pocket expenses. If we take the monthly hormonal costs and add them to the costs of pharmaceuticals typically associated with the ongoing mid to later life aging processes, these costs can have a great impact on the fixed income of older transgenders. It is also important to realize that, within the trans-population, different sub-populations will have different healthcare related problems. For example, female-to-male transsexuals who have had mastectomy will always have the problem of secrecy within the healthcare system. *"Either his chest scars are obvious, or his genitals give him away. Thus, accessing normatively sexed and gendered healthcare services is nearly impossible,"* points out Barry. Barry continues

> Add to this the difficulty of FTMs who have taken only hormones but could not afford or do not want surgeries. Billy Tipton comes to mind as one who never accessed healthcare in his lifetime, and probably died prematurely because of it. There are scads of FTMs who suffer in isolation because they refuse to subject themselves to medical scrutiny, possible mistreatment, and ridicule. Also, there is Robert Eads who recently died of medical neglect, after seeking help from at least 20 doctors who refused to treat him for ovarian cancer.

Witten, Eyler, and Weigel (1999) discuss issues of elder care for the transgenders, transsexuals, and cross-dressers. Related health cost issues face intersex individuals. For example, Cheryl Chase, former Executive Director of the Intersex Society of North America (ISNA, 2002), points out that the expense of treating osteoporosis in agonadal intersexed individuals can be frequently problematic. Moreover, Judy Bradford points out that, *"for lesbians, even ones with substantial incomes, there is a fear of ending up in a place where there are no gays, especially once you spend down your resources to be able to enter a nursing home facility."* For transgenders, this problem is magnified, not just in the lack of appropriate care facilities, but also in the lack of medical knowledge currently available on how to manage mid to late life healthcare issues in the transgendered population. For the cross-dressing population, Lance points out that the issues may not be quite as medically dire. Lance points out that being a cross-dresser is like walking the line between hetero and transgendered. *"As long as I live as a 'het,' I'm okay."*

Lance is not worried about retirement. For the intersexed population, midlife is a time when they are coming out and coming to grips with what has happened to them. *"The surgery designed to 'fix their genitals' almost always creates shame (surgery is used to hide intersex bodies), damage to sexual function and feelings of betrayal by trusted adults,"* says Chase. Chase goes on to say that, *"In fact, the people we have spoken with experience early genital surgery as mutilation."* These problems must be treated and there are few therapists willing to deal with the intersex population or who even know how to handle their problems.

However, for the cross-dressers, secrecy may be a big issue. The impact on the marital status, on the family and on the social ecology of the cross-dresser could be profound. Secrecy is also a critical issue for the intersexed population. Chase tells the following story:

> A college student visited the university clinic for back pain problems. When the doctor discovered that she had been treated for the intersex condition he wrote, in capital letters on her chart, 'Ambiguous Genitalia.' The student stopped attending the clinic because of the reasonable expectation that she would be treated as a freak.

Chase continues with the statement *"Such treatment is frequent, not an uncommon story. It makes you feel like a freak and it keeps you away from medical care."*

While secrecy affects all who have non-normative bodies they cannot hide, like transsexual and intersex people, secrecy was, in one form or another and to one degree or another, an important issue to all of the discussants. Secrecy for the purposes of marital stability, for the purposes of receiving appropriate healthcare, for job security, and hence financial stability were all-critical to the lives of all who sat around the table. Transgenders have no legal recourse against discrimination, nor are they included in hate crimes legislation. Emergent from these themes is the little addressed issue of the mid-life issues [concerns] of the significant others (SOFFAs), the partners (Cooke-Daniels, 1995), the spouses, and the children in LGBTI families. The interplay of aging and non-traditional sexualities, coupled with non-traditional family structures can have a great impact on the social ecology of a relationship.

Intergenerational issues were also a priority around the dinner table. Nearly everyone had one or more elder parents/relatives about whom they were worried. For some, showing up as the "new" self could create problems for the other family members as well as for themselves. Rebecca asked, *"What happens at a funeral? Everyone knows they had a son. How do I show up and explain myself? How do we handle the life crisis issues?"* Marissa's brother has a brain tumor. *"My parents have forbidden me to come home. They will not let me talk to him. I can't go to see him. I can't go to the funeral. How am I supposed to handle this?"* Lance's parents don't even know about Lance. The resultant crisis, should they ever find out, was clearly a very disturbing prospect to Lance.

It was a somber table when the discussion finally closed. We had started in the sunlight and ended in darkness. I asked for last thoughts. Kristin said, *"LGBT people are in denial about aging, their own mortality."* Heads nodded in assent. Tracy added, *"LGBT immortality syndrome?"* More heads nodded in agreement. However, perhaps Paula made the most telling statement of all:

"Just because you don't open the mail doesn't mean you don't owe the bills. You need to pay towards your future in installments."

DISCUSSION

From a macro-sociological perspective, it is well documented that "health" is intimately tied to position in the power hierarchy. That is, top people live longer than bottom people. Marmot's (1986) now well-known Whitehall study of more than 10,000 British civil servants over a two decade period serves to document this fact by pointing out that there "was an obvious 'gradient' in mortality from top to bottom" of the study hierarchy (Evans et al., 1994; Marmot, Kogevinas, & Elson, 1987). Hertzman (2001) further elaborates upon this phenomenon by stating that, " . . . examples show that major shifts in the health status of whole populations over time do not necessarily depend upon the implementation of public health or medical control measures against specific diseases." They point, instead, to "a profound linkage between health and the social environment including levels and distribution of prosperity in a society." Hence, social environment as mediated by position in the power hierarchy profoundly affects health status.

Tightly integrated with this status in the hierarchy or "socio-ecological embedding" is the "critical role of early experience in influencing health and well-being over the course of the life cycle (ibid.)." Our research, and the research of others, has demonstrated that the transgender and intersex community have a socio-ecological environment that carries with it implicit issues surrounding violence and abuse. These issues are not only historic for a given individual, but must also be dealt with on a day-to-day basis. We have demonstrated that the impact of psychosocial, biomedical, temporal-cultural issues all have an impact on the life course of a transgender and/or intersex individual and that these factors impact the generative processes of aging as a human being.

The impact of our previous discussion is not localized only to the current cohort of transgender and intersex persons. It extends into the future generations to come. For example, in 1999, in the United States, the size of the age 65 years and older population was 34.7 million individuals. This sub-population represents approximately 13% of the total population of the United States. There were 4.2 million people who were over age 85 years. The age 65 years and older population is projected to reach over 70 million individuals over the next three decades. Centenarians, individuals 100 years old or more, represent a special component of the aging population. They are the fastest growing segment of the aging population, the second fastest being the 85-plus-year-old population segment. For centenarians, the current estimate is 50,000-75,000 individuals. This group is expected to reach 834,000 by the year 2050. Moreover, 90% of the centenarians are women and 10% are men. This prevalence rate is approximately the same or a little higher than that of other industrialized countries. Based upon estimates of the demographics of the U.S. population as a whole and of the demographics of the transgender and intersex populations, it is possible to construct a reasonable demographic of the aging transgender and intersex populations. Back of the envelope calculations demonstrates that the numbers of potentially older transgender and intersex persons is not negligible (Witten, 2002b). Furthermore, if we allow for the more broad interpretation of transgender as including cross-dressing, non-surgical, gender queer, and non-Western gender, then these estimates would increase substantially. Additionally, it is important to recognize that issues associated with transgender and intersex persons must, by their very nature, include the numerous lives that these people touch such as former partners, parents, children, current partners, friends, employers and employees, as well as random individuals on the street. Thus, the issues that remain unresolved in the mid-life will be carried forward into the late life, further confounding the developmental, biomedical, and socio-cultural issues of that later stage.

These life cycle stages are further confounded by all of the standard demographic and socio-economic variables such as socio-economic status and race. A recent study (Battle, Cohen, Warren et al., 2002), just released–through the NGLTF–gives one of the first and largest glimpses into a national, multi-city sample of Black gay, lesbian, bisexual, and transgender people. The study examines family structure, sexual identity, political behavior, experiences of racism and homophobic bias, and the policy priorities of more than 2,500 Black GLBT people that attended Black Gay Pride celebrations in nine cities during the summer of 2000. Support for racial differences can also be seen by examining the data of the WTNAS. Results from the Washington Transgender Needs Assessment Study (2000) document significantly lower educational levels, 42% unemployment, and significantly lower income earning levels (48% of the WTNAS respondents state that they could not afford care, 29.6% state that they have either no insurance or insurance that does not cover the transgender healthcare related needs). Additionally, in the WTNAS study, 37% of those employed worked as service industry workers, 14.5% as private sector office workers, 5.5% as sex industry workers, and the rest in other categories, with only 9% working as private sector professionals. Clearly, the type of employment will have significant impact on the later life issues, not only of regular aging, but of transgender related aging as well.

For those who are elders on a fixed income, transgender medicines and interventions can be problematic at best, as they are not covered under Medicare

(Cahill & Jones, 2001). Additionally, current estimates (Crystal et al., 2000) show that expenditures averaged 19.0% of income, for full-year Medicare beneficiaries alive during all of 1995. Higher burden subgroups, included those in poor health (28.5% of income), older than age 85 (22.4%), and with income in the lowest quintile (31.5%). Financial breakdowns for the TLARS show that, for female-to-male transsexuals (n = 32 in the first wave of the study), the bulk of the respondents made less than $30,000/year with a significant amount making less than $20,000/year. Note that this inequity is true despite the fact that the population is not under educated. The overall study population is similarly educated and more well off due to the preponderance of executive males in the population.

The fact that Wave 1 of the TLARS study is a best-case scenario is again born out by the results of the WTNAS study showing that only 6% of the WTNAS respondents had college degrees and another 6% had graduate or professional degrees. Results of the WTNAS study are similar to the TLARS female-to-male transgender component. However, the WTNAS reports additional critical information in that 19% of all of the WTNAS participants reported that they had been evicted during their lifetimes, and 64% stated that they were evicted for non-payment of rent.

To put the impact of the additional medical (pharmaceutical) treatment into perspective, the post-operative male-to-female transsexual is typically taking at least one gender-related medication. Typically, this medication is not covered under insurance. The average charge for this hormonal medication can range from between $40 and $100/month. Given the already meager fixed income available to a large portion of the transgender population, this additional medical burden can be oppressive. Pre-operative or peri-operative transgenders are typically taking upwards of two prescriptions per month, increasing their fiscal burden proportionally more. In addition to the medication charges, there are additional gender-related medical charges including psychological evaluations, ongoing physiological tests for liver damage or other hormonally mediated damage, medical intervention due to unexpected medical interactions of hormones with other age-related medications, interactions with current HIV/AIDS medications, and other unforeseen medical complications. It is of particular importance to note that the portion of the population of age greater than fifty years old is the fastest growing portion of the population with respect to incurring AIDS/HIV. Given that HIV/AIDS is a growing problem (Bockting, Rosser, & Coleman, 1999) in the transgender population (more so in the sex industry workers at this time), given the increasing success of drug cocktails that prolong the lives of HIV/AIDS victims, it is not unreasonable to assume that the transgender population will have a growing number of individuals who are on age-related prescriptions such as high blood pressure medicines, cardiac related medicines and/or pulmonary medicines, simultaneously on hormones, and in need of HIV/AIDS drugs all at the same time. Moreover, given the demonstrated preponderance of the lack of medical coverage in both the WTNAS and TLARS surveys, given the large proportions of the population with marginal to no income, and given the stigma associated with being transgendered–as seen by the data on violence, abuse, and hate crimes presented earlier–it is not unreasonable to project (based upon the cited research references with respect to social support networks, socio-economic status, etc.) that the long-term quality of life and the success at meeting the HP2010 goals will be marginal to non-existent given the current federal policies with respect to the transgender population in general and the elders of that population in particular.

This combination of socio-economic factors negatively impacts all facets of the transgender population's daily lives. It is clear that there is increased stress due to violence/abuse, fiscal impoverishment, healthcare delivery stress, lack of insurance stress, and stigma associated with self-identifying with the transgender population. The scientific literature in Gerontology and Geriatrics has repeatedly demonstrated that these factors have a significant negative impact on health, quality of life, functional capacity, mental status, etc. Low-income levels lead to inability to purchase necessary hormones, increasing the likelihood of illegal hormone purchase and use of dirty needles that can lead to HIV/AIDS. Concomitant low-income levels lead to poor housing and subsequent increased risk for substance abuse, depression, suicidal behavior patterns, and risky sexual behaviors such as participating in sex industry work. Moreover, the stigma of transgender makes access to assisted living and nursing home facilities beyond the reach of many and is certainly a fearful situation for most. This further diminishes the potential elder care facilities available to the aged of the transgender population. Little is known about elders in the intersex community. It is not unreasonable to argue that there will be both significant similarities and differences between the two communities. However, there is no reason to doubt that unresolved issues in an intersex person are also carried forward in time and will need to be dealt with in the later years.

CONCLUSION

In this paper we have presented a study of the mid-life issues of the transgender and intersex communities using the socio-ecological grounding of violence and abuse across the lifespan as a framework within which the transgender/intersex person must not only navigate, but also eventually emerge. Using the sociological argument of lifespan health effects as mediated by power inequality in the socioeconomic/political hierarchy of society, coupled with the inherent violence and abuse suffered by the transgender/intersex community, we have demonstrated that these populations are at risk for significant problems, in a variety of areas; risks that may well exceed those of the "normative" control populations. Within this framework, we have examined the similarities and differences between the transgender/intersex countersystem and the "normative" population aging dynamics. Based upon the results of both quantitative data and qualitative field interviews, we have illustrated the validity of the countersystem and demonstrated how examining that system allows us to develop a richer understanding of the complexities of middle and later life-cycle dynamics. We have seen how the stigma and social isolation of being trans- and/or intersex identified leads to significant social isolation and that this isolation, coupled with the generative processes of aging, the concomitant risks associated with the transgender/intersex lifestyle, and the fiscal insecurity associated with these lifestyles are profound covariates with respect to what would be expected life cycle issues for a normative control individual. We have briefly addressed the little information available on cross-cultural factors in mid-life cycle processes by examining the results of the TLARS study (Caucasian, upper SES) and of the WTNAS study (Black, lower SES) and demonstrated that the TLARS study provides an upper bound for how good things can get, thereby allowing us to postulate that things are at least that bad or worse in other populations. There are little to no data on international populations, with respect to mid-to-late life aging issues in the transgender and intersex communities (Witten et al., 2003). This author's anecdotal experience with these communities in Europe and Asia supports the conjecture that things are significantly worse, for the most part in most countries, when compared to the United States. This is particularly true in Thailand and the Philippines where most transpersons are street sex industry workers and there is a high incidence and prevalence of HIV/AIDS.

Launching phases may be disrupted by children who, having to deal with the parent's identity change, cut communications with that parent or the family as a whole, thereby isolating the parent from the future interaction with the child, future potential for needed family support from that child during late mid-life to late-life transformation, and decreased social support network through familial isolation, not only of the child but of the potential grandchildren as well. Married couples, in which one of the pair identifies and transitions to transgendered, now must deal with not just the task of becoming a couple again, but redefining what–if any–the relationship will be. Thus, the whole construct of the family must now be redefined (Boenke, 1999), not just the normative relationships between the members. What does it mean for the former "Dad" to now be female and how does the adult child create an adult relationship with the person who is now "Dad and yet not Dad?"

The dynamics of marriage of the children, new relationships for the transgendered parent and the non-transgendered parent are now altered. The person who once was "Dad" and is now female, or the person who once was "Mom" and is now male, may choose to re-partner with a partner of the same or opposite sex, thereby creating a new sexuality with which the adult child must now deal. Confounding this new development are the issues of explaining the changes to potential grandchildren who may or may not be old enough to comprehend the changes or care about them. Marriage of the adult child now is no longer about getting the parents to accept the new partner, it is now also about helping the partner to deal with coming into a family in which a "parent-in-law" is now a transgendered person.

For intersex persons, family may well be yet another non-normative structure. Children might be adopted. They might find out about their parent as a result of having to deal with the hospitalization of that parent or gender identity confusion that leads to transgender on the part of the intersex parent. The intersex adult may well be dealing with issues arising from surgical sexing that was undesired and that may have had a profound effect on the intersex person's life history. Thus, the intersex child is also potentially dealing with the conflict between the morality of taking care of the elder parent and dealing with the anger towards that parent or parents for having the intersexed child surgically sexed.

Mortality issues are also confounded by transgender and intersex issues. Both transgender and intersex individuals are now, at this time of their life, dealing with elderly parents who may or may not be accepting of changes, who may or may not have been accepting of past changes, and who may now need help from the transgender or intersex child either on an infrequent or chronic basis. Clearly, unresolved issues can create conflict between the expected morality of taking care of the parent and the hurt and anger/hatred of the child for lack of love, acceptance, support, and even disinheritance. Additional complications can include the parent's demand for help and concomitant refusal to allow the child to appear before the parent in the child's new identity. Death of a parent can remove all chances of the adult child's receiving acceptance, acknowledgement, or of being able to resolve issues associated with not just normative life issues, but issues related to being transgender and/or intersex identified.

Individuals who transition in mid-to-late life are placing themselves at financial and social risk, as we have seen in the previous qualitative examples.

Such a risk can impact a family in which the primary wage earner, who might also be transgender or intersex identified, is now outed and loses his/her (zee's) job as a consequence of that outing (whether voluntary or not). Hence, the previous family structure is now destabilized, not just through the actual issues of transgender/intersex, but through the subsequent loss of financial support and perhaps the social isolation as well. It is particularly important to take note that, during the launching phase, there is an increase in spirituality and religiosity (Jones, 1996) of the mid-life parent. Many of these transgender and intersex individuals now, because they are "out," no longer have access to the traditional spiritual dwellings of their past lives as most traditional religions and spiritualities see non-normative sex, gender, and sexualities as not only unacceptable, but a sin. One study participant told this author that she (male-to-female, postoperative transsexual, 33 years old, Caucasian) wanted to attend her former Baptist Church. She was told that the only way that she could be a member of the parish was if she realized that she had (a) sinned and if she (b) promised to remain celibate. Thus, the transgender/intersex person is frequently isolated from family, friends, job, and spiritual support network.

Transgender and intersex persons must go through a great deal to survive. Those that manage to live long lives as transgendered or intersexed persons must have developed coping and survival strategies that were highly effective in the face of all that is against them. Understanding these coping and survival strategies can potentially benefit the normative population, particularly if these strategies can be extended to any individual in the mid-to-later stages of the life cycle. Understanding how members of the community manage to live fulfilling lives can also help us to better understand the abilities of the human being to deal with complex difficult situations and to resolve them in a fashion that can allow the person to not just simply survive, but to also have a satisfactory quality of life.

NOTES

1. All names have been changed and all individuals have had a chance to read their descriptions and commentary and to approve their anonymity or to alter details so that they feel comfortable with the description. No ages or sex/gender/sexuality descriptions are altered.

2. We say that intersex is body oriented as it is currently determined to be a genetic disorder. This is not to say that there are no psychological issues associated with the intersex conditions. Similarly, it may be that transgender will be found to have a strong genetic component. However, currently it is considered of the mind.

3. A recent Finnish study has demonstrated that the distribution of psychological disorders among a small cohort of pre/post-operative transsexuals is no different than that from a random selection of the population (as based upon MMPI responses).

While this is a small study and needs to be replicated, it clearly points to the fact that GID is not a disorder that should be "stigmatized."

REFERENCES

Adelman, M. (1987). *Long Time Passing: Lives of Older Lesbians.* Boston, MA: Alyson Publishing.

Ahmed, S.M. (1999). Reaching out to the underserved: A collaborative partnership to provide healthcare, *J. Health Care for the Poor and Underserved*, 10(2): 157-168.

American Psychiatric Association (2000). *Diagnostic and Statistical Manual of Mental Disorders 4th Edition-DSM IV-TR.* Washington, D.C.: American Psychiatric Association Press.

Aronow, W.S., Ahn, C., & Gutstein, H. (2002). Prevalence and incidence of cardiovascular disease in 1160 older men and 2464 older women in a healthcare facility. *J. Gerontology. Med. Sci.*, 57A(1): M45-M46.

Asscherman, H., Gooren, L.J.G., & Eklund, P.L.E. (1989). Mortality and morbidity in transsexual patients with cross-gender hormone treatment, *Metabolism.* 38(9): 869-873.

Ayala, J., & Coleman, H. (2000). Predictors of depression among Lesbian women. *J. Lesbian Studies*, 4(3): 71-86.

Barrett, A.E. (1999). Social support and life satisfaction among the never married. *Research on Aging*, 6: 46-72.

Barusch, A.S. (1997). Self-concepts of low-income older women: Not old or poor, but fortunate and blessed. *Int. J. Aging and Human Development*, 44(4): 269-292.

Bass, D.M., & Noelker, L.S. (1987). The influence of family caregivers on elders' use of in-home services: An expanded conceptual framework. *J. Health and Social Behavior*, 21: 184-196.

Basu, A.M. (2000). Gender in population research: Confusing implications for health policy. *Population Studies*, 54: 19-38.

Battle, J., Cohen, C.J., Warren, D., Fergerson, G., & Audam, S. (2002). *Say it loud: I'm black and I'm proud.* New York, N.Y.: NGLTF Press. [Available at *http://www.ngltf.org*].

Bear, M. (1989). Network variables on determinants of the elderly entering adult residential care facilities. *Aging and Society*, 9: 149-163.

Bengtsson, T., & Lindstrom, M. (2000). Childhood misery and disease in later life: The effects on mortality in old age of hazards experienced in early life, southern Sweden, 1760-1894. *Population Studies*, 54: 263-277.

Bernard, M., Phillips, J. Machlin, L., & Davies, V.H. (2000). *Women Ageing: Changing identities, changing myths.* London: Routledge.

Bockting, W.O., Rosser, S., Coleman, E. (1999). Transgender HIV prevention: Community involvement and empowerment. *Int. J. of Transgender*, 3(1+2): *http://symposion.com/ijt/hiv_risk/bockting.htm.*

Boenke, M. (Ed.) (1999). *Trans Forming families: Real stories about transgendered loved ones.* Imperial Beach, CA: Walter Trook Publishing, Co.

Bowles, S. (1995). A death robbed of dignity mobilizes a community. *Washington Post* (10 December), Metro Section. B01.

Brecher, E. (1984). *Love, sex, and aging.* Boston: Little-Brown.

Butler, S.S., & Hope, B. (1999). Health and well-being for late middle-aged and old lesbians in a rural area. *J. Gay and Lesbian Social Services*, 9(4): 27-46.

Cahill, S., & Jones, K.T. (2001). *Leaving our children behind: Welfare reform and the LGBT community*. Washington, D.C.: NGLTF [Available at *http://www.ngltf.org*].

Cahill, S., South, K., & Spade, J. (2000). *Outing Aging: Report of the NGLTF Task Force on Aging*. Washington, D.C.: NGLTF. [Available at *http://www.ngltf.org*].

Carter, B., & McGoldrick, M. (Eds.). (1999). *The expanded family life cycle: Individual, family and social perspectives*. Needham Heights, MA: Allyn & Bacon.

Cassell, J. (1998). *The Surgeon in the Woman's Body*. Cambridge, MA: Harvard University Press.

Choudhury, S., & Leonescio, M.V. (1997). Life-cycle aspects of poverty among older women. *Social Security Bulletin*. 60(2): 17-36.

Christmas, C., O'Connor, K.G., Harman, S.M. et al. (2002). Growth hormone and sex steroid effects on bone metabolism and bone mineral density in healthy aged women and men. *Journal of Gerontology: Medical Sciences*, 57A(1): M12-M18.

Clark, F., Carlson, M. et al. (1996). Life domains and adaptive strategies of a group of low-income, well older adults. *Amer. J. Occupational Therapy*, 50(2): 99-108.

Colton, H. (1983). *The Gift of Touch*. New York: Seaview and Putman.

Cook-Daniels, L. (1995). Lesbian, gay male, and transgender elder abuse. [Available at *http://www.amboyz.org/articles/elderabuse.html*].

Crystal, S. Johnson, R.W., Harman, J., Sambamoorthi, & Kumar, R. (2000). Out-of-pocket healthcare costs among older Americans. *J. Gerontology*. 55B(1): S51-S62.

Cucinotta, D., & Ravaglia, G. (1998). *Cognitive and Affective Disorders in the Elderly*. Amsterdam: Elsevier Science Ireland.

Currah, P., & Minter, S. (2000). *Transgender Equality*, NGLTF Policy Institute, N.Y.

Czikszentmihali, M. (1977). *Finding Flow*. New York, NY: Harper-Collins.

DeJong, G.F. (2000). Expectations, gender, and norms in migration decision-making. *Population Studies*, 54: 307-319.

Dempsey, C.L. (1994). Health and social issues of gay, lesbian, and bisexual adolescents. *Families in Society*, 75(3): 160-67.

Devor, H. Transsexualism, dissociation, and child abuse: An initial discussion based on non-clinical data, *J. Psych and Hum Sexuality*, 6 #3 (1994) 49-72.

Docter, R.F. (1985). Transsexual surgery at 74: A case report. *Arch. Sexual Behavior*, 14(3): 271-277.

Doyal, L. (2001). Sex, gender, and health: the need for a new approach. *British Medical Journal*, 323: 1061-1063.

Dressler, W.W., & Bindon, J.R. (1997). Social status, social context, and arterial blood pressure. *Amer. J. Physical Anthropology*, 102(1): 55-66.

Elkins, R., & King, D. (1996). (Eds.) *Blending Genders: Social Aspects of Cross-dressing and Sex-changing*. New York, N.Y.: Routledge.

Ettner, Randi. (1999). XVI International Meeting, Harry Benjamin International Gender Dysphoria Association. London, U.K., August 20, 1999.

Ettner, R. (1999). *Gender loving care: A guide to counseling gender-variant clients*. New York, N.Y.: W.W. Norton and Company.

Evans, R.G., Barer, M.L., & Marmor, T.R. (1994). (Eds.) *Why are some people health and others not? The determinants of health of populations.* Hawthorne, N.Y.: Aldine De Gruyter.

Everard. K.M., Lach, H.W., Fisher, E.B., & Baum, M.C. (2000). Relationship of activity and social support to the functional health of older adults, *J. Gerontol.,* 55B(4): S208-S212.

Fausto-Sterling, A. (2000). *Sexing the Body.* New York, N.Y.: Basic Books, Inc.

Feinberg, L. (1996). *Transgender Warriors.* Boston, MA: Beacon Press.

Fernandez, M.E. (1998). Death suite costs city $2.9 million; Mother of transgendered man wins case. *Washington Post* (12 December 1998), Metro Section, page C01.

Ferree, M.M., Lorber, J., & Hess, B.B. (Eds.). (1999). *Revisioning Gender.* Thousand Oaks, CA: Sage Publications.

Fox, N. (1994). *Postmodernism, sociology, and health.* Toronto, Canada: University of Toronto Press.

Fulmer, E.M. (1995). Challenging biases against families of older gays and lesbians. In *Strengthening Aging Families: Diversity in Practice and Policy* (Eds.) Smith, G.C., Tobin, S.S., Robertson-Tchabo, E.A., & Power, P.W. Thousand Oaks, CA: Sage Publications.

Fulmer, E.M., Shenk, D., & Eastland, L.J. (1999). Negating identity: A feminist analysis of the social invisibility of older lesbians. *J. Women and Aging,* 11(2/3): 131-148.

Gannon, L., Luchetta, T., Rhodes, K., Pardee, L., & Segrist, D. (1992). Sex bias in psychological research, *American Psychologist,* 47(3): 389-396.

GLMA. (2000). *Healthy People 2010: Companion Document for Lesbian, Gay, Bisexual, and Transgender (LGBT) Health.* U.S. San Francisco, CA. Gay and Lesbian Medical Association. [Available at *http://www.glma.org*].

Golant, S.M. (2002). Geographic inequalities in the availability of government-subsidized rental housing for low-income older persons in Florida. *The Gerontologist,* 42(1): 100-108.

Goodnow, C. (2000a). Task force is studying effects of cross-gender surgery on kids, 13 March 2000. *Seattle Post-Intelligencer.*

Goodnow, C. (2000b). A tragically maimed boy, raised as a girl, comes to terms with his identity, 13 March 2000, *Seattle Post-Intelligencer.*

Grant, A.M. (2001). Health of socially excluded groups: Lessons must be applied, *British Medical Journal,* 323, 1071.

Greenberg, Julie A. (1998). Defining male and female: Intersexuality and the collision between law and biology, *Arizona Law Review,* 41(2): 265-328.

Griffen, P. (1989). Gender roles in physical education, *CAPHPER Journal,* 55: 23-26.

Grossman, A.H., D'Augelli, A.R., & S.L. Hershberger. (2000). Social support networks of Lesbian, Gay, and Bisexual adults 60 years of age and older, *J. Gerontol.,* 55B(3): P171-P179.

Hagerty, B.K., Lynch-Sauer, J., Patusky, K., & Bouwsema, M. (1995). An emerging theory of human relatedness, *Image,* 25: 291-296.

Harding, S. (Ed.). (1987). *Feminism & Methodology.* Bloomington, IN: Indiana University Press.

Havey, A. (1997). *Gay mystics.* New York, N.Y.: HarperCollins Publishers.

Healthy People 2010. (2000). U.S. Government Printing Office, Superintendent of Documents, P.O. Box 371954, Pittsburgh, PA. [Available at *http://www.glma.org* or *http://www.health.gov/healthypeople/Document/tableofcontents.htm*].

Hertzman, C. (2001). Health and human society. *Scientific American*, 89 (6): *http://www.americanscientist.org/articles/01articles/Hertzman.html*.

Hopper, S.V. (1995). The influence of ethnicity on the health of older women. *Clinics in Geriatric Medicine*, 9(1): 231-259.

Hull, K.E. (2001). The political limits of the rights frame: The case of same-sex marriage in Hawaii. *Sociological Perspectives*, 44, pp. 207-232.

Hutchinson, E.D. (1992a). *Dimensions of human behavior: Person and environment.* Thousand Oaks, CA: Pine Forge.

Hutchinson, E.D. (1992b). *Dimensions of Human Behavior: The Changing Life Course.* Thousand Oaks, CA: Pine Forge.

Intersex Society of North America. (2002). *http://www.isna.org*.

Jacobs, S.E., & Cromwell, J. (1992). Visions and revisions of reality: Reflections on sex, sexuality, gender, and gender variance, *J. Homosex.*, 23: 43-69.

Jones, J.W. (1996). *In the middle of this road we call our life: The courage to search for something more.* San Francisco, CA: HarperSanFrancisco.

Kaminski, E. (2000). Lesbian health: Social context, sexual identity, and well-being, *J. Lesbian Studies*, 4(3): 87-101.

Kanuha, V. (1990). Compounding the triple jeopardy: Battering in lesbian of color relationships. Special issue: Diversity and complexity in feminist therapy: I, *Women and Therapy*, 9(1/2): 169-184.

Kehoe, M. (1989). *Lesbians over Sixty Speak for Themselves.* New York: The Haworth Press, Inc.

Keller, E.F., & Longino, H.E. (Eds.). (1996). *Feminism and Science.* Oxford, England: Oxford University Press.

Kirk, S., & Rothblatt, M. (1995). *Medical, Legal, and Workplace Issues for the Transsexual.* Watertown, MA: Together Lifeworks.

Kleinman, A., & Sung, L.H. (1979). Why do indigenous practitioners successfully heal? *Soc. Sci. & Med.* 13B: 7-26.

Kockott, G., & Fahrner, E.-M. (1988). Male-to-Female and Female-to-Male transsexuals: A comparison, *Arch. Sex. Behav.*, 17(6): 539-546.

Kraaij, V., Arensman, E., & Spinhoven, P. (2002). Negative life events and depression in elderly persons: A meta-analysis. *Journal of Gerontology: Psychological Sciences*, 57B(1): P87-P94.

Krause, N., & Shaw, B.A. (2000). Role-specific feelings of control and mortality, *Psychology and Aging*, 15(4): 617-626.

Kubzansky, L.D., Berkman, L.F., & Seeman, T.E. (2000). Social conditions and distress in elderly persons: Findings from the MacArthur studies of successful aging, *J. Gerontol.*, 55B(4): P238-P246.

Kurtz, M. Lesbian wedding allowed in Texas by gender loophole, *Seattle Post-Intelligencer*, 7 September 2000.

Laferrier, R.H., & Hamel-Bissell, B.P. (1994). Successful aging of oldest old women in the Northeast Kingdom of Vermont, Image: *The Journal of Nursing Scholarship*, 26(4): 319-323.

Lang, F.R., & Baltes, M.M. Being with people and being alone in late life: Costs and benefits for every day functioning.

Langevin, R. (1983). *Sexual Strands: Understanding and Treating Sexual Anomalies in Men*. Hillsdale, NJ: Lawrence Erlbaum Associates.

Lemay, P., Dauwalder, J.-P., Pomini, V., & Bersier, M. (1996). Quality of life: A dynamic perspective. In *Nonlinear Dynamics in Human Behavior*, Sulis, W. & Combs, A. (Eds.). Singapore: World Scientific Press.

Levin, J.S. (1994). (Ed.). *Religion in Aging and Health*. Thousand Oaks, CA: Sage Publications.

Levin, J.S. (2001). (Ed.). *Religion in Aging and Health*. Thousand Oaks, CA: Sage Publications.

Liebig, P.S. (1996). Area agencies on aging and the National Affordable Housing Act: Opportunities and challenges, *J. Appl. Gerontol.*, 15(4): 486-500.

Littleton & Prange. (2000) LITTLETON v. PRANGE, San Antonio Court of Appeals, San Antonio, TX 2000 (definition of sex for the purposes of marriage).

Litwin, H. (2001). Social network type and morale in old age. *The Gerontologist*, 41(4): 516-524.

Litwin, H., & Landow, R. (2000). Social network type and social support among the old-old. *Journal of Aging Studies*, 14: 213-228.

Logan, J.R., & Spitze, G. (1994). Informal support and the use of formal services by older Americans. *J. Gerontol. Soc. Sci.*, 49: S29-S34.

Lombardi, E.L., Wilchins, R.A., Priestling, D., & Malouf, D. (2001). Gender violence: Transgender experiences with violence and discrimination. *J. Homosexuality*, 42(1): 89-101.

Lundh, U., & Nolan, M. (1996). Aging and quality of life 2: Understanding successful aging, *Brit. J. Nursing*, 5(21): 1291-1295.

Lyng, S. (2000). Class lecture notes in Medical Sociology, Virginia Commonwealth University, Richmond, VA.

Magai, C., & McFadden, S.H. (1996). *Handbook of Emotion, Adult Development, and Aging*. San Diego, CA: Academic Press.

Mager, A.K. (1999). *Gender and the Making of a South African Bantustan*. Portsmouth, N.H.: Heinemann.

Manton, K.G., Singer, B.H., & Suzman, R.M. (1993). *Forecasting the Health of Elderly Populations*. New York, NY: Springer-Verlag.

Marmot, M., Smith, G., Stansfeld, S., Patel, C., North, J., White, L., Brunner, E., & Feeney, A. (1991). Health inequalities among British civil servants: The Whitehall II Study. *The Lancet*, 377: 1387-1393.

Martin, A.D., & Hetrick, E.S. (1988). The stigmatization of the gay and lesbian adolescent. *J.Homosexuality*, 15(1-2): 163-83.

Mathieson, K.M., Kronenfeld, J.J., & Keith, V.M. (2002). Maintaining functional independence in elderly adults: The roles of health status and financial resources in predicting home modifications and use of mobility equipment. *The Gerontologist*, 42(1): 24-31.

Morley, J.E. (2002). Drugs, aging, and the future. *J. Gerontol.*, 57A(1): M2-M6.

Newman, P. et al. (1999). Understanding the diverse needs of the Medicare population: Implications for Medicare reform, *J. Aging and Social Policy*, 10(4): 25-50.

Pesquera, A. (1999). Court to decide what's changed in sex operations. *San Antonio Express News*, September 3, 1999.

Pinquart, M., & Sorenson, S. (2000). Influences of socio-economic status, social network, and competence on subjective well-being in later life: A meta-analysis. *Psychology and Aging*, 14(2): 187-224.

Posner, J.D., McCully, K.K. et al. (1995). Physical determinants of independence in mature women, 76(4): 373-380.

Pryzgoda, J., & Chrisler, J.C. (2000). Definitions of gender and sex: The subtleties of meaning. *Sex Roles*, 43(7/8): 553-569.

Rautio, N., Heikkinen, E., & Heikkinen, R-L. (2001). The association of socio-economic factors with physical and mental capacity in elderly men and women. *Arch. Gerontol. and Geriatrics*, 33: 163-178.

Reker, G.T., & Chamberlain, K. (Eds.). (2000). *Exploring existential meaning: Optimizing human development across the lifespan*. Thousand Oaks, CA: Sage Publications.

Ritzer, G. (1992). *Sociological Theory*. New York: McGraw-Hill.

Rivera, J. (1994). Domestic violence against Latinas by Latino males: An analysis of race, national origin, and gender differentials, *Boston Coll. Third World Law J.*, 14: 231-57.

Robbins, S.P., Chatterjee, P., & Canda, E.R. (1998). *Contemporary Human Behavior Theory: A Cultural Perspective for Social Work*. Boston: Allyn and Bacon.

Roberts, J., Snyder, D.L., & Friedman, E. (Eds.), (1996). H*andbook of Pharmacology of Aging*, 2nd Edition, Boca Raton, FL: CRC Press.

Robinson, K. (2000). Older Americans 2000: Key indicators of well-being. Hyattsville, MD: Federal Interagency Forum on Aging-Related Statistics. [Available from *http://www.agingstats.gov*].

Rowe, J.R., & Kahn, R.L. (1997). Successful aging. *The Gerontologist*, 37(4): 433-440.

Russell, S.T., Franz, B.T., & Driscoll, A.K. (2001). Same-sex romantic attraction and experiences of violence in adolescence. *American Journal of Public Health: Lesbian, Gay, Bisexual, and Transgender Health*, 91(6): 903-906.

Sands, R.G. (2001). *Clinical Social Work Practice in Behavioral Mental Health: A Postmodern Approach to Practice with Adults*. Needham Heights, MA: Allyn and Bacon.

Satterfeld, S.B. (1988). Transsexualism. Special Issue: The sexually unusual: Guide to understanding and help. *J. Soc Work and Hum Sexuality*, 7(1): 77-87.

Schulz, R., & Heckhausen, J. (1996). A lifespan model of successful aging, *Amer. Psychologist*, 51(7): 702-714.

Slusher, M.P., Mayer, C.J., & Dunkle, R.E. (1996). Gays and Lesbians Older and Wiser (GLOW): A support group for older gay people, *The Gerontologist*, 36 (1): 118-123.

Smith, J.H., & Mahout, A.M. (Eds.). (1994). *Psychoanalysis, Feminism, and the Future of Gender*. Baltimore, MD: Johns Hopkins University Press.

Sobsey, D. (1994). *Violence and Abuse In the Lives of People with Disabilities: The End of Silent Acceptance?* Baltimore, MD: P.H. Brookes.

Solarz, A.L. (Ed.). (1999). *Lesbian Health: Current Assessment and Directions for the Future*. Washington, D.C.: National Academy Press.

Spradley, J., & McCurdy, D.W. (2000). *Conformity and conflict: Readings in cultural anthropology*. Needham Heights, MA: Allyn and Bacon.

Stallings, M.C., Dunham, C.C., Gatz, M., Baker, L.A., & Bengston, V.L. (1997). Relationships among life events and psychological well-being: More evidence for a two-factor theory of well-being, *J. Appl. Gerontol.*, 16(1): 104-119.

Strawbridge, W.J., Cohen, R.D., Shema, S.J., & Kaplan, G.A. (1996). Successful aging: Predictors and associated activities, *Amer. J. Epidem.*, 144(2): 135-141.

Stotland, E., & Canon, L.K. (1972). *Social psychology a cognitive approach.* Philadelphia: W.B. Saunders Company.

Swingle, P.G. (1968). *Experiments in social psychology.* New York: Academic Press.

Timiras, P.S., Quay, W.B., & Vernadakis, A. (Eds.) (1995). *Hormones and Aging.* Boca Raton, FL: CRC Press.

Tirrito, T. (2000). The spirit of collaboration: Social work/The Church/Older adults, *Social Thought*, 19(3): 59-76.

Turner, J.S. (1996). *Encyclopedia of Relationships across the Lifespan.* Connecticut: Greenwood Press.

Turrell, G., Lynch, J.W., Kaplan, G.A. et al. (2002). Socioeconomic position across the lifecourse and cognitive function in late middle age. *Journal of Gerontology: Social Sciences*, 57B(1): S43-S51.

Valentine, D. (2000). *"I know what I am": The category "transgender" in the construction of contemporary United States American conceptions of gender and sexuality.* Doctoral Dissertation, New York University.

Van Baarsen, B. (2002). Theories of coping with loss: The impact of social support and self-esteem on adjustment to emotional and social loneliness following a partner's death in later life. *Journal of Gerontology: Social Sciences*, 57B(1): S33-S42.

Velkoff, V.A., & Kinsella, K. (1998). Gender stereotypes: Data needs for ageing research. *Aging International.* 24(4): 18-38.

Vitt, L.A., & Siegenthaler, J.K. (Eds.). (1996). *Encyclopedia of Financial Gerontology.* Connecticut: Greenwood Press.

Watt, G. (2001). Policies to tackle social exclusion. *British Medical Journal*, 323: 175-176.

Waxman, B.F. (1991). Hatred: The unacknowledged dimension in violence against disabled people. *Sexuality and Disability Journal*, 9(3): 185-199.

Weiss, G.L., & Lonnquist, L.E. (2000). *The Sociology of Health, Healing, and Illness.* New York: Prentice-Hall.

Whipple, B., & Scoura, W.K. (1989). HIV and the older adult, *J. Geron. Nursing*, 15: 15-18.

Witten, T.M. (2001a). Trans/Inter-Sexuality. Submitted to: *Sexual Lives: Towards a Theory and Reality of Human Sexuality.* New York: McGraw-Hill Publishers.

Witten, T.M. (2001b). The transgender/intersex experience: Living in the quantum shadow. A presentation at the International Lesbian and Gay Conference, Oakland, CA.

Witten, T.M. (2002a). Midlife issues of aging in the LGBT community: A roundtable discussion. *Outword*, XX(yy): 98-97.

Witten, T.M. (2002b). On the epidemiology and demography of transgender and intersex: A white paper. TranScience Research Institute Preprint Series, 2: WP-2002-01. [Available at *http://www.transcience.org*].

Witten, T.M. (2002c). Geriatric care and management issues for the transgender and intersex populations. *Geriatric Care and Management Journal*, 12(3): 20-24.

Witten, T.M., & Eyler, A.E. (1997). HIV, AIDS and the elderly transgendered/transsexual: Risk and invisibility, presentation at the 1997 Gerontological Society of America, Cincinnati, OH.

Witten, T.M., & Eyler, A.E. (1999). Hate crimes against the transgendered: An invisible problem. *Peace Review*, 11(3): 461-468.

Witten, T.M., Ekins, R.J.M., Ettner, R., Harima, K., King, D., Landén, M., Nodin, N., P'yatokha, V., & Sharpe, A.N. (2003). Transgender and Transsexuality. In Ember, C.R. & Ember, M. (Eds.). *The Encyclopedia of Sex and Gender: Men and Women in the World's Cultures*. New York, N.Y.: Kluwer/Plenum, in press.

Witten, T.M., & Eyler, A.E. (2003). Spirituality and aging in the transsexual and transgendered community, in preparation.

Witten, T.M., Eyler, A.E., & Weigel, C. (2000, Winter). *Transsexuals, Transgenders, Cross-Dressers: Issues for Professionals in Aging*, OutWord. [Available at *http://www.asaging.org/LGAIN/outword-063.htm*].

Wolinsky, F.D., Coe, R.M., Miller, D.K., & Prendergast, J.M. (1985). Correlates of change in subjective well-being among the elderly. *Journal of Community Health*, 10: 93-107.

Xavier, J.M., & Simmons, R. (2000). *The Washington Transgender Needs Assessment Survey*, personal communication.

Zhang, Z., & Hayward, M.D. (2001). Childlessness and the psychological well-being of older-persons. *J. Gerontol.*, 56B(5): S311-S320.

Discrimination in the Workplace:
The Firing of a Transsexual

Phyllis E. Berry
Karen M. McGuffee
Jeffrey P. Rush
Susan Columbus

SUMMARY. The purpose of this study is to compare the benchmark cases of Audra Sommers, a transsexual who was fired from her job on April 25, 1980, to more recent cases to determine if workplace discrimination and laws have changed for transsexuals since 1980. To explore these issues, we conducted personal telephone interviews with two transsexuals and examined pertinent legal cases since the Sommers' cases. Our two case studies revealed that they had not experienced discrimination in their workplaces. In regards to the court cases, we found conflicting results–sometimes the courts determined that sex and gender are synonymous in terms of the Civil Rights Act of 1964, Title VII protec-

Phyllis E. Berry, PhD, Karen M. McGuffee, JD, Jeffrey P. Rush, DPA, and Susan Columbus, BS, are affiliated with the University of Tennessee at Chattanooga, Chattanooga, TN 37403-2598 (E-mail: Phyllis-Berry@utc.edu).

Address correspondence to: Criminal Justice Department, 615 McCallie Avenue, Chattanooga, TN 37403.

An earlier version of this paper was presented at the 1998 annual meetings of the Academy of Criminal Justice Sciences, Albuquerque, New Mexico.

[Haworth co-indexing entry note]: "Discrimination in the Workplace: The Firing of a Transsexual." Berry, Phyllis E. et al. Co-published simultaneously in *Journal of Human Behavior in the Social Environment* (The Haworth Social Work Practice Press, an imprint of The Haworth Press, Inc.) Vol. 8, No. 2/3, 2003, pp. 225-239; and: *Sexual Minorities: Discrimination, Challenges, and Development in America* (ed: Michael K. Sullivan) The Haworth Social Work Practice Press, an imprint of The Haworth Press, Inc., 2003, pp. 225-239. Single or multiple copies of this article are available for a fee from The Haworth Document Delivery Service [1-800-HAWORTH, 9:00 a.m. - 5:00 p.m. (EST). E-mail address: docdelivery@haworthpress.com].

Journal of Human Behavior in the Social Environment, Vol. 8(2/3) 2003
http://www.haworthpress.com/web/JHBSE
Digital Object Identifier: 10.1300/J137v8n02_13

tion, while other times they ruled they are not the same. Implications of the findings are discussed. *[Article copies available for a fee from The Haworth Document Delivery Service: 1-800-HAWORTH. E-mail address: <docdelivery@haworthpress.com> Website: <http://www.HaworthPress.com> © 2003 by The Haworth Press, Inc. All rights reserved.]*

KEYWORDS. Transsexual, transgender, sexual orientation, employment, discrimination

INTRODUCTION

Equal Opportunities for Everyone

Most Americans would probably agree with the statement that "everyone in our society deserves an equal opportunity to become successful based on one's individual merits and efforts." However, some members of our society are denied these opportunities due to legal forms of discrimination, which are allowed to be practiced in the workplace.

The Civil Rights Act of 1964, Title VII, made it unlawful for employers to refuse to hire or discharge a person based on their race, color, religion, sex, or national origin. For individuals attempting to bring sexual orientation discrimination claims under Title VII, it depends upon how the class is defined. Under the proposed theory of recovery, it is not individuals who are discriminated against due to sexual orientation who are protected, but rather individuals who are discriminated against because of sex. An individual who is the victim of sexual orientation discrimination must show that the harm suffered was from a sex-based classification (Schroeder, 1998). Some employers have attempted to escape liability by arguing that they were not engaging in sex discrimination, but rather sexual orientation discrimination (Flynn, 2001).

In 1973, the Rehabilitation Act also made it illegal for the federal government to deny employment opportunities with the federal government to persons having mental or physical handicaps. Other groups, such as gays, transvestites, and transsexuals, which have declared themselves to be victims of discrimination in the workplace, have turned to the courts for help. The Civil Service Reform Act of 1978 established that homosexuality and private homosexual conduct could not be used to disqualify persons for federal employment and that employees in the protected civil service could not be disciplined or terminated except for legitimate, work-related causes.

The purpose of this study is to compare recent workplace experiences and court cases of transsexuals to determine if their experiences differ from that of Audra Sommers (AKA, Timothy Kevin Cornish), a pre-op transsexual who was fired from her job in 1980, when she refused to use the men's restroom. This study will examine the following research questions: (1) Do transsexuals in the workplace now experience less discrimination than did Audra Sommers in 1980? (2) Have transsexuals, since the Audra Sommers' cases, been able to find relief through the courts in regards to workplace discrimination?

Definition of Transsexual

The term transsexual is defined in the Diagnostic and Statistical Manual of Mental Disorders of the American Psychiatric Association (3rd edition) as an individual who has feelings of inappropriateness about their anatomic sex, wishes to rid themselves of their own genitals and to live as a member of the opposite sex, has continuously felt this way for at least two years and does not have a coexistent mental disorder such as schizophrenia or a genetic abnormality. Transsexualism is a gender identity disorder involving a sense of belonging to a particular sex, not only biologically, but psychologically and socially as well (Gooren, 1997). In more modernist terms, transsexuality is defined as someone who is in transition from becoming one sex to the other (Roen, 2002).

LITERATURE REVIEW

Being feminine or masculine is similar to belonging to any social or cultural group. It is like being a part of a cult, with pressures to conform to gender norms. People who are "either/or" gender are forced to remain silent and get by (pass); hence, this "passing" becomes a form of social control. Passing lends itself to silence, invisibility, lies, self-denial, and the loss of one's power (Bornstein, 1995). Some transgendered and transsexual people, who would prefer not to have attention drawn to their gender, are forcibly outed by others who become aware of their uniqueness (Roen, 2002). Being out and proud, versus passing, may cause serious repercussions in the lives of many "either/or" gendered people (Roen, 2002).

For some, transgenderism has become a political movement that seeks to challenge the belief that people can only be classified into dichotomous sexual categories of either male or female (Roen, 2002). For others, building rights for sexual diversity begins with a broad-based effort toward claiming core rights for sexuality as a key aspect of all human beings (Miller, 2001). Still others claim that sexuality is "socially constructed," based upon specific historical processes that produce different sexualities (Macintosh, 1998; Weeks, 1995).

If sex and gender are more than just dichotomous variables, then how does one "become" a transsexual? While, to a certain extent, both sex and gender are socially constructed, the genetic-endocrine heritage theory states that the inner "sexual" identity is genetically arranged in the prenatal state, whereas, the outer "gender" identity is socially constructed during the postnatal experiences. A transgendered experience can occur when there is no agreement between the mind and body. In conflicts such as these, the mind takes precedence in determining gender identity (Diamond, 2000).

Many countries in Europe have passed special legislation for transsexuals. The first to pass such legislation was Sweden in 1972. Germany followed in 1981, Italy in 1982 and the Netherlands did so in 1985, with Turkey following in 1988 (Weitze & Osburg, 1998). The German Transsexuals' Act provides two options for legal relief. The first option simply entails changing the individual's first name. The second option requires that the individual must have undergone sex reassignment surgery and has adapted his/her external appearance to be that of the desired gender. Both options require that the individual produce two independent expert opinions that state that the individual has met the criteria for transsexualism (such as, having lived as a transsexual for at least three years) and that the condition is lasting in nature (Weitze & Osburg, 1998). Other restrictions apply, such as the individual must be at least 25 years of age, not married, and be permanently incapable of reproduction. Usually individuals do not have to have legal permission to begin hormone treatment and surgery; however, two physicians must approve requests for castrations (Weitze & Osburg, 1998).

In the United States we take a lot of our rights for granted. One area of rights that is starting to become challenged is, "Do people have the right to choose their own sex?" Marques and Silva (1997) approached this question from Brazilian law. Brazil's constitution guarantees their citizens the right to privacy and to a self-image. Marques and Silva (1997) questioned whether this also applied to the legal rights of transsexuals after sex reassignment. Like the United States, Brazil has no special legislation for transsexual persons, and this creates difficult situations for transsexuals (e.g., in marriage, adoptions, work, etc.). In Brazil, when sex determination mistakes happen, as in cases of intersexuality (physical defects), the birth register is changed to reflect the newly discovered true sexual status of the person. However, when a person's sex change is due to medical intervention, as in the case of a transsexual, it has been suggested that the person should be registered as a quasi third gender, namely a transsexual, in order to avoid misunderstandings within society (Marques & Silva, 1997).

Setting a Precedent–The Background

In 1986, William A. Blackwell, a cross-dresser and transvestite, filed a suit against the Treasury Department with the U.S. District Court for the District of Columbia. He claimed he had been denied employment because he was a transvestite and that transvestitism was a mental handicap covered by the 1973 Rehabilitation Act. After the case went to appeals court, it was decided that refusal to hire an applicant because of perceived transvestitism would violate the Rehabilitation Act if indeed the employer knew the applicant was a transvestite. However, in Mr. Blackwell's case, he had not specifically mentioned to his employer that he was a transvestite, therefore, there was no way to know if he had suffered from this sort of discrimination, so the appeals court affirmed the lower court's decision, and the case was dismissed (Leonard, 1993).

In July 1990, the Americans With Disabilities Act declared that regardless of whether medical professionals classified transvestitism, homosexuality, or transsexuality as a mental impairment, those found to be suffering from these "impairments" do not have protection from discrimination in employment or public accommodations under the federal law (Leonard, 1993).

However, if our society embraces the belief that everyone should have equal opportunities and protection under the law, it begs the question, "Does this include homosexuals, transvestites, and transsexuals?" To answer this question, this article examines the case of Audra Sommers, a transsexual.

The Audra Sommers' Cases

The case of Audra Sommers, a pre-op (before sex reassignment surgery) transsexual, is provided to show a relationship between legal inscriptions of identity based on cultural motives and accounts, and the lack of protection from workplace discrimination for such identified individuals. At birth, Audra was born a boy and given the name of Timothy Kevin Cornish.

On April 22, 1980, Audra began working at Budget Marketing, Inc., as a clerical worker in Polk County, Iowa. Before she began her employment, Audra had undergone hormonal therapy and was dressing and acting as a woman, although she had not yet undergone sex-reassignment surgery. The first two days of her employment passed uneventfully without any complaints being voiced regarding her performance. However, on the third day, another employee of Budget Marketing, Inc., who knew Audra as a man, recognized Audra. Soon, this acquaintance had spread the word that Audra was actually a man, and the other women starting complaining that they did not want Audra using the women's restroom. Audra, however, refused to use the men's restroom. Audra was dismissed from the company on April 25, 1980 (Leonard, 1993).

Audra, believing her civil rights had been violated based on sex discrimination, filed charges with the Equal Employment Opportunity Commission (EEOC). Even though the EEOC decided they could not help Audra, they provided her with a letter authorizing her suit in the U.S. District Court for the Southern District of Iowa.

Her suit was dismissed, however, due to the fact that her claim was not specific enough and lacked jurisdiction subject matter against the company. She was advised by Chief Judge William C. Stuart to amend her complaint and specify whether she was claiming discrimination based on being a male, female, or transsexual, and to specify whether or not she had undergone sex-reassignment surgery. Audra's amended complaint stated that she had been discriminated against due to being a female person with an anatomical man's body. She claimed that the term "sex" should be interpreted under Title VII of the Civil Rights Act of 1964 to include a person who is anatomically male, but psychologically female (Leonard, 1993).

Budget Marketing, Inc. submitted an affidavit from a physician claiming that the medical profession recognized persons such as Audra as males, and therefore, reaffirmed its motion to have the case dismissed. Audra, in turn, introduced affidavits from two physicians stating that currently the medical profession considered persons like Audra to be females.

Judge Stuart treated the motion to dismiss as a motion for summary judgment and granted the motion, based on the Voyles v. Ralph K. Davies Medical Center case, a federal court case that refused to grant relief to a transsexual plaintiff. The judge explained that Congress had not intended for the Court to determine a person's sex based upon the psychological makeup of an individual while ignoring the individual's anatomical classification. Because she was anatomically male, the court declared Audra a male, and therefore, she had not been discriminated against when she was fired for refusing to use the men's bathroom (Leonard, 1993).

Audra appealed her claim to the U.S. Court of Appeals for the Eighth Circuit, but again the court ruled that she was not protected from discharge under Title VII of the Civil Rights Act of 1964. The court explained that Congress had intended for the term "sex" to mean either male or female, and transsexualism did not fall within the protection of the Act. Although the court was sympathetic towards Audra's plight, it felt powerless to act (Leonard, 1993).

Audra then filed charges against Budget Marketing, Inc. with the Iowa Civil Rights Commission, claiming disability discrimination. However, the Commission refused to consider her complaint. She then sought relief through the Polk County District Court, but the district court upheld the Civil Rights Commission's decision. Finally, she appealed to the Supreme Court of Iowa (Leonard, 1993).

The unanimous Supreme Court of Iowa, with Justice Louis W. Schultz writing, dismissed Audra's claims. Although, the court did agree that transsexuals suffered from a serious problem of gender disorientation which may be due to medical and psychological disturbances, the court decided that transsexuals could not be considered as persons with disabilities under the Civil Rights Act (Leonard, 1993). Justice Shultz wrote:

> The condition must independently come within the definition of impairment before attitudes of others can be said to make the condition a substantial handicap. Because transsexualism lacks the inherent propensity to limit major life activities of the listed examples of mental impairment, the commission could reasonably conclude it is not a mental impairment under the statute or rule. (Leonard, 1993)

The court did agree that transsexuals faced discrimination. However, it is not due to impairment, but rather it is because *they are considered undesirable* (emphasis added). Although the courts recognized that Audra's sexuality was the reason she was fired from her job, they would not recognize the fact that this was exactly the same type of discrimination the legislators were trying to prevent when they included sex in the statutes (Leonard, 1993).

Applying the Societal Reaction Perspective to These Cases

The decisions made in Audra's cases were based upon explicit interpretations of the civil rights laws, rather than upon any implied interpretations that Congress may have actually intended. To emphasize this point, interpretive sociology, using the societal reaction perspective, is used to analyze this case.

The societal reaction perspective, based on Max Weber's interpretive sociology, stresses the importance of subjective meanings in everyday social life. One variant of interpretive sociology is symbolic interactionism. According to Herbert Blumer, human beings not only interpret but also react to the actions of others (Pfohl, 1994).

Reaction theorist Howard Becker was concerned with how deviants became labeled as such, and suggested that a given act cannot be considered deviant just because it is commonly thought of as such. Instead, the process by which an act becomes labeled deviant must be considered. Becker suggested that deviant labels come from powerful moral entrepreneurs who lobby for the deviantization of certain behaviors (Pfohl, 1994). Erving Goffman extended the societal reaction perspective to people who become negatively labeled based on how they look and act. Such persons then become stigmatized and must endure social problems that others do not encounter (Pfohl, 1994).

The societal reaction perspective, or labeling theory, helps one to have a more comprehensive sociological understanding of deviance by requiring that attention be paid to the interactive dynamics between the people who condemn nonconformity and those who are being condemned (Pfohl, 1994). In the case of Audra Sommers, she presented herself for work as a woman, even though she was anatomically male. This act in and of itself did not create a problem. It was only when an acquaintance spread the word that "she" was actually a "he" that her problems began. Now the interactive dynamics of the situation had changed, and the other employees of Budget Marketing, Inc. considered Audra deviant.

Audra interpreted the firing as an act of sexual discrimination because she psychologically considered herself to be female. She even supplied the court with two physicians' interpretations that persons like her are considered females. However, the judge ruled that Congress had not intended for the court to dismiss an individual's anatomical classification. Audra appealed to the U.S. Court of Appeals for the Eighth Circuit, but again the court agreed with the lower court's interpretation of sex as being either male or female, based upon the anatomical classification of the individual.

Audra then claimed she was a victim of disability discrimination and filed charges with the Iowa Civil Rights Commission. The Commission refused to even consider her complaint, so she sought relief from the Polk County District Court. However, the court sided with the Commission's decision. Audra's last appeal was made to the Supreme Court of Iowa, where an unanimous court agreed that although transsexuals did suffer from a serious problem of gender disorientation, which may in fact be due to medical and psychological disturbances, this disability lacked the propensity to limit major life's activities and would not be considered as a mental impairment under the statute or rule. The court further agreed that transsexuals did face discrimination, but not because they are impaired, but rather because they are undesirable.

In all of these situations, the powerful moral entrepreneurs of the court refused to examine Audra's situation in a creative, interpretive way. Instead, they chose to interpret her acts as deviant and labeled her as an undesirable. Because of being labeled as such, she was therefore denied protection under the law from discrimination. The court refused to consider the possibility that Audra's stigma had limited her major life activities and thus, hindered her opportunities for success. Even though the courts were in the position to bring about social change, they chose not to, and consequently, even today, certain groups still face discriminatory employment practices.

INTERVIEWS WITH TWO TRANSSEXUALS

The purpose of this research was to answer the following research questions: (1) Do transsexuals in the workplace now experience less discrimination than did Audra Sommers in 1980? (2) Have transsexuals, since the Audra Sommers' cases, been able to find relief through the courts in regards to workplace discrimination? To help answer the first question, we decided to try and interview some transsexuals about their workplace experiences. By word of mouth, we were able to locate two transsexuals who were willing to talk with us. We conducted unstructured telephone interviews to gather personal data about these two cases.

Our first case involved a pre-op transsexual named "Zipora" (not her real name). Zipora is a 21-year-old, Puerto Rican "male" who has been taking hormones since the age of 16. She has lived in the United States for six years. Her parents are divorced, and her mother and siblings live in the southeast region of the United States. They support Zipora's decision to become a woman; however, her father does not. Zipora has the breasts and the "hair of a woman," as well as a "voice of a woman." Her penis is shriveled and "does not function." Her female roommate (who has never known her as a "man") said that, "she is more of a woman than most women I know." The roommate also stated that, "Zipora looks like a model and is accepted as a female among all of our friends–men and women alike." Zipora has had plastic surgery to have her nose reshaped and made more feminine and is planning on having additional surgery to complete her transformation into a woman in about two years. Money is a factor, however, and she is trying to find the money to have the surgery. The only place where she found it to be fairly inexpensive is in Thailand, where the surgery will cost around US $5,000.

Zipora reported that she is accepted as a woman wherever she goes and indicated that when she applied for her current job, at a computer company, her employer, thought he would be meeting a "he." When she told him that "he" was actually a "she" he said, "Okay," and the interview proceeded as usual, with her being hired for the job. Zipora stated that she has not experienced any discrimination (either overtly or covertly) on the job and that she has been up-front with her co-workers from the beginning, explaining to them that she is a pre-op transsexual. She uses the ladies room at work and is rarely hassled about it.

Our second transsexual was Niki (not her real name). Niki is a middle aged, post-op transsexual. Although Niki agreed to be interviewed, she did not seem to be as open to discussing her situation. All she would tell us about her working situation is that she is a professional. Niki stated that she had the respect of her colleagues prior to her surgery and that she still has their respect. She stated that she carries herself like a professional and dresses as such. She feels that if you carry on like a circus character, you will, in essence, be treated that way. She did make it a point of telling us that she used to be an "upstanding" male member of her community and has children. Niki told us that she has not had any difficulty with colleagues, friends, or relatives.

Niki shared with us that if we saw her on the street, we would never know that she once was a man. Niki is about 5'9" tall and weighs around 150 pounds. She wears a size 12, works out daily and carries herself as a woman.

Why did the work experience of Audra differ so vastly from the work experiences of Zipora and Niki? Are their experiences just unique, or have times changed? Or have the laws that protect the rights of transsexuals changed since the Sommers' cases? To answer these questions we examined pertinent legal cases that had occurred since the Sommers' cases.

Developments in the Law (Since the Sommers' Cases)

Since the opinions in the *Sommers'* cases, the United States Supreme Court decided the case of *Price Waterhouse v. Hopkins*, 490 U.S. 228 (1989). The plaintiff (a female) in *Price Waterhouse* filed suit under Title VII of the Civil Rights Act of 1964, as amended, 42 U.S.C. section 2000e et seq., charging that Price Waterhouse had discriminated against her on the basis of sex discrimination in its decision not to repropose her for partnership after her candidacy was held for reconsideration earlier. The Supreme Court held that Price Waterhouse violated Title VII when, in its evaluation of Hopkins, it relied on gender role stereotypes of how a woman is to look and act. Evidence presented at the lower court included comments from partners describing Hopkins as "macho," suggesting that she take a "course at charm school," "walk more femininely, talk more femininely, dress more femininely, wear make-up, have her hair styled, and wear jewelry." In determining that some of the partners reacted negatively to Hopkins' personality because she was a woman based on the above statements, the Court stated that, "a person's gender may not be considered in making decisions that affect her." The Court continued to say, "Title VII even forbids employers to make gender an individual stumbling block to employment opportunities."

Although the plaintiff in the *Price Waterhouse* case was not transsexual, based on the *Price Waterhouse* case, it appears the term "sex" as used in Title VII entails more than anatomy thereby allowing transsexuals to prevail under Title VII claims. However, some courts have recognized the *Price Waterhouse* case to include transsexuals and some have not.

In the case of *Dobre v. National Railroad Passenger Corp.*, 850 F. Supp. 284 (E.D. Penn. 1993), the plaintiff, a transsexual, sued her employer under Title VII, as well as under state law, for sex discrimination while in the process of becoming female. In this case, Dobre contends the employer would not allow her to dress as a female, use the women's restroom, use her female name, or allow her to have a desk in view of the public. Without delving into the facts of the case, the court dismissed the claim, stating that "Title VII prohibits an employer from taking adverse employment actions because of an employee's 'sex,'" and, "The term 'sex' as used in U.S.C. section 2000e-2(a) is not synonymous with the term gender," citing *Holloway v. Arthur Anderson & Co.* 566 F.2d 659, 662 (9th Cir. 1977), which rejected the appellant's argument that Title VII prohibits discrimination based on gender (which would encompass discrimination based on transsexualism).

The court concluded the allegations of the Plaintiff did not support a claim that she was discriminated against as a female and therefore failed to state a claim upon which relief could be granted. In this case sex is interpreted to mean biological sex. Or in other words, for a person to be considered a woman, the person must have the anatomy of a woman.

Likewise, in *Underwood v. Archer Management Services, Inc.*, 857 F. Supp. 96 (D.C. 1994), the plaintiff, a transsexual, sued her employer under the District of Columbia Human Rights Act claiming her termination was due to her personal appearance and sex and/or sexual orientation. In its decision to dismiss the complaint for failure to state a claim, the court found that under the Act and under Title VII, "sex" used in these provisions do not include discrimination based on transsexuality.

Similarly, in the case of *Davis v. Sheraton Society Hill Hotel*, 907 F. Supp. 896 (E.D. Penn. 1995), the court found that discrimination based on gender is not protected under Title VII. In this case, Davis, a non-transsexual male, sued for reverse sex discrimination under Title VII and the Pennsylvania Human Relations Act claiming that derogatory comments were made by co-workers about his attire and his employer refused to return him to his prior position at work upon his return after a medical absence. Although the court did not grant summary judgment on the issue of Davis's work position under Title VII, it granted summary judgment on the issue of sex discrimination stating that the co-workers' comments "do not refer to Davis's sex, but to his gender, and discrimination based on gender is not protected under Title VII."

Although some cases have followed the pre-*Price Waterhouse* line of reasoning denying transsexuals sex discrimination claims under Title VII, some have considered *Price Waterhouse* but have concluded they are inapplicable to their fact scenarios. For instance, In *Broadus v. State Farm Ins. Co.*, 2000 U.S. Dist. LEXIS 19919 (W.D. Mo. 2000), Plaintiff, an African-American transsexual, sued under the Americans With Disabilities Act (for physical impairments he suffered), and under Title VII claiming co-worker sexual harassment and negative treatment by management due to his physical appearance. In granting summary judgment to the defendant regarding all issues, the court recognized *Price Waterhouse* as prohibiting stereotyping which plays a role in employment decisions under Title VII; however, it stated that, "It is unclear however, whether a transsexual is protected from sex discrimination and sexual harassment under Title VII."

Finally, in *Oiler v. Winn-Dixie Louisiana, Inc.*, 2002 U.S. Dist. LEXIS 17417 (E.D. La. 2002), Plaintiff, a transvestite, brought an employment discrimination action under Title VII and the Louisiana state statute alleging Winn Dixie terminated him due to his lifestyle as a cross dresser while off work. After taking into consideration past cases defining "sex" differently than gender and discussing *Price Waterhouse*, the court found that his actions were not similar to the plaintiff's in *Price Waterhouse*. The court reasoned the plaintiff in *Price Waterhouse* never pretended to be the opposite sex, and therefore, that case is inapplicable. Additionally, the court reasoned that since neither the United States Supreme Court nor Congress had clearly expanded the definition of "sex" to include sexual identity disorders, sexual preference, orientation or status, then this court would not do so either. The defendant was granted summary judgment.

On the other hand, some cases have found viable claims for transsexuals. For example, in the case of *Maffei v. Kolaeton Industry Inc.*, 626 N.Y.S.2d 391 (N.Y. App. Div 1995), the plaintiff, a transsexual, brought an action against his employer alleging discrimination based on sexual orientation under state law. In denying the defendant's motion for summary judgment, the court held that although Title VII cases had not allowed transsexuals relief, these cases were "unduly restrictive and should not be followed in interpreting our New York City statute." The plaintiff was allowed to proceed under state law. Similarly, in *Rentos v. OCE-Office Supplies*, 1996 U.S. Dist. LEXIS 19060 (S.D.N.Y. 1996), the court denied the defendant's motion to strike the plaintiff's complaint of employment sexual discrimination finding that, like Maffei, although Title VII cases failed to provide relief for transsexuals, New York allowed relief and plaintiff was entitled to a hearing on the merits.

In *Schwenk v. Hartford*, 204 F.3d 1187 (9th Cir. 2000), the plaintiff, a transsexual, sued under Title VII and the Gender Motivated Violence Act, 42 U.S.C.S. section 1398 (d)(1) as a result to defendant's alleged attempt to rape her. In denying the defendant's motion for summary judgment, the court reasoned that the earlier judicial approach denying transsexuals claims under Title VII taken by federal courts had been "overruled by the logic and language of *Price Waterhouse*." The court stated that under Price Waterhouse, 'sex' under Title VII encompasses both sex–that is, biological differences between men and women–*and* gender. Discrimination because one fails to act in the way expected of a man or woman is forbidden under Title VII. Indeed, . . . the terms 'sex' and 'gender' have become interchangeable." The court found Plaintiff was entitled to a hearing on the merits.

In *Enriquez v. West Jersey Health Systems*, 342 N.J. Super. 501, 777 A.2d 365 (2001), Plaintiff, a transsexual, filed a complaint for wrongful termination of employment based on the New Jersey Law Against Discrimination. After reviewing cases prior to *Price Waterhouse* holding Title VII did not apply to transsexual claims, and cases following *Price Waterhouse*, the court con-. cluded that the reasoning in *Maffei, Schwenk*, and *Price Waterhouse* (as well as other cases), was "more closely connected to our own state's historic policy of liberally construing the LAD," citing *Fraser v. Robin Dee Day Camp*, 44 N.J. 480, 486, 210 A2d 208 (1065). The court later added, "Sex is comprised of more than a person's genitalia at birth," quoting Taylor Flynn, Transforming the Debate: Why We Need to Include Transgender Rights in the Struggle for Sex and Sexual Orientation Equality, 101 Colum. L. Rev. 392, 415 (2001). The court concluded that "the word 'sex' as used in the LAD should be interpreted to include gender, protecting from discrimination on the basis of sex or gender." The plaintiff was allowed to proceed on the sex discrimination claim as well as other claims.

DISCUSSION

Based on the brief analysis of these few cases defining rights of transsexuals under Title VII, it is readily apparent that the courts are not uniform in their approach to this issue. Also, we found that the two transsexuals we interviewed, in contrast to the experiences of Audra Sommers, did not feel like they had experienced workplace discrimination due to their transsexualism. These two cases were not meant to represent the experiences of all transsexuals, but rather they were used to open the way for new discoveries. The United States is a complex, pluralistic society consisting of diverse cultures with corresponding vocabularies that provide multiple motives and accounts, some of which get institutionalized into laws (Ben-Yehuda, 1990). "Complex pluralistic societies are characterized by a multiplicity of centers, each one enveloped by a particular symbolic-moral universe that demarcates its moral boundaries" (Ben-Yehuda, 1990). In our society, the law is capable to promote or constrain social change. At this point, the courts have interpreted the law differently, giving conflicting signals in regards to transsexual rights in the workplace.

Who should judge a person's gender–the courts, the medical field, society, or the person? Should there be more than two categories of gender protected under Title VII? Is gender socially constructed, thus superceding biological sex? If so, how can the conflict between anatomical sex and socially constructed gender that is embodied by transsexuals be resolved? Or should transsexuals be treated under the medical model, that treats transsexuals as pathological?

As we wait for these questions to be answered, there are people whose lives and livelihoods are being affected in the workplace due to some people still considering them to be "undesirables." In contemporary American society, it is necessary to create a society that guarantees basic individual human rights. Becoming a transsexual goes beyond the medical procedure necessary to change a person's sex from one sex to another. It includes legal problems, such as changing one's name, birth certificate, issues of marriage, adoption, inheritance, etc. The time has come for human rights claims regarding gender to be addressed by Congress. Should transsexualism be included in sex discrimination under Title VII? Or should it be included under gender discrimination and should gender discrimination be included under Title VII? Congress should amend Title VII to prohibit discrimination for transgendered individuals. This is not a radical idea, but rather a solution that provides equality for these individuals.

REFERENCES

Ben-Yehuda, N. (1990). *The politics and morality of deviance: Moral panics, drug abuse, deviant science, and reversed stigmatization.* Albany, NY: State University of New York Press.

Bornstein, K. (1995). *Gender outlaw: On men, women, and the rest of us.* New York: Vintage.

Diamond, M. (2000). Sex and gender: Same or different? *Feminism & Psychology, 10,* 46-54.

Flynn, T. (2001). Transforming the debate: Why we need to include transgender rights in the struggles for sex and sexual orientation equality. *The Columbia Law Review.*

Gooren, L. (1997). Transsexualism, introduction, & general aspects of treatment. Retrieved from the World Wide Web: http//www.sx4all.nl/~txbreed/gooren.html#intro.

Leonard, A. (1993). *Sexuality and the law: An encyclopedia of major legal cases.* New York: Garland Publishing.

Macintosh, M. (1998). The homosexual role. In P. Nardi & B. Schneider (Eds.), *Social Perspectives on Lesbian and Gay Studies* (pp. 68-76). New York, NY: Routledge.

Marques, C. L., & da Silva, E. R. (1997). Legal aspects of transsexualism in Brazilian law: A private law approach. *The International Journal of Transgenderism, 1,* Retrieved April 8, 2002, from the World Wide Web: http://www.symposion.com/ijt/ijtc0105.htm.

Miller, A. M. (2001). Uneasy promises: Sexuality, health, and human rights. *American Journal of Public Health, 91,* 861-864.

Pfohl, S. (1994). *Images of deviance and social control: A sociological history, 2nd ed.* New York: McGraw-Hill, Inc.

Roen, K. (2002). *"Either/or" and "both/neither": Discursive tensions in transgender politics.* Chicago: Chicago Press.

Schroeder, T. A. (1998). Fables of the deconstruction: The practical failures of gay and lesbian theory in the realm of employment discrimination. *American University Journal of Gender, Social Policy, & the Law.*

Weeks, J. (1995). History, desire, and identities. In R. Parker & J. Gagnon (Eds.), *Conceiving sexuality* (pp. 33-50). New York, NY: Routledge.

Weitze, C., & Osburg, S. (1998). Empirical data on epidemiology and application of the German transsexuals' act during its first ten years. *The International Journal of Transgenderism, 2.* Retrieved April 8, 2002, from the World Wide Web: http://www.symposion.com/ijt/ijtc0303.htm.

CASES

Broadus v. State Farm Ins. Co., 2000 U.S. Dist. LEXIS 19919 (W.D. Mo. 2000).

Davis v. Sheraton Society Hill Hotel, 907 F. Supp. 896 (E.D. Penn. 1995).

Dobre v. National Railroad Passenger Corp., 850 F. Supp. 284 (E.D. Penn 1993).

Enriquez v. West Jersey Health Systems, 342 N.J. Super. 501, 777 A.2d 365 (2001).

Holloway v. Arthur Anderson & Co., 566 F.2d 659 (9th Cir. 1977).

Maffei v. Kolaeton Industry Inc., 626 N.Y.S.2d 391 (N.Y. App. Div. 1995).

Oiler v. Winn-Dixie Louisiana, Inc., 2002 U.S. Dist. LEXIS 17417 (E.D. La. 2002).

Price Waterhouse v. Hopkins, 490 U.S. 228 (1989).

Rentos v. OCE-Office Supplies, 1996 U.S. Dist. LEXIS 19060 (S.D.N.Y. 1996).

Schwenk v. Hartford, 204 F.3d 1187 (9th Cir. 2002).

Sommers v. Budget Marketing, Inc., 667 F.2d 748 (8th Cir. 1982).

Sommers v. Iowa Civil Rights Commission, 337 N.W.2d 470 (Iowa 1983).

Underwood v. Archer Management Services, Inc., 857 F. Supp. 96 (D.C. 1994).

Voyles v. Ralph K. Davies Medical Center, 403 F. Supp. 456 (N.D. Cal. 1975), affirmed without opinion, 570 F.2d 354 (9th Cir. 1978).

STATUTE

Civil Rights Act of 1964, Title VII, 42 U.S.C. sec. 2000e-2(a) (1988).

Index

AA. *See* Alcoholics Anonymous (AA)
Abuse
  of GLB adolescents in rural areas,
    139-140
  physical, in lesbian relationships,
    161-163,162t
  psychological, in lesbian
    relationships,
    161-163,162t
Abusive behavior
  jealousy and, in lesbian
    relationships, 163-164,
    164t,165t
  in lesbian relationships, 162-163,
    164t
  sex role identity and jealousy as
    correlates of, 153-169.
    See also Lesbian
    relationships, abusive
    behavior in, sex role identity
    and jealousy as correlates of
Accreditation Standards, 77
ACLU, 22,23
Acquired immunodeficiency syndrome
    (AIDS), 41,43,44,45,46,47,
    48,49,50,51,64
  as risk factor for GLB adolescents,
    120
ADA. *See* Americans with Disabilities
    Act (ADA)
Adams, H.E., 2
Adolescent(s)
  GLB
    described, 131-132
    prevalence of, 112
    risk factors of, 111-129
      family issues, 113-114
      HIV/AIDS, 120-122
      implications for practice
      within social

        environment,
        122-124
      peer issues, 115-116
      school issues, 115-116
      substance use, 117-118
      suicidal behavior, 118-120
    in rural areas, 129-144
      described, 132-134
      study of
        abuse from others in,
        139-140
        coming out in, 138
        data analysis in, 137
        data collection in, 136-137
        discussion of, 141-142
        formal supports in, 141
        instrumentation in, 136-137
        interactions with parents in,
        179
        isolation in, 137-138
        methodology of, 134-137
        results of, 137-141
        suggestions to other
        adolescents in,
        140-141
        supportive adults in, 140
  homosexual, coming out of, 93-110
    as crisis, 101-104
    study of
      clinical implications of,
      104-110
      introduction to, 94-96
      literature review in, 96-100
    suggestions to, from GLB
      adolescents in rural areas,
      140-141
AIDS, 41,43,44,45,46,47,48,49,
    50,51,64
  as risk factor for GLB adolescents,
    120-122

   241

BOOK ORDER FORM!

Order a copy of this book with this form or online at:
http://www.haworthpress.com/store/product.asp?sku=5043

Sexual Minorities
Discrimination, Challenges, and Development in America

____ in softbound at $29.95 (ISBN: 0-7890-0235-3)
____ in hardbound at $49.95 (ISBN: 0-7890-0230-2)

COST OF BOOKS _____

POSTAGE & HANDLING _____
US: $4.00 for first book & $1.50
for each additional book.
Outside US: $5.00 for first book
& $2.00 for each additional book.

SUBTOTAL _____

In Canada: add 7% GST. _____

STATE TAX _____
CA, IL, IN, MN, NJ, NY, OH & SD residents
please add appropriate local sales tax.

FINAL TOTAL _____
If paying in Canadian funds, convert
using the current exchange rate,
UNESCO coupons welcome.

❏ BILL ME LATER:
Bill-me option is good on US/Canada/
Mexico orders only; not good to jobbers,
wholesalers, or subscription agencies.

❏ Signature _____

❏ Payment Enclosed: $ _____

❏ PLEASE CHARGE TO MY CREDIT CARD:

❏ Visa ❏ MasterCard ❏ AmEx ❏ Discover
❏ Diner's Club ❏ Eurocard ❏ JCB

Account # _____

Exp Date _____

Signature _____
(Prices in US dollars and subject to change without notice.)

PLEASE PRINT ALL INFORMATION OR ATTACH YOUR BUSINESS CARD
Name
Address
City   State/Province   Zip/Postal Code
Country
Tel   Fax
E-Mail

May we use your e-mail address for confirmations and other types of information? ❏ Yes ❏ No We appreciate receiving
your e-mail address. Haworth would like to e-mail special discount offers to you, as a preferred customer.
We will never share, rent, or exchange your e-mail address. We regard such actions as an invasion of your privacy.

Order From Your **Local Bookstore** or Directly From
The Haworth Press, Inc. 10 Alice Street, Binghamton, New York 13904-1580 • USA
Call Our toll-free number (1-800-429-6784) / Outside US/Canada: (607) 722-5857
Fax: 1-800-895-0582 / Outside US/Canada: (607) 771-0012
E-mail your order to us: orders@haworthpress.com

For orders outside US and Canada, you may wish to order through your local
sales representative, distributor, or bookseller.
For information, see http://haworthpress.com/distributors

(Discounts are available for individual orders in US and Canada only, not booksellers/distributors.)

Please photocopy this form for your personal use.
www.HaworthPress.com   BOF04